P9-CQJ-710

LIBERATION

DEVELOPMENT
& SALVATION

RENÉ LAURENTIN
Translated by Charles Underhill Quinn
ORBIS BOOKS, Maryknoll, New York

ABBREVIATIONS

AAS *Acta Apostolicae Sedis*, Rome: Vatican, 1909–

ASS *Acta Sanctae Sedis*, Rome: Vatican, 1865–1908

DC *Documentation Catholique*, 5 Rue Bayard, Paris–8ᵉ

DENZINGER, H. *Enchiridion symbolorum*, 32nd edition, revised by A. Schönmetzer, Fribourg: Herder, 1963

ICI *Informations Catholiques Internationales*, 163 Boulevard Malesherbes, Paris–17ᵉ

PG *Patrologiae cursus . . . Series graeca*, Paris: Migne, 1857–1866

PL *Patrologiae cursus . . . Series latina*, Paris, Migne, 1844–1864

Other abbreviations used are explained in the text when necessary. For the biblical quotations, the text of the Revised Standard Version of Holy Scripture has been generally followed.

Originally published by Editions du Seuil, Paris, 1969.

COPYRIGHT © 1972 ORBIS BOOKS, MARYKNOLL, NEW YORK 10545

LIBRARY OF CONGRESS CATALOG CARD NUMBER: 72-156970

DESIGN BY LA LIBERTÉ & RAYNER

MANUFACTURED IN THE UNITED STATES OF AMERICA

CONTENTS

Preface, vii

DEVELOPMENT AND LIBERATION, ix   DEVELOPMENT, A CULTURAL
PROBLEM, xiv   THEOLOGY OF THE FUTURE & OF HOPE, xv

Introduction, 3

PART I: THE CHURCH AS A LIVING COMMUNITY, 5

1: Development, a Postconciliar Movement, 7

THE LIFE OF THE CHURCH AS A THEOLOGICAL LOCUS, 7   DEVELOPMENT
IN THE LIFE OF THE POSTCONCILIAR CHURCH, 8   A GENUINE MOVEMENT,
15   A MOVEMENT ON AN ECUMENICAL SCALE, 18   DEVELOPMENT, A
FRONTIERLESS MOVEMENT, 23

2: The Sources of the Movement, 24

OFFICIAL SOURCES OF DEVELOPMENT, 24   THE PIONEERS, 26   LOOKING
BEYOND THE PIONEERS, 35

PART II: THE QUESTION BEING EXAMINED, 37

3: The Word "Development," 39

EARLY USAGE OF THE TERM, 40   THE TERM IN THE DICTIONARIES, 42
THE MAGISTERIUM, 45   THE FOUR LEVELS OF VOCABULARY, 47   THE
LIMITATIONS OF A WORD, 50   CONCLUSION TO THE WORD STUDY, 52

4: Is There a Theology of Development? 54

ESCHATOLOGY OF CONTINUITY, 55   THE PERSPECTIVE OF DISCONTINUITY,
57   CONCLUSION, 59

v

PART III: SOURCES FOR ANSWERING THE QUESTION, 61

5: The Scriptural Evidence, 63
THE NEGATIVE EVIDENCE, 63   TEMPORAL PROSPERITY & ESCHATOLOGY,
64   BIBLICAL ANTHROPOLOGY INTEGRATES THE BODY, 68   THE GOD
WHO IS GOOD, CREATOR OF A GOOD WORLD, 69   MAN COMPLETES
CREATION, 71   REDEMPTION RESTORES CREATION, 74   THE ESSENTIAL
COMMANDMENT, 76

6: The Rights of the Poor, 83
THE POOR IN THE OLD TESTAMENT, 84   THE MEANING & IMPORT OF
LAWS FOR THE POOR, 88   PATRISTIC AND LATER TRADITION, 95

7: The Magisterium and Development, 102
AN EARLY USAGE OF "DEVELOPMENT" BY PIUS XII, 102   DEVELOPMENT
IN MATER ET MAGISTRA, 103   PACEM IN TERRIS & DEVELOPMENT, 105
THE COUNCIL & DEVELOPMENT, 106   POPULORUM PROGRESSIO &
DEVELOPMENT, 108   TOWARD A NEW STAGE FOR DEVELOPMENT, 112

PART IV: SOME ANSWERS TO DEVELOPMENT PROBLEMS, 115

8: Why Development Relates to Salvation, 117
A NEW FACE FOR AN OLD OBLIGATION, 118   THE NEW NAME OF PEACE,
121   A SCANDAL THAT MUST END, 122   A REMEDY FOR CERTAIN
UNHEALTHY DISSOCIATIONS, 122   CONCLUSION: THE RECONCILIATION
OF CONTRARY OPTIONS, 127

9: The Ambiguities of Development, 134

10: Violence as a Contemporary Problem, 150
THE REALITY OF VIOLENCE TODAY, 150   HISTORICAL VARIATIONS, 153
THE PRINCIPLES OF VIOLENCE, 155   BIBLICAL PRINCIPLES OF VIOLENCE,
156   THE PHILOSOPHICAL PROBLEM OF VIOLENCE, 160   FORMS &
LIMITS OF VIOLENCE, 163

11: The End and the Means, 167
THE FINALITY OF DEVELOPMENT, 167   THE CRITERIA OF DEVELOPMENT,
173   THE MEANS FOR DEVELOPMENT, 177

12: Some Norms for Development, 180
TECHNICAL PRECISION, 180   POLICY, 181   PROPHECY, 184   PARTICI-
PATION & COMMUNICATION, 186   DEVELOPMENT & LITURGY, 188

13: Mission and Development, 200
CONTRAST OF IDEAS, 200   THE MOVEMENTS CONCUR, 201   RECONCILIA-
TIONS & CONVERGENCES, 203   DIFFERENCES & COINCIDENCES, 207

14: A Last Word, 210
Notes, 217
Bibliography, 235

PREFACE

It is time, now that this American edition is being published, that a step forward be taken. At Medellín, the Latin American bishops saw in the development program a new "exodus" for their people. An exodus rich in issues and ideas, moreover. It is more than two years since the publication of *Développement et salut* (May 1969) and the National Theological Congress in Mexico (November 1969) and with what I have already written in mind, I find I must call attention to certain matters.

Development and Liberation

First of all, the word "development" has been rapidly devalued as a result of abuses done in its name. Indeed, it becomes more and more obviously true that "development aid" for the establishment of industries or even "development funding" results in chaining the underdeveloped peoples to foreign economies and integrating them into alienating systems and structures. Prescinding from the question of good or bad will, these systems effectively concentrate wealth and brain power to the detriment of underdeveloped countries.

In this respect, use of the expression "developing countries" is hypocritical and false. For the situation in these countries is not getting better but is worsening in many ways. The process is inexorable for the following reasons especially:

a) Exports from the underdeveloped countries (90 percent raw materials) are constantly decreasing, and exports from the developed countries (64 percent products of industry) are constantly increasing. Brazil is a classic example: in 1937 she had to export 14 sacks of coffee in order to import one automobile; in 1967, she had to export 40. Economists from the UN and CEPAL acknowledged that this so-called economic model of the underdeveloped countries ("primary exporter type" as they call it) is achieving underdevelopment rather than development.

b) Capital exported by the wealthy countries does not remedy this situation. Private investments, which do have the advantage of providing work, have a twofold drawback. First, they seek maximum results in a minimum of time, in accordance with the law of profit which is one of capitalism's incentives. Private investments thus unbalance the economy in the countries where they have taken root. Secondly and above all, what comes out of the underdeveloped countries is ultimately more consequential than what goes in. From 1951 to 1961, according the UN conference report on Trade and Development (Geneva 1964), the value of foreign capital invested in Latin America was 9.5 billion dollars, but the profit return to the investors outside Latin America was 13.4 billion—or a 3.8 billion dollar loss to the underdeveloped countries.

c) Development aid in the form of gifts or loans constitutes a more favorable contribution. But it is insufficient. As has long been pointed out, the developed countries ought to devote 1 percent of their revenue to such aid. Paul VI has reiterated it several times since 1963, but such aid is far from that percentage. And what is worse, it has even diminished if we evaluate it in real, and not nominal or monetary terms.

In addition, the same economic determinism is dissipating internal capital in the underdeveloped countries. From 1946 to 1962, 5.4 billion dollars were sent abroad by the great indigenous wealthy families of Latin America. And that capital did not in any way depend on outside trade. It originated, like its exporters, in the underdeveloped countries.

Even if we prescind from this clandestine dollar drain, the loan balance is negative. From 1951 to 1961, for instance, the United States exported $2,900,000,000 in investments and $3,384,000,000 in gifts and loans, making a total of $6,284,000,000 in capital for various enterprises. During this time, however, $6,875,000,000 were returned to the U.S. in earnings and $1,554,000,000 in loan reimbursements, interest payments, and royalties; a total of $8,329,000,000, which is a net loss of more than $2 billion dollars for Latin America. Paradoxically, the underdeveloped countries are exporters of capital to the developed nations!

We are touching here on the phenomenon of concentration, the law of the system, which causes a good number of students from the Third World to settle in the developed countries (not only in North America but also in Europe) for their training, as a result of aid given to these countries. Here again, aid translates as a hemorrhage on the one hand and a concentration of assets on the other.

People sometimes counter these findings with an undeniable fact: production indexes are increasing, therefore the underdeveloped countries are, albeit insufficiently, in a process of developing.

This conclusion calls for reservations on many accounts:

The rate of absolute growth of the underdeveloped countries must be tallied with the rate of their population growth. For all these countries taken together, the population rate was 2.3 percent on the average between 1950 and 1967. For this period then, the growth index is not 4.8 percent (according to the most favorable calculations), but 4.8 percent less 2.3 percent, or 2.5 percent. This is infinitesimal for a period of 18 years. Furthermore, this seemingly positive note is neutralized and even reversed by the phenomena mentioned above.

But the deterioration is due especially to the dependence resulting from the establishment of development processes that are introduced by outside assistance.

On the most material level, the external public debt of the underdeveloped countries reached the height of 45.7 billion dollars (exactly $45,742,000,000) by June 30, 1968. The payments made by these countries, on the grounds of what has been called "service of the debt," are constantly on the rise: from $2,314,000,000 in 1961 to $4,018,000,000 in 1968. Today, two-thirds of public aid are used to reimburse back payments. Such indebtedness is alienating.

In this respect, the *under*developed countries today are not in the situation of the *un*developed nations. The latter have developed within their own context, and in accordance with their own laws, not under the onus and direction of others.

Let us add that the interest rates have risen constantly: from 3 percent in 1964 to 3.1 percent in 1965, and 3.3 percent in 1968;

and the repayment time lessened from 28.4 years to 24.8 years during that same three-year period.

Finally, there are strings attached to this aid. For example: 80 percent of the monies exported as loans and gifts to the countries of Latin America have to be spent in the United States for purchases whose nature and price are stipulated by contract so as to make possible the disposal of surplus goods by the U.S. In this context, "aid to underdeveloped countries" is manifestly an aid in overcoming the financial and commercial crises of the developed capitalist countries. It is accomplished by disposing of surplus goods in accordance with economic regulators that do not always correspond to real needs. And it explans the remark of Dom Helder Camara in a conference he gave in the United States: "We do not want your help, we want your justice."

It also explains other significant facts: Brazil made the best strides in her economic growth at a time when foreign aid was less: 1950–54, when the participation of foreign capital in the total investment was barely 8.2 percent and 1955–56 when foreign capital was only 2 percent. China, deprived of foreign aid and in the throes of enormous internal difficulties, has nevertheless achieved a growth rate that is far higher than that of Latin America. And thanks to a consciously organized "insular" situation, Japan began the development which brought her to a state analogous to that of England, the pilot country in economic development in the nineteenth century.

We can understand why the underdeveloped countries are countries in a bind since they are dependent on ideas of development that originated abroad and are foreign to their aspirations, to their own culture, and often to their needs. And they are satellized by the rich countries. Robert MacNamara, former U.S. Secretary of Defense, noted that "25 percent of the population of the world holds 75 percent of the world's wealth." This disproportion has in no way lessened since his statement; the gap has widened between the mean standard of living in North America or Europe and that in India or Brazil.

Development, as it has been realized so far, is concentrating wealth and brainpower in a kind of a metropolis-satellite structure which is profitable for the metropolis but deadly for the satellite. In this respect, underdevelopment manifests itself as a by-product of development.

This is why the expression "Third World" is more and more untenable, for the underdeveloped world does not have the reality of a "third world" between that of capitalism and socialism. It has no autonomous existence. It is satellized in one world or the other. It is the fringe and the more or less enslaved periphery of the developed world.

But that is not all: this metropolis-satellite structure tends to reproduce itself in accordance with the same economic laws and in all echelons within the underdeveloped countries themselves. Rich and developed areas empty and colonialize the others. In Brazil the South is impoverishing the North as Professor Duarte Lago Pacheco of São Paulo University pointed out:

> It is erroneous to say, as people say here: São Paulo is a locomotive pulling twenty empty cars (the twenty states of Brazil). If São Paulo is a locomotive, this locomotive is fed by the twenty cars that come after it, and they are the ones transporting the coal to feed the locomotive.
>
> This phenomenon of internal colonialism is intimately connected with external colonialism of which it is merely the projection: the colonialism of São Paulo over the northeast is in fact that of the great American or European firms found there: Ford, Volkswagen, Philips of Brazil, etc.

In fact, the development in process today in Brazil (at a rate which in certain respects is happily being accelerated) involves only 30 percent of the population. The rest of the people are marginalized and held in subjection by the dictatorial police-state regime. Their destitution is growing, and the death rate is accelerating. To speak of "development" in this particular "world" is laughable.

It is important to recall (and to publish) these analyses which are not in the French edition, *Développement et salut,* because I had already made them a few months earlier in a book called *L'Amérique latine à l'heure de l'enfantement.*

This reminder is necessary as background and also to explain the crisis in vocabulary.

Just as the word "charity," which was used to denote individual help given to the destitute in the nineteenth century, has come to ring false because it stood for a kind of almsgiving that was just enough to maintain destitution—the breeding-place of revolt—so also has the word "development" harbored false hopes, and neutralized the forces that mobilize the people. It has not only slowed down the processes of necessary liberation, but it has strengthened alienations.

Certainly, more often than not, the intentions were good, but the fact is that they were ineffective and even counterproductive; i.e., producing the contrary effect, or *controproducenti,* to use the expressive Italo-Spanish word.

The word "development" today is being increasingly replaced by the word "liberation," for the basic reason that liberation from the system that maintains underdevelopment is the prerequisite if there is to be any development at all.

This idea of liberation offers another advantage. It reflects a very rich biblical notion. God is the liberator of Israel, the *Goel,* to use the Hebrew expression (Isaiah 43:14; 44:6, 24; 47:4; *cf.* Jeremiah 50:34). According to the old Hebrew law this term stood for the close relative who had the right to defend his family, either to save the family's threatened patrimony (Leviticus 25:23 *ff.*), or to liberate a "brother" who had fallen into slavery (Leviticus 25:46–49). The term therefore implies the assertion of a bond of kinship between Yahweh and Israel, by reason of the covenant. God revealed himself in the human event that liberated Israel from a state of bondage to other men. He is, more radically, the liberator from sin, through his death. But two things cannot be forgotten: sin is the opposite of charity and justice. Liberation from sin requires the abolition of human situations of injustice and oppression, according to the theology of the prophets themselves whose words take on very pointed meaning in the reality of the underdeveloped peoples of today:

> I will rejoice in Jerusalem,
>   and be glad in my people;
> no more shall be heard in it the sound of weeping
>   and the cry of distress.
> No more shall there be in it,
>   an infant that lives but a few days,
>   or an old man that does not fill out his days, . . .
> They shall not build and another inhabit;
>   they shall not plant and another eat. . . .
> They shall not labor in vain,
>   or bear children for calamity, . . .
> While they are yet speaking, I will hear . . .
>
> (Isaiah 65:19–24)

Liberation will not be brought on stage *Deus ex machina* fashion, but through the action of human freedoms enlightened by the ra-

tionality of the intelligence and immersed in the realism of a political policy. Liberation cannot be realized without struggle and contradiction—a struggle for the sake of justice and love to establish the
very inner life of human realities. Today, as in the time of Abraham
or the exodus, it is in the inner working of a human plan that God
can reveal himself among men.

I should therefore be tempted today to rewrite the present book
published under the French title *Développement et Salut* (Development and Salvation) and replace the first word by *Liberation*.

But this would then be a different book. And it would be a shame
to sacrifice the word "development."

The word is still irreplaceable. In the full sense given it by Paul
VI (whose misunderstood demands are made plain throughout this
book) it remains valid and unassailable.

Moreover, the word "liberation," which is used so frenetically
and ambiguously today, is also threatened with the devaluation at-
tendant on other misuses of language. If liberation is used as a drawing-room slogan or as the by-word of an armchair theologian, like
development it becomes a hoax. It gives the illusion that the word
itself is enough to destroy the systems and forces of oppression in
order to solve the problem. What has to be done, actually, is to con-
struct and invent better forms. Furthermore, a purely anarchical
notion of the word "liberation" without any viable development
project would merely reinforce the established disorder. The worst
kinds of dictatorship have a good case for claiming to be guarantors of
order when faced with actions that are impotent and chaotic.

If we wish to avoid these new devaluations, let us be careful about
the limits and the full sense of the word "liberation."

First of all, liberation is a first step, a stage. What is important
is to see in advance what will be done with liberty, and to effect a
human development worthy of the name. Freedom is not an absolute. Every freedom is limited in many ways—by the freedom of
others, by the internal necessities of each being who must become
responsible for himself, by the demands of discipline and toil. Freedom evolves in the midst of tensions and contradictions inherent in
every human development (R. Colin, "Contradiction et développement," in *Développement et civilisations*, no. 39-40, March-June
1970, pp. 2-3).

If the word "liberation" were touted unconditionally without
serious analysis and without a political policy worthy of the name, it

would merely specify a destructive power and catalyze massive opposition against it. Anarchy plays into the hands of reaction.

True liberation ought not only to destroy oppressive forces and structures, but also to generate viable structures of freedom, creativity, and communication. In these matters, many socialist regimes have not succeeded in creating original structures. Instead they have pirated hierarchical and bureaucratic processes from capitalism.

Liberation must be realized on all levels: economic, political, cultural, and human. It requires exacting reflection on all these levels.

It must be a radical liberation from the sin which is at the root of evil. Without this regeneration from sin through the love *(agape)* which God reveals, there will be no genuine fellowship among men.

Insistence upon the word "liberation," then, concretizes and reevaluates the sense of the word "salvation." This change in emphasis is an invitation also to underline two themes asserted in this book: the necessity for analyses of the situation and the necessity for commitments in the political order. Thinking along these lines is today promoting reflection on the theology of revolution; i.e., on the value of the Gospel as a principle of active renewal of meaning and with the conversions and breakthroughs that implies (J. Comblin, *Théologie de la révolution*, Paris: 1970).

Development, a Cultural Problem

I also feel the need today to stress what has been said about the *cultural* aspect of development (especially, pp. 170–173). My trip to Asia has since confirmed for me the essential importance of this factor.

—Development is intrinsically connected with culture and must come about in authenticity. What so impressed me in Japan is the adventure of a people that have brought about their development by remaining faithful to their own culture. This is one of the keys to success.

—Negatively, and in a more general way, we can notice increasingly the rise everywhere of military wars, the more radical economic wars and especially the cultural wars which are developing instinctively and by chance (between the USSR and China whose cultures are irremediably at loggerheads despite common ideology and concerns, and between China and Tibet, between North America and Latin America, between England and Hong Kong and other territories where we find an artificial subculture being exported). I shall not develop this problem since I have treated it elsewhere, in the conclusion of my *Flashes sur l'Extrême-Orient.*

Illich correctly sensed the necessity for developing a Latin American culture. He denounced the alienation produced by the export of foreign models, on the level of the schools and universities, as well as economic and religious realities. Will people understand what he means?

Theology of the Future and of Hope

Finally, this study on development has led me to weigh the importance of a "theology of the future" and of hope in the manner of Jürgen Moltmann. It is superfluous to stress this in the Preface to an American edition since this is one of the dominant currents in theology in the United States. It is even more important than the theology of "secularization" which in some way provides the negative side of the problem. Certainly, man in search of liberation cannot rid himself of his past, with which he makes his future in a necessary continuity. He cannot forget revelation. But salvation is not a return to the past, it is a flight forward. It is the construction of a world of justice and human fellowship in which God can dwell in the heart of relations between men.

God is not yet the God who is "all in all things." Mankind must become the "place" where he is fulfilled in the world. This is the mission of human freedom. Christian hope is not scorn for the world, nor an escape into another world. It sets the seeds and establishes the roots of that world to come which is to be revealed on the last day; the world of love. Thus hope has earthly roots. It is connected less with man's dreams than with his action.

In speaking in this way about what has to be done, we touch on one of the limits of this book. Its purpose is to show the importance and the interest of development, its situation in relationship to the Gospel, to the Church, and to the world in order to clarify the meaning of the values concerned. But this theoretical introduction does not dispense anyone from learning the techniques and the political options relevant to the particular area in which his responsibilities lie.

In this period of reconversion, the connections between theory and praxis are in crisis. More and more, people understand the inadequacy and often the deceptiveness of a purely abstract theology, which would be an intellectual alibi on the margin of any plan of salvation.

This excessive trust in language and the misuse of language (which people thought actually effected the "good" it spoke about) have given rise to very radical reactions. A number of Christians who face the problems of "liberation and development" are allergic to any theological language.

The first group, of theoreticians, is involved in a criticism of the structures which are at present paralyzing the upward thrust of culture and development. That includes the structures of the Church, implicated as she is in the present system of economic and political power, language, and thought, which leads to alienation. Their theology is purely critical; it is or seems to be purely destructive and negative.

This stress on criticism is partly unavoidable today, and is due to the following situation: the preeminent theological "place" is the life of the Church in which the Holy Spirit vivifies Christ and his Gospel. When dealing with development, the life of the contemporary Church often presents internal contradictions between *intention* and reality; between the aspirations for justice and an integration within the oppressive forces of this world to which the Church has sociological, financial, political, and diplomatic ties. Often in the Church the mystique of liberation remains on the level of abstract language, while outside the Church among men of good will, we find a dynamism which comes from the liberating power of the Gospel. It is in this way that the theology of the life of the Church is today necessarily a critical theology. But let us not remain at that stage! Criticism is easy, but art is difficult. It is the practice of development and faith that must be promoted in a positive way.

A second group senses the same difficulties but on the level of action. Often, they find themselves swept up in a revolutionary process, for the following reasons: in the circles in which they are involved they note that their good intentions are powerless. Even if they are neutral, even if they do good, even if they negotiate with the powers of this world for the defense of the poor who are dying from under-development, they are still interdependent on the structures that maintain antidevelopment. Indeed they contribute to their maintenance—in Latin America particularly. A number of them move on to Marxism because in it they see a force which is not implicated in the system that must be left behind. They find in Marxism not only the support and the solidarities necessary for any action (a support which they sought elsewhere in vain), but also an instrument of political analysis external to the oppressing system, as well as the sense of an effective plan of action. For this reason, they commit their faith in the liberation of men and their thirst for salvation, although not without deviation.

The courageous reflection of the former and the courageous action of the latter, both born out of evangelical conviction, call for respect and understanding. May both groups be strong enough in their faith to preserve in this night through which we are passing at present, the deep bond with Christ and the Spirit. May they thereby rise above the ambiguities or deviations in which they may find themselves.

May it also be possible for men who maintain above all else their fidelity to the visible Church to go beyond those ambiguities, compromises, or deviations in which the Church herself may be implicated in order to contribute to the promotion of a genuine liberation and a real development, no matter what the cost.

The burst of faith which is smothered under the injustices of present-day society will not be something merely verbal. Words will take on meaning only in a plan that is *lived*. Hence the importance of a "theology of the future," which will be a theology in *praxis*. One of the concerns of this theology will be to discern the appearance of valid models whose diffusion would work wonders for the present situation and catalyze the emergence of methods worthy of the name. Is not the present crisis in the Church both a crisis of meaning (i.e. of faith) and of method?

R.L.

LIBERATION
DEVELOPMENT
& SALVATION

INTRODUCTION

This book was born of a grave problem in Latin American life. In April 1968 the Mexican Theological Society asked me to chair a session that was aimed at preparing a national congress on the theme: Development and Salvation. The central question was well put: Does development have any significance in relation to salvation as proclaimed by Christ?

I should certainly have refused such a vast subject had I been able to resist the forceful persuasion of my Mexican friends.

For one thing, I am not an economist and I felt overwhelmed by economics, this basic aspect of the problem. Was such a demand not inspired by a mistaken confidence in theology's capacity of treating *de omni re scibili?* Has theology not remained sterile when it set out to deal with the social order from abstract principles? For another thing, isn't approaching these problems "from on high," so to speak, a method contrary to nature? Trees grow up from their roots, or, to quote one Christian woman's declaration: "Pots boil from the bottom up, not from their cover down, even if the cover is a miter." A letter from Roland Colin, director of IRFED, confirmed for me the validity of this objection from his own experience: "Theology and development cannot meet on the theoretical plane; or, at least, a purely theoretical encounter is not very meaningful for men concerned with development."

In addition, a wall seems to have been raised for the theologian on his own territory. Christ spoke of *salvation,* but never mentioned a

3

word about *development*. Not only did he avoid the question; but he seemed to say we should not be concerned with it: "Look at the birds of the air: they neither sow nor reap nor gather into barns, and yet your heavenly Father feeds them" (Matthew 6:25–34; Luke 12:22–31).

At a time when certain people are reproaching the Church for whoring with the world, this question might seem to be merely a secularist mirage, or else the Trojan horse of those who would like to breach the defenses and reduce theology to the human sciences and politics. Can we even speak of a "development theology"?

However, some reflection on this essential question proved stimulating and fruitful within the context of the basic concerns of our time: stopping the deadly injustice of underdevelopment, promoting development in a unified world, reestablishing the unity of love of God and love of men, the unity between theology and life, and setting up contacts between the Church and the world in accordance with the blueprints drawn up by John XXIII and the Council.

The reception given the first part of this present study, on July 24–25 in Querétaro, Mexico, was both encouraging and rewarding, as were the contacts I had with Father A. Lesort, who invited me in his discerning way to resume the study and branch out from what was a purely Mexican perspective. So was my consultation with specialists in a field which in many respects was new for me: they were chiefly Roland Colin and V. Cosmao of IRFED; F. Bezi, M. Chaumont, and A. Lecointre from the Institute for Developing Countries (University of Louvain), Father Houée, director of ISSEO at the University of Angers, Father de la Chapelle, assistant secretary of Justitia et Pax; and J. Canal, and Dr. Anne Retel (who had been entrusted with the health survey in Senegal in 1958 by Lebret). And among the theologians, I must mention H. Cazelles, Father Chenu, Father Mérimée, and André Laurentin. I also learned much from my conversations with Bishop Delhaye at the Louvain Colloquium (November 1968). These contacts brought out an obvious fact: the theological "place" of development is the very life of the Church.

This study, then, begins with a fact of the present day: the development movement. It will then consider the issue both linguistically and fundamentally. It will consult Scripture, tradition, and the magisterium and will finally attempt an answer to these questions: In what way does development affect men's salvation in Jesus Christ? Why must Christians become involved?

Part One

The Church as

A Living Community

DEVELOPMENT—
A POSTCONCILIAR
MOVEMENT

1

No one spoke of the "development[1] of peoples" in the Church before the last war. And for the decade immediately afterwards this problem was of concern to only a few specialists among Christians. But today it is one of the most frequent if not one of the most fundamental themes of teaching and Christian action, in all levels of society, from the grassroots on up.

The Life of the Church as a Theological Locus

Our investigation will start out from this new fact, for the life of the Church is the *locus* of any sound theology.

It is out of the life of the early communities and for them that the whole theology of the New Testament was born: the Epistles, obviously; Revelation, addressed to the Seven Churches; and the Gospels which were born out of the communities' memory in order to evolve a catechesis. The same is true for the theology of antiquity: letters, homilies, apologetical essays all originated in the life of the community, as explanations and defenses of the churches. I do not mean that life, looked upon in its subjectivity, is the source of doctrine. That source is the Word of God. But this word was entrusted to the Church: *ecclesia* (etymologically, "the assembly"), in order that it might be lived within it. It is in her life and her memory that the

7

word is preserved in words and actions, and the actions go beyond
words. This is how she lives, survives, is rejuvenated by the Holy
Spirit, and, in accordance with the needs of the times and of history,
develops. For theology itself is subject to development. Newman
proved this against the rigidities that ruled in his time.

We may seem to be off the track by mentioning dogmatic development at the beginning of a book whose object is basically economic
development. However, the two concepts are not strangers to one another, since doctrinal development is bound up with the pace of cultural development. And we shall be led to a study of this correlation.

For the moment, I merely wish to point out the two aspects of
this idea and to avoid any ambiguity: where I use the word "development" without modifier, I am referring to the second phenomenon:
human development whose most obvious and most studied incentive
is economic growth.

Since development is not an abstract notion or the object of a
revelation from on high, but rather a dynamic and earthly process,
any theological discussion of it and even what the magisterium has to
say only have meaning if they are relevant to the life situation. And
this is a crucial reason for starting out from this point.

Development in the Life of the Postconciliar Church

For the course of our investigation and for clarity's sake, it seems best
to consider first of all the Roman Catholic Church. Such a course will
seem narrow and clerical to many readers, but we shall find ourselves
going beyond this starting point rather quickly. Indeed, development
has become of prime importance in the life of the postconciliar
Church.

The fifty-fourth Semaine sociale de France (July 11-16, 1967) was
devoted to this theme.[2] The same was true for the Sixth World Congress of Catholic Jurists (Dakar, December 5-11: *Le Monde,* December 7 and 15-16; *La Croix,* December 11). Development was the subject of one of the longest and most publicized resolutions at the Congress of the Laity in Rome in October 1967.[3] In 1961, the University
of Louvain founded an Institute for the Study of Developing Countries which initiated a colloquy of the International Federation of
Catholic Universities that met in Paris on October 4-5, 1968; in
November 1968, it launched the review *Culture et Développement.*[4]

The Gregorian University, whose Institute of Social Sciences has a "development section" (section 3) has just created a study center on this same subject, within the framework of the theology faculty.[5] At the Catholic University of Angers, ISSEO (Institut des sciences sociales économiques de l'Ouest) was founded to serve the development of that region of France which had been neglected because of its remote location in the European "Far West."

Recent years have seen, on the grass-roots level, a multiplication of group fasts for the benefit of the Third World. In Germany, Adveniat, which organizes these actions, collects considerable sums each year. This is quite a meaningful thing in a country where Hitler had instituted collective frugal meals in order to develop armaments. The Christians have reconverted this custom to serve peace. The communitarian impulse that had been corralled into the service of the will for power has become redirected into gifts of self for the service of mankind.

Adveniat, founded in 1961, and Caritas Internationalis, founded in 1950 (it coordinates 84 national committees), have been brought into CIDSE (Cooperation Internationale pour le Développement socio-economique), established on July 18, 1968 at Rome. It federates Christian organizations whose purpose is to help the Third World.[6] The financial capacity of this federation comes close to that of the largest international organizations. Its aim is expressed in its statutes:

1. To study the ways and means of promoting cooperation in aid for socioeconomic development, etc.
2. To promote the creation of new development aid organizations, etc.
3. To give them technical assistance on demand.

A number of religious orders, the Jesuits for example,[7] have set up development assistance organizations. Twenty-one of them are federated in SEDOS (Servizio di Documentazione e Studi, Via dei Verbiti, 1, Rome). They had their first congress in March 1969. About the same time, a round table of all Catholic organizations was projected, not as a reenforcement for "confessionalization" but in order better to coordinate their services to the underdeveloped countries.

A list of all the organizations of this type throughout the world was drawn up by the OCDE.[8] It has fourteen hundred pages and lists thousands of Christian institutions. Obviously such a catalogue puts all organizations on the same level, the outstanding and the incidental, the good and the mediocre, the effective and the illusory, and even the harmful, but wheat always grows mixed in with the weeds.

NONRELIGIOUS INVOLVEMENT IN DEVELOPMENT

What is actually happening far surpasses what can ever be catalogued. The idea of development produces vocations of new and varied kinds which do not lend themselves to statistics. As a matter of fact, many Christians are involved in these nonreligious organizations. Their involvement is in the spirit of service and not of infiltration. More and more, since the Council, people understand that the Church must not control everything, that she must be a servant and be poor. Other people are inventing new methods and formulas that no longer have any particular religious tag. IRAM (Institute of Research and Application of Development Methods)[9] is a case in point. It sets up "enthusiasm"-teams in agricultural areas, serving the development policy proper to each country of the Third World, with a concern for stimulating from within the possibilities inherent in "local cultures" in every sense of that term. CINAM (Society for Industrial Studies and Territorial Adjustment) which originated within the sphere of influence of Economie et Humanisme, is working in the same spirit. Similar instances are those of the International Center for Rural Development and the Inter-African Cooperative for Development. The latter is of African foundation (Togo, Dahomey, and the Cameroons) and was initiated by a former Young Christian Worker from Togo. He, Bernard Akapo, is young and capable and has refused cabinet posts in order to keep to his own work with freedom in regard to official or international organizations. Whatever the price for that freedom, what is important to him is that concerned people take charge of their own development in agriculture, fishing, and crafts.

THE HIERARCHY AND DEVELOPMENT

The Church's hierarchy has taken up this concern not only officially but efficaciously. This is something new. Of course the Church has had her "poor" and took care of them through her "good works." But each day those "good works" became more obsolete. Ultimately their function seems to have been the easing of Christian consciences without solving the problems of the poor. A new concept of charity became urgent, since it was discredited by such debasement. Today the Church is committed to a new attitude. There is no longer any question merely of gifts and ecclesiastical organizations destined to assist individuals, families, or small groups.[10] The basic objective is to modify the structures that keep the poor poor. With this in view, many bishops' conferences have stimulated Catholics' participation in this collective movement. Yet it was well after many others in Latin America and Europe had done so that the bishops' conferences of Holland and the United States prepared documents on this theme, in 1969.

DEVELOPMENT IN LATIN AMERICA

In Latin America this movement has come to the forefront and has brought about an institutional metamorphosis.

It is here that a new method of doing things was born and has proliferated: the giving—or sale at a nominal price—of church lands so that development programs can be realized.[11] Problems have cropped up since this method has diminished the wealth of the ecclesiastical institution. What was more, the income from such properties had been supporting useful social endeavors, and until now it has been a principle of good management that every institution depended upon capital and lived off the income from it.

At times Church authorities go still further. They sacrifice church structures—their repair, embellishment, or even construction —in favor of development projects. Bishop Dammert Bellido of Cajamarca in Peru, one of the prelates who have made this choice, explained this in a letter to Senator R. Puga, who had offered to give him a credit of $37,000 for the restoration of his cathedral.[12]

> I have other preferences. There is a priority for certain works of mercy that require an immediate solution . . . a prison (the one at present is a pig-sty); the canalization of the San Lucas River which, with its black water, is infecting the people; keeping the new hospital going and modernizing the old one. . . .
> It is very outstanding and noble of you to be concerned about the restoration of my cathedral, the spiritual center of the diocese, but Christians, according to St. Paul, are also the temples of the Holy Spirit, and when it comes to doing works of mercy, visiting the sick, or receiving the complaints of the prisoners . . . we must not falter.

The example was followed in Holland, quite creatively, with the Carmelites deciding to stop the beatification of one of their members,

in order to give the money they saved to "Third World development." The sum was computed at some $90,000.[13]

Does this imply a turning away from the sacred? Or is it rather a
reconverting to the sacred? Is it horizontalism? Is it not rather a reaction against the myth that puts God far up in the sky and removed
from men—in order better to situate him among men, within the interpersonal relationships that are developing right there among them?
This movement is characterized by a transition from an ethic of do-
goodism to an ethic of participation, of true paternalism in the service
of men valued for themselves, and as responsible signs of the Incarnate
Word (Matthew 25:34-46).

The movement also brings the Church into a context of realism
and solidarity which is very well expressed by the reaction of Latin
American militants[14] to a European manifesto on the position of a
Christian "toward capitalism, Marxism, and the Third World":
"Where are these people who drew up the manifesto, since they
merely confront the phenomena of their time and don't involve
themselves from within?"

It was in Latin America, on August 24, 1968, that Paul VI officially approved those disputed activities that were seemingly "impoverishing the Church":

> We are informed of the generous gestures made in certain
> dioceses which have put at the disposal of needy peoples the land
> which they still controlled, *in accordance with* well-thought-out
> plans for agrarian reform. . . . This is an example that deserves
> to be praised and even imitated wherever it is prudent and pos-
> sible (DC. Sept. 11, 1968, No. 1524, col. 1527).

Throughout the continent, organizations for study and implementa-
tion of development have been founded. After pioneer initiatives in
Colombia (Sustatenza and Fe y Alegría), we find in particular:

ILADES (Latin American Institute for Economic and Social Development) and DESAL (Economic and Social Development for Latin
America), founded by Father Vekemans in Santiago de Chile.

IEPAL (Institute of Study for Latin America) and the Centro
Fabro of the Jesuits in Montevideo.

ICODES (Colombian Economic and Social Institute), founded
in 1964 by the Rev. Gustavo Pérez, and IDES (Institute of Social Doctrine and Study) at Bogotá.

ESRAD (Center for Socio-Religious Statistics and Studies Applied to Development), founded August 24, 1967 in Ecuador.

CIAS (Center for Investigation and Social Action), founded by the Jesuits in Buenos Aires.[15] It gave rise to the formation of centers with the same name in the large cities of the continent—Bogotá, Quito, and Caracas, principally. The object of these centers is not only the publication of magazines and books, but any activity which prepares the way for development in all areas.[16]

To this we should add the social action department of CELAM,[17] and the national commissions set up by the bishops' conferences in each country, as well as the local commissions connected with the Roman commission on Justice and Peace.[18]

On March 28, 1968, the Mexican episcopate wrote a pastoral letter on development for the first anniversary of the encyclical *Populorum progressio*. The Mexican theological society gave substance to this text by organizing a national congress on the same theme. Held from July 12 to July 14, the congress was not limited to four days of speeches, for the theme involved a praxis, and before that a conversion. This is why seven months went into its preparation—of the documentary research, publication of basic works, interviews with many different people, distribution of a bulletin, preparatory regional sessions. The congress was thus able to realize its threefold objective:

Analysis of the situation and awakening of consciences;
Prophecy: that is, the interpretation to and in Mexico of the fact of development at this particular moment of her history, in the light of God's plan of salvation;
Finally: conversion to this fact of development.

The objective is to create on a countrywide scale, far beyond the jurisdiction of the Church and yet with a certain religious prudence, a movement promoting coherent development suitable for the whole of Mexico.[19]

In April 1968 at São Paulo, the Christian Family Movement held a symposium of experts on Family and Development. Father Comblin of Recife, one of the theologians most involved in the problem,[20] was a major participant.

In May 1967, the Brazilian episcopate worked out a basic document on this question[21] and Dom Helder Camara launched a movement for all of Latin America which he first called "a movement of

liberating moral pressure," and then, "Action, Progress, and Peace";
its axis is development, beginning with the formation of consciences
which is its necessary root.[22] The Eucharistic Congress at Bogotá
centered on the theme of feeding men. One entire day, presided over
by the pope himself, was devoted to development (August 23, 1968).[23]

As the Medellín assembly drew near (August 25-September 8,
1968), groups of priests and laity multiplied statements[24] on this subject: documents that were often committed and energetic. For example, the directors[25] representing five million unionists wrote:

> What is lacking in Latin America is a prior social revolution
> that can create objective and subjective conditions for a full de-
> velopment of our people and a definitive liberation of the Latin
> American man.

The Medellín assembly gave this theme a central place. It was the
crucial point of the working document.[26] And supported by Paul VI's
discourse[27] at Bogotá, it remained so in the final conclusions. The
assembly's program was even formulated as the "Presence of the
Church in the present-day transformation of Latin America." And its
objective was "the promotion of men and the continent toward values
of justice, peace, and conjugal love." The preliminary statement,
from which we extract the following keynote, is specifically focused on
development,[28] which is called, in terms inspired by the Bible, a new
Easter. (The quoted words were used by the pope in his closing
address to the Council.):

> Just as Israel, the ancient people, felt God's salvific presence
> in the past when he freed them from bondage in Egypt, when he
> led them across the sea and brought them to the conquest of the
> land, so we too, the new people of God, cannot fail to sense his
> saving presence when we are dealing with "a true development
> that is the passing of each one of us from inhuman life conditions
> to more human conditions."

Six of the sixteen documents of Medellín are devoted to that theme.
And that theme permeates the others.

Even the bishops of Colombia, who represent the bastion of organized conservatism in Latin America, and who dissociated themselves from the conclusions of Medellín, felt the need to commit themselves on this point[29] and ask for a "profound structural change."

A more significant fact, since it is found at the grass-roots level,
among the youth, is this: the Latin American students (who are leav-

ing the Church or—now—may even be born outside the Church) are manifesting a concern for development and thereby for the Church. The school chaplains whom I met in Latin America had taken to this new phenomenon; nevertheless another fact has neutralized it. The many warnings Paul VI gave at Bogotá against revolution and violence produced the feeling that the way opened by the Church risks being a blind alley. Obviously the Latin American students did not ask the pope to canonize violence, but their twofold disappointment is due to this: that he did not denounce, as such, the institutionalized violence, so obvious to their eyes, and that instead, in addressing the poor, he censured any violent action aimed at liberating them. Will the more subtle conclusions of the Medellín assembly be enough to show to what extent the ways to a solution still lie open? It would be premature to give a firm answer to this question.

A Genuine Movement

The action for development has the characteristics of a movement: a collective spontaneous impulse that is both convergent and sustained and originates in an imperative historical necessity. This postconciliar movement shows traits analogous to the preconciliar movements at whose confluence was located the very springboard for the ecclesiological, biblical, liturgical, missionary, and ecumenical movements of Vatican II.[30] The appearance of those currents, brought about by the protracted need to compensate for the excesses of the Counter-Reformation, was at first quite disconcerting at a time when the Church gave the appearance of a timeless and changeless monolith in which there was no room for movements and even less for those of the grass-roots variety.

But the Council took note of the phenomena. It identified their origin in the Holy Spirit who, since the first Pentecost, has created the necessary historical conversions, beginning with the transition from the regime of the law to the regime of grace, from the Judeo-Christian communities to the evangelization of the nations. The Church is placed in history to serve a mankind in evolution. It is normal therefore that she experience new values and needs from within, that she react like every living being to situations that arise both from within and from without. Let us be specific. The action

of the Holy Spirit is not an intervention from without, but something
from within the body of Christ, within the freedoms it awakens to
their own life and their own initiative. This action is even less a new
revelation, for revelation was completed at the end of apostolic times.
It stimulates and develops powers that had been neglected or become
dormant.

Like the preconciliar movements, the postconciliar movement
for development is characterized by a return to poorly understood
sources in order to understand how to meet new needs.

These are the needs of a world torn apart, a world thrown off
balance by fatally unjust inequities, but a world that is still the bearer
of a grand plan and at the summit of cosmic creation. This imbalance
is therefore less an illness than it is a difficult growing-up. A unified,
accelerated world has become aware of its unity, of the urgent need to
build itself up materially and culturally. More precisely, it is faced
with an inescapable alternative: to build itself up or be destroyed; to
grow in the direction of the explosion and human disintegration of
which the atom bomb is the symbol, or else to grow in accordance
with the measured combustion of human warmth in which the values
of justice and love among men unfold. The movement was also produced from within by the hazily felt need for the Church to emerge
from her aggressive isolation toward earthly and secular realities, and
to get away from her hermetic alibi of "sacred" for a handful of rites.

Consequently, the sources to which Christians are returning are
two—a renewed perspective of the obligation for charity consistent
with contemporary problems and a revealing look at the cosmic role
of Christ as found in Saint Paul.

Like the preconciliar movements, the postconciliar movement
for development is characterized by a quest that is not without its
gropings and problems—all arising from the relationship between the
Church and the world. We shall return to this point.

Like the preconciliar movements, the postconciliar development
movement is not an isolated thrust. It is part of a whole closely connected with the structure of Vatican II. Its internal connection with
the grass-roots community movements has been studied elsewhere.[31]

The community movement incarnates the basic promise of Vatican II. It is at the core of the dogmatic constitution *Lumen gentium*:
remake the Fellowship Church, the Church as an existing people.

The development movement responds to a second major idea of
Vatican II, a complementary idea evoked by the constitution on the

Church in the Modern World: set up a new relationship with the secular realities. Resituate the Church so that she is no longer in an ivory tower "facing" the contemporary realities of human life but *in the midst of* men in search of salvation and able to assume, to discern, and to animate the world plan from within. It is a fact that grass-roots communities become spontaneously involved in development. It is also a fact that development action takes on communitarian forms, chiefly in matters of rural development.

Like the preconciliar movements, the development movement implies a conversion of mentality. The originators of the biblical movement stopped looking at Holy Scripture as an arsenal for apologetic use. They looked at it for itself and attempted to grasp its original meaning by using all the resources of textual, literary, and historical criticism. Similarly, those involved in the development movement looked at the reality of the world, not as a bloc of forces from which the Church has to maintain a respectable distance, or which she should dominate, but as the creation of God himself: a continual creation in which even today he gives us "life, movement and being" (Acts 17:28), and also "the true light that enlightens every man . . . coming into the world" (John 1:9). There is no longer any question of treating the world of men as a means; we must enter into the world's own purpose—what God evokes from within and for which men are striving. A Christian, even a priest, or a theologian, may no longer stay on his pedestal above the world, with the pretense of being like God, "knowing good and evil" (Genesis 3:5), that is, endowed with an inexhaustible and sovereign knowledge. Rather, a Christian must be within the very core of this creation, humbly seeking.

This is the Christian attitude of people devoted to development. How can we be made to understand this attitude, this conversion? It is all the harder since faith is a living search, not a possessed and ready-made and dominant truth. It does not dazzle with words but is committed to action, to an encounter with men, for the establishment of justice. What is striking with "development" Christians is the unity of their lives. Religion is not something apart, but the very crux of their service for men, the fabric of life. Two letters from laymen involved in development will allow us to better understand this spirit and exigency which are both evangelical and technical:

> There is no longer any question of thinking you're superior to the poor because you're rich, because you're better dressed; the only superiority is loving God and others. . . .

No more question of "having the poor with you." Cutting down on the organizations that presuppose this "having" is a good thing, since we are beginning to look upon love for others in a different way.

Taking part in a development project is not charity. It's a duty in justice and an operation of the intelligence.

The other letter is on more technical ground:

Practical development compels us each day to begin with the heart of reality before we can grasp its meaning, to try to control the course of things, but by first plunging in, since through our effort they are taking the shape of a new destiny. . . .

As the human sciences become integrated in development they make us day after day discover the capital importance of the phenomena of language, of ways of speaking, and on a broader scope, of communication, for a world struggling for the totalization of man's conquests for the service of all men. We are measuring the operational usefulness of developments in linguistics, symbology, and cybernetics. A theology that is receptive to development ought even more forcefully to look into the significance of these phenomena in relation to its own aims.

We see that the frontiers of our investigation, which had been directed toward the movement for development within the life of the Church, have been exceeded. And at the same time we can understand the originality of this postconciliar movement compared with the preconciliar movements which, in differing degrees, remained within the ecclesial sphere. To say that this outcome is a result of the Catholic development movement would still be too narrow and monopolizing. The development movement did not originate in the Catholic Church and it has not spread centripetally as a result of her preaching. She perceived it in the world at large. She joined it. The convergence therefore comes from sensing wider horizons. And it is important to point this out.

A Movement on an Ecumenical Scale

The development movement exists on an ecumenical scale.

In July 1966, this was one of the central themes of the first world conference organized at Geneva by the "Church and Society" department of the World Council of Churches.[32] The spontaneous convergence between the Catholic Ecumenical Council and the World Council of the other Churches has not turned into a rivalry as it had in the past. It has led to close collaboration. The result was the cordial founding of SODEPAX (Joint Committee on Society, Development and Peace). The constitution of this group, which brought together representatives of the World Council and the Catholic Church, was decided upon at the Geneva assembly between July 18 and 20, after several preparatory meetings at Rome in January and in Zagorsk in March 1967. The first official meeting took place at Beirut, April 20–27, 1968, where on the eve of New Delhi,[33] a clear statement was made on the obligations of the developed nations to form a development strategy. The second meeting was held at Rome on May 21–23, 1968.[34] This group was well represented in Uppsala at the Fourth General Assembly of the World Council (July 4 and 20, 1968), where Sections III and IV were devoted to the same problems: Economic and social development, and toward justice and peace in international development.[35]

The report on development is situated explicitly in an extension of what had gone before: from Paul VI's encyclical to the Beirut text. It had the intention of extending and completing the previous reports. It related them to the Uppsala theme: "Behold, I make all things new" (Revelation 21:5; *cf.* A. Wenger, *Upsal le défi du siècle aux Eglises*, Paris: Editions du Centurion, 1968, p. 133).

The report first of all diagnoses our present failure (*ibid.*, p. 134):

> The first decade of development has become the decade of disillusionment. . . . Most of the industrialized countries have tended to reduce the amount of their financial commitments for the welfare of the developing countries. . . . They show repugnance at modifying their trade structures, the structure of their investments and their financial and technical assistance to an extent appropriate to the needs of development in two-thirds of the world. . . . A neo-isolationism is in the process of gaining ground in many countries. All of this is happening in a time when we have the technical ability to eliminate destitution.

The report next (p. 135) clearly states the need for changing the structures which are perpetuating and aggravating the crisis:

> Both the industrialized countries and the developing nations started out their economic cooperation with erroneous ideas. They thought that a simple transfer of capital and technical assistance would automatically give rise to a process of autonomous growth. But effective world-wide development requires that radical structural transformations be worked out on the

levels of the developing nations, the industrialized countries and ultimately in the international economic system. . . . On all three levels, it is necessary to insert a new dynamism of human solidarity and justice into the economic and social processes.

In several developing countries ruling groups are monopolizing national production and diverting for their own profit the resources coming from abroad.

The international economic system is so constructed that financial assistance is often neutralized by the inequitable structures of trade exchange, by the abnormally high returns from private investments and by the burden of repayment of debts.

For their part, the industrialized countries will have to modify their production structures and their investment policy and encourage the adoption of a new international division of labor, with the aim of giving to the countries in debt outlets for their new exports. The assistance is dynamic to the extent . . . that it leads to autonomous growth. . . . This is why, if we favor the industrialized countries devoting at least 1% of their gross national product to helping the developing countries, we think that they must do so within the framework of an equitable system of trade exchange and investments.

Finally, the Uppsala report proposes a development strategy "in permanent collaboration with the Roman Catholic Church." To this effect, it formulates rules of action and strategy, first for the Churches (*ibid.*, pp. 142-43):

Elucidate the biblical view of the unity given by God to mankind . . . and draw from it the concrete consequences for universal human solidarity and the proper administration of the earth's resources. . . .

That each Church devote a part of its regular income for development assistance. . . .

Explore how it is possible to set up international foundations as a result of which gifts and other Church funds would be carefully invested for development.

See to it that all political parties give a place of priority in their programs to development.

Use their influence with the governments of industrialized countries, etc.

The document proposes guidelines for "each Christian":

1. Be aware of . . . the destitution belts and the Christian responsibility concerning economic justice . . .
2. Pray . . .
3. Engage in dialogue . . . form groups devoted to . . . a constructive effort at education and commitment.

4. Insist with the educational authorities upon . . . information on development in school programs.
5. Get involved in community development projects.
6. Make the development question of prime importance in electoral choices and other political commitments.
7. . . . Set aside for development assistance . . . a percentage of one's income, etc.

The report finally asks that theology integrate its effort with the commitment to development, in order to "understand the *meaning* and the goal proposed to the people" (p. 146).

The text thus concludes as it began, because it is *in the name of faith itself* and of the authenticity of the Christian life that the assembly committed itself to this field. One reporter, André Philip, on July 8, 1968 formulated this in biblical terms (Genesis 4:8–10):

> The Holy Spirit calls to us through events, and if we are to respond to the call of the Third World, it is because today God has us by the throat, is shaking us mercilessly, and asking us: "Cain, what have you done with your brother?"

The report reflects the same idea in terms inspired by a remark of Dr. Willem Adolph Visser 't Hooft:

> The Church's vocation is to work for the establishment of a responsible world society and to call men and nations to repentance. To be self-satisfied in the face of the destitution in the world is to be guilty of heresy in the order of behavior.

At a moment when dialogue and negotiation were marking time in the Churches, particularly on matters like intercommunion and mixed marriages, the question, the challenge posed by the urgent needs of a world in crisis, led the Churches to examine more thoroughly their prime responsibilities to face up to a salvation that is to be realized on earth. They were more vividly conscious of this fact at Uppsala.

Development has become one of the privileged areas of ecumenical cooperation, in a mood of necessary and stimulating complementarity. In the discussions of this diverse gathering, one would look in vain for a sign of denominational lines.

What we have noted at the summit of ecumenism, we find also at the base, in many initiatives throughout the world. For example, the joint work of ministers and priests in the vast and wretched suburbs of Buenos Aires publicly aired the question: *Is it possible to evangelize separately when we have accomplished development together?*[36] Ecu-

menical convergence such as this is all the more harmonious since it
is situated on new terrain which has not been encumbered by the
polemics of the Renaissance.

It is the sign of a new stage of action. Preconciliar Catholic movements were aimed at offsetting the inflexibility shown in the past
toward Protestant positions; they were a rediscovery of values that had
been obscured by polemics. Thus, for example, the biblical movement
rediscovered the primary value of Scripture while Protestantism softened the exclusivity of its axiom *Scriptura sola,* against which Catholics
often aligned themselves so unilaterally. In short, there was a *coming
together* on common ground *from opposite attitudes.* In the matter of
development, there is a discovery together of a relatively new area, in
which the various denominations can forget themselves in their service
of others. What is more, the Beirut meeting[37] led to the superseding of
ecumenism itself, which is evident in the conclusion:

> The program should be ecumenical, not in the interest of
> ecumenism itself, but rather . . . [in the interest] of a task to be
> brought to a satisfactory conclusion.

Ecumenism, like the Church, has returned to the evangelical law of the
giving of self: "Do not let your left hand know what your right hand
is doing" (Matthew 6:3). In other words, the donor must accept the
fact that he is a means and not set himself up as an end. The gift is
not destined to enhance the good conscience, glory, and power of the
giver, except in the long run and without his knowledge.

Thus the postconciliar movements show both their convergence
with the preconciliar movements and the disappearance of denominational lines in a new area of activity.

On this level of ecumenism, the changing of attitudes, a characteristic of the movement, differs with different denominations. Unlike
Catholics, Protestants do not need to encounter the realities of the
world, but they do have to specify how these "elements of the world"
are of concern to the Churches today.

What is important is that the conversion is convergent, that it involves us in forward progress along the same road, that it calls for a
restructuring of the Churches; which is explained very well in this
extract from one of the first documents of the joint SODEPAX group
(SDEP Geneva: Dec. 3, 1968, p. 3, no. 01):

> The work envisaged is aimed at a transformation of mental-
> ity, structures and cultures, in the direction of mankind's collec-

tive taking in charge of his destiny. The Churches are resolutely committed to this movement, and in order to involve their members they are brought to a rethinking of their teaching and preaching, a reinvestigation of their sources in order to evolve a global view that gives coherence and meaning to this process and in order to communicate an inspiration which can stimulate its dynamism.

Thus the various denominations expand beyond their own narrowness.

Development, a Frontierless Movement

It is not only the frontiers between Christian denominations, but the Christian and religious frontiers themselves that are being obliterated by the sweep of the movement.

There is no point in attempting to describe the movement in all its dimensions, for not only is it an old and vast phenomenon but also one full of contrasts. Concern for human development takes on different forms and names in divergent ideologies. Also it would be a questionable simplification if we were to limit ourselves to a description of what is most accessible and most documented—what came out of the San Francisco conference when the UN was founded in 1945.

What we must remember is that development, this secular phenomenon, has never been and must not be a Christian monopoly, any more than the evangelical vocation of Christianity is only to build itself up within its own little world. The movement is the universal service of all men by all men of good will. It is a detoxicifying cure for the Churches to leave behind their narrowly ecclesiastical concerns in collaboration for a universally human cause whose very object excludes all frontiers.

The Christian movement to which we have given a closer look converges on a worldwide scale in the aspirations of all men of good will for justice, peace, and unity by means of development. The movement's originators, including John XXIII and the Council, did not set themselves up as teachers. They attempted to read this yearning in men's hearts, to perceive its evangelical value, to organize it, and to promote it. This movement, then, is inscribed on the heart of contemporary life as the Church divests herself of any desire for domination and rediscovers her evangelical vocation as "leaven" in the dough (Matthew 13:33; Luke 13:21).

THE SOURCES
OF
THE MOVEMENT

2

No movement is ever a chance happening. It is the result of impelling force, of historical necessity. Where then did the development movement come from?

Official Sources of Development

PAUL VI AND DEVELOPMENT

Once again our investigation focuses on an awakening within the Catholic Church. Within this framework, our first answer to the question seems clear. The movement is connected with Paul VI's encyclical[1] *Populorum progressio* (March 26, 1967).

As a matter of fact, the statement and the action of the pope were an important factor in giving impetus to the movement—all the more so since this has been one of the strong points of the present pontificate. That encyclical is not an isolated act; it was prepared for in many allocutions and has been followed by many others: the one the pope made on June 20, 1967, for example, to the Committee for Progress in World Nutrition.[2] The question has an important place in his message to Africa (October 29, 1967).[3] It is the central theme of the allocution addressed on January 19, 1968 to the so-called "good will mission" which represented the group of seventy-seven countries that met in Algiers in 1967 to draw up a joint statement from the countries of the Third World for the New Delhi conference of March 15, 1968.[4]

The pope was represented in the international conferences that dealt with this question. Mr. Leon de Rosen represented the Vatican at the Athens meeting of December 1, 1967.[5] Archbishop Giuseppi Caprio headed the Holy See's delegation to the second United Nations Conference on Trade and Development, where he delivered a statement on February 6, 1968.[6]

Certainly Paul VI's strong insistence has stimulated this universal current. At the time that the Virgin Mary represented the focal point of the pontificate of Pius XII, the bishops and those in authority felt obliged to do something about it. By the same token today they find themselves obliged to do something about development, which has become one of the crucial aspects of the present pontificate. But, as in the time of Pius XII, action taken at the top has its limitations. And where the groundwork has been done, improvised preliminaries meant to express the official will of the sovereign pontiff are more or less artificial. The result can even be counterproductive, a term which implies eliciting inadvertently a counter-reaction to the very cause that people intend to serve. The action that authority takes, as important as it may be for authentification, coordination, and stimulation, presupposes something more in order to be productive.

THE COUNCIL AS A SOURCE OF DEVELOPMENT

In any event, *Populorum progressio* is not a starting point. It is categorically and explicitly situated as a consequence of the Council (no. 1):

> The development of peoples. . . . On the morrow of the second Vatican ecumenical council, a renewed awareness of the message shows the Church's duty to place herself in a position to serve men by helping them to grasp all the dimensions of this grave problem and by convincing them of the urgency of acting with solidarity at this decisive turning point in the history of mankind.

Compare Number 3 where the pope refers explicitly to the constitution *Gaudium et spes* which is also mentioned in *Populorum progressio's* notes 7, 10, 12, 14, 20, 24, 34, 38, 42, 53, 59, or twelve times altogether: more than *Mater et Magistra* (four times in notes 6, 30, 35, 49), and *Pacem in terris* (once in note 65).

The Pastoral Constitution on the Church in the Modern World, in which the notion of development is so prominent, as we shall see on closer examination, is the last born and the final project promulgated by the Council[7] on December 7, 1965. On the following day, the closing day, the Church's commitment was signified at the offertory by the gifts set aside for development projects in Bethlehem, in India, Cambodia, and Pakistan.[8] The Council's constitution *Gaudium et spes* (no. 90) asked for the creation of an organizational body that would coordinate initiatives in this area. And this is the reason why in January 1967 Paul VI established the Justice and Peace commission,[9] for which he maintains special concern and interest.[10]

THE ROLE OF JOHN XXIII IN DEVELOPMENT

Even the Council is not a starting point. It expressed a central idea of John XXIII, his firm desire to renew the Church's relationship with the world in a style that included receptivity, optimism, dialogue, cooperation, and involvement from within. *Mater et Magistra* (May 15, 1961) and *Pacem in terris* (April 11, 1963) played pilot roles for the Council.

However, it was not in the charters and instructions of the authorities or the official organizations, nor in the top-level decisions that the movement originated. All that they all did was to take on, guarantee, organize, and amplify something that already existed as petitions, research, and nascent realities. They clarify and give scope to the movement, but they are not its source.

The Pioneers in Development

At the beginnings of every movement there are pioneers from whom come the first awakenings and the first prophetic acts.

MANUEL LARRAIN

Such a key move was made on the threshold of Vatican II, before the opening of the Council—and before Schema 13 was even thought of. It was initiated by a bishop of Chile. He, Dom Manuel Larraín, who died in 1966, was also one of the first secretaries and first presidents of CELAM.[11]

As early as June 1962, in agreement with Cardinal Silva Henríquez of Santiago de Chile, he turned the church lands over to a development plan for which he also set up all the technical assistance and the educational training necessary. For he saw that it would be useless to give lands to people unqualified to take over their cultivation.

The blueprint had been completed in 1961; it set a pattern. Latin America was thus demonstrating its capacity for renovation, for inscribing truly prophetic realities in the lives of men, without either documentation or theorizing. In the earth and in people's hearts, there was sown a seed capable of flowering limitlessly in thought, action, and union. In this deed which so captured people's minds, even though it had been conceived outside of any spirit of propaganda, we find all the elements of a conversion that characterizes the development movement: the Church renouncing her self-aggrandizement in order to empty herself, in order to give—without any egoism, however sacred—in accordance with the spirit of Christ's own kenosis (Philippians 2:7-8). She made the transition from right perceptions to commitment; from words to actions; from gifts that salve the donor's conscience to gifts which genuinely serve the aims of the recipient; from material sacrifices to educational accomplishments that develop for the victims of underdevelopment awareness, responsibility, and a sense therefore of their own values. For ultimately people can escape from deprivation only by taking their destiny in their own hands. In this Manuel Larraín and the Church of Chile were pioneers.

LOUIS LEBRET

But the first dynamic mover, the man who realized the depth of the problem and gave expression and form to it in the field, the man who gave the Council the idea, the experiences, and the formulas which already were convincing, the man who worked for the swift and almost premature determination of these demands by the magisterium was Father Louis Lebret.[12] He died in 1966 in the midst of drafting the encyclical *Populorum progressio,* which was delayed for several months by his death.

The economist, François Perroux, professor at the College de France, wrote of him: "The man has an historical dimension and significance."

Louis Joseph Lebret was born at Le Minihac-sur-la-Rance into a family of Breton seamen and farmers. His first vocation pushed him irresistibly to the sea. At the age of eighteen, six months after the beginning of World War I, he entered the École Navale at Brest. Ranked eleventh on entering the academy, one of the most difficult in France, he was graduated third in his class. Louis Lebret was shaped in the hard school of the war and the sea—the sea where without respite one must combine technical precision and a sense of improvisation; but where one must also understand men when one is in charge of them.

In 1923, a naval officer and an instructor at the École Navale, he ended his naval career in order to follow God's call. He entered the Dominicans. For him this was no escape from the world but a way to meet in God all human reality.

In 1930, Father Lebret founded the Jeunesse maritime chrétienne as a result of his concern for combining Christian commitment and the service of man in his everyday context. Firsthand knowledge of the bitter destitution unleashed by the economic crisis of the Great Depression induced him to set up the Secrétariat social maritime. But he soon understood that that was inadequate and set out upon a total reorganization of the fisheries. He plunged into labor union, economic, and legislative activities, and started numerous surveys of the fishing industry and the French and foreign seafood markets. Together with Ernest Lamort, a union activist, he founded the Fédération française des syndicats professionels de marins. He rescued fifty thousand families from destitution and saved the trade. And it was then that he heard a leading Communist say: "What you did for the fishing trade we want to do everywhere."

Undoubtedly the Communist was referring there to the value of a struggle for the establishment of structures capable of freeing men from their alienation.

Lebret had put into effect fully, within the human context, what was later made explicit in *Populorum progressio*. And the encyclical would have had nothing to make explicit had Lebret not first put it into effect.

Let him give his own balance sheet of this first phase, for the style is the man—direct, thoughtful, demanding, and technical (*Dynamique concrète du développment,* Paris: Editions ouvrières, 1961; Foreword dated Nov. 1, 1960 at Saigon, p. 7-8):

> From 1929 to 1945, one of my chief concerns was to find a way for the French maritime fisheries to effect a difficult transition from a less mechanized and industrialized phase to one that was more "productive," but without that necessarily causing too great an exodus of the coastal population. I was firmly convinced that development of the maritime fisheries by an increase of the raw product need not result in a poorer quality of fish or in a decline in the number of people involved. The problem was a really difficult one since the excessive motorization and industrialization were a serious threat to the reproduction of the fish. Further-

more, the old fishing methods had to give way inevitably to new techniques. The situation was complicated by the flooding of the market with foreign fish which were an overflow from countries with a higher production rate at the time of the world economic crisis, and which were thus able to find a ready sale in France.

The successive analyses I then made of the French shoreline and the European littoral, and my studies of the condition of the international market, showed me both the economic and human aspects of the one same branch of activity. This constituted a first approach to a method by which economic and social facts could be distinguished. The study was conducted town by town and fishery by fishery and was especially directed to all the population localized in many large, medium size, and small ports whose markets were variously regional, national, or international. Competition between the ports and fisheries also interfered; and the networks of production, packaging, and distribution were extremely complex and in rapid evolution. Important innovations were appearing: cooperative fishing, the use of motorboats for tuna fishing and of cold-rooms for on-board preservation; tuna preserved in its natural state like salmon, the unexpected use of marine algae; transportation in refrigerated trucks and even by air, etc.

The role of the distributor at the central market of Les Halles in Paris was diminishing on account of the ease of telephonic communication, and the control port of Lorient-Keroman had been created. Trawlers were able to reach deeper seas; the great fishing was no longer off Iceland and Newfoundland but off Greenland. Morocco became a serious competitor in the canning of sardines. Men's lives were also transformed. Industrialized fishing required the crews to do unfamiliar work, but the resultant earnings were far superior to what they were in coastal fishing. Fishing villages were becoming depopulated when they were not suitable to become seaside resorts. Actually the fishermen were unorganized and, in most of the ports, were incapable of adapting rapidly enough to the new working conditions.

Through our analyses of the structures of production and marketing in the fisheries as a whole and singly and through a series of negotiations, we were able to bring about the consolidation of the unions and the greatest general reorganization of the French maritime fishing industry since the Ordonnance of 1681. Thus a handful of men, observing and interpreting the facts and then organizing the people involved in a given industry, was able to exert a decisive influence.

The study center, Economie et Humanisme, was foreshadowed in this difficult confrontation. It was born as a result of the conviction that it is possible to direct an economic and

technological evolution in a direction favoring men, if we begin
by studying the dominant complex reality, work out a doctrine,
and form a collective force intent on putting it into practice.

It was in 1942, during the war, that Louis Lebret founded the Economie et Humanisme center. Its quite transparent name could have
been used as the title of the encyclical *Populorum progressio* since it
asks how to put economy in the service of men, and how to integrate
man within it. For economy is not merely dealing with cost account-
ing for money and merchandise. It is also a question of human reality,
which is an integral and fundamental part of economy—health,
education, training for a trade, and general education. Properly
understood, economy must integrate all that; it must balance the productivity demanded of the individual against the wear and tear of his
work, his limitations as a worker, his normal diet, and his housing.
All these coefficients are no less important than market values and
must be translated into an economic quantity and calculated on a
group scale in accordance with their dynamics and structure. François
Perroux[13] worked in this area and also on the explanatory theory of
"progressive economy." For Father Lebret this man was in economic
sciences what Ernest Lamort had been in unionism, and, both
through Lebret and directly, Perroux was one of the sources of inspiration for the encyclical *Populorum progressio*, even though his name
does not appear.

As a complement to Economie et Humanisme, and in order to
harmonize the economy of the "developed countries," Father Lebret
subsequently founded (1958–60) IRFED (International Institute of
Research and Formation for Harmonized Human Development)
which aimed at working out the doctrine and forming organizational
nuclei for the developing countries.

After 1945–46 his initiatives found a following abroad. Since
from the outset he had arrived at the essentials of human reality
through evangelical love, Lebret easily made the transition without
intending to do so from the affairs of Breton fisheries to those of the
world.

On the eve of World War II, he was invited to virtually every
corner of the globe to put his doctrine into practice, first in Latin
America and then in Africa and Asia. "These are my laboratories," he
often said with a smile.

These laboratories for which he recruited researchers and composed practical guide lines are established all over the world: Belgium,

Holland, Germany, Denmark, Norway, England, Algeria, Tunisia,
Italy, Scotland, Ireland (1933–39); after the war in Spain and Luxem-
bourg (1945–51), Brazil, Uruguay, Argentina, Chile (1945–51), Colombia (1955), Japan, the Philippines, Hong Kong, Vietnam, India, Iran
(1952–57), Morocco, Senegal, Malagasy Republic (1955–58), Rwanda
and Venezuela (1964).

He worked quickly and calmly. He arrived fortified with solid
documentation and customarily began his investigation by flying over
the region under study in a private plane with the assistance of a
geologist and a topographer. From this vantage point he formed his
first hypotheses. Then he went into the field to see men and study
figures. He jotted everything down in the small notebooks he always
had with him, and every evening he read them "in order to put his
ideas in order," no matter how late into the night he had been working. He then set up the necessary research teams and as far as possible
saw to it that the nationals of the particular country were in responsible positions at the top. He knew how to pick and train men. His confidence in them was at once total and demanding. It was this stimulating confidence, perhaps, that most struck the people working with
him. Finally, on the basis of data uncovered and tabulated systemati-
cally, he reached conclusions which he set up as options, since every
kind of development is achieved through choices and sacrifices—and
not making any choice often means choosing the worst. Father Lebret
was without peer in helping politically responsible people to put their
option into effect. He never had ready-made solutions, but he would
propose a number of workable choices and then help those in charge
to set up their plans accordingly. He went to the Third World as an
insider and with the requisite methods, yet methods that were not
authoritarian. "He wasn't a demagogue like the rest, admitting of no
argument when it came to matters of technique," one observer of his
work told me.

His investigations (which were the fundamental aspect of his
work) are still for the most part unpublished. His work is inscribed
chiefly on work in the field and in men's hearts. The consultations he
gave in many countries humanized their economy. Urban projects in
São Paulo, Rio, and Belo Horizonte bear the mark of his influence.
And all over the world I have met men whose lives have become meaningful, thanks to him. The groups he founded for research or development—or inspired—are working harder than ever. Indeed, they flourish. Thus, unlike Teilhard, who was a solitary originator of another

kind of change in a synthesis of man and faith, Lebret was not a
man alone. He not only had disciples around to assist him but also
others who carried on his work afterwards. The organizations and re-
views founded by him still continue; the initiatives he took have
gained followers and are proliferating. He is no isolated innovator.

Africa was a turning point for him—specifically Senegal in 1958,
where he uncovered the unsuspected cultural dimensions of development. Latin America had kept him within a style of culture with
which he was familiar. "African-ness, in Senghor's sense" made a very
vivid impression on him. He humbly felt himself left behind by the
cultural experiment of a different civilization, but through his global
perceptions he committed others to it. This was the origin of the
"civilization and development" research undertaken by IRFED. This
openness, this willingness to become immersed in human realities was
essential with Lebret and it did not age and wither. Implicit in what
he had founded was the flowering of the future. This is also the seed
and the root of what he did from the beginning, as he himself explains
(*Journées missionaires de la Tourette,* L'Arbresle (Rhône): Editions
ouvrières, 1947, p. 7; Emile Poulat, *Naissance des prêtres-ouvriers,*
Paris: Casterman, 1965, p. 526):

> On the one hand when one has become aware of the destitu-
> tion of these coastal populations and the catastrophe awaiting
> them, anguish grips the heart; on the other hand, when one's
> previous study and the competence one has acquired give oppor-
> tunities for accomplishing something effective, commitment and
> leadership are essential.

On the technical plane, although lacking the mathematical model
which he could not quite bring into focus, his growing and convergent
investigations led him to propose a "concrete dynamic of development" which directs the economy of the Third World and the world
at large to the service of man. In his book *Dynamique concrète* he had
these (and only these) words set in large type (p. 44):

> Civilization's problem is above all a problem of stabilizing
> man within a generalized regimen of human economy and of har-
> monized integral development.

His main ideas were themselves condensed in simple formulas. These
axioms express the *finality* of development—being more human:
"Have enough to be more" or again, "Have more to be more."

Lebret insisted on the *means*, which are necessarily demanding and scientific:

> Intelligence by itself is oppressive and love alone is not efficacious. The love of men must be intelligent, painstaking, and technical.

In his last years he expressed this basic idea even more simply: "I understood that mercy operates through structures."

Hence his concern with "substituting an economy of needs for the economy of profit," according to François Perroux's formula.

Lebret also insisted on *human resilience* (*Journées*, pp. 53–54; Poulat, *op. cit*, pp. 535–36):

> The members of a given group of men have to be brought to a point of taking total charge of themselves, by themselves, in order that they themselves may resolve the problems of their spiritual and material lives.

Thus Lebret, who was working for economic reforms at the level of heads of state, was also one of the chief inspirers and counsellors of the priest workers at the end of World War II, one of the men who knew in 1946 how best to situate the problems of the relationship between missionary action and development action.[14]

We can understand therefore how spontaneously receptive he was to the broadest kind of ecumenism, which he himself lived in depth at Dakar in his relations with President Mamadou Dia, a Muslim—a relationship which resulted in mutual enrichment. This explains words he whispered on the day of his death, in a state of semi-consciousness, after the last rites: "Broaden ecumenism beyond the Christian world."

This was all of one piece with him, for everything started from faith: an eyes-open faith, a faith integrated with human realities. He broke through the encircling sterility of abstract principles that characterized "Catholic moralism" in social matters, even in the great encyclicals. He shattered the infernal circle of the do-gooder in order to establish an efficacious charity—a charity which functions through structures and involves participation. At the price of wearisome labor, he roused a fundamental awareness. That, indeed, is why he seems to have been the prime mover, the person who twenty years before Vatican II, instigated the change without which the Council would have been only half able to function.

Opposing economic formulas that alienated man and promoting those that free him, he was by this fact a stranger to the caricature of God that some people use to cover up repression, but he was inhabited by the God who liberates. Thus he began in the field, without polemics, to give a convincing answer to the real questions posed by Marxism.

His life was not an easy one, since he had to navigate against the current—against the methods and options imposed by the powers of this world: those powers to whom he refused to sell himself, even in the guise of intangible forms theoretically free of any "strings." He was most strict in this regard even under pressure.

His last words sum up all this—love of God, love for men, relentless work on the moving landscape of human realities: "Life is beautiful. You've got to navigate for others. It's the way to show the Father you've understood him."

All of Louis Lebret's "sources" are here: God, men, and the sea.

We have underlined a difference between him and the other great originator, Pierre Teilhard de Chardin. And it would be easy to emphasize the contrasts between the two men: the Jesuit and the Dominican, the paleontologist and the economist, the poet and the leader of men, the thinker and the doer; the one concerned with understanding the meaning of evolution, the other with directing it from within; the one specializing in the study of the most distant past, and the other devoted to the realistic construction of the world of tomorrow. Nevertheless, it was the necessary analogy between these two men that inspired *Schema 13*: the one from beyond the grave, the other in his lifetime and through his active collaboration—two scholars in human sciences, two prophets, two pioneers. Both achieved a synthesis, until then unknown, between their faith and a new dimension of human change. For Teilhard, that dimension emerged from paleontology and moved toward the future and final development of the world; Lebret perceived it in the economic development with which contemporary man freely builds his world now. In March 1955 Teilhard wrote[15] from New York:

> Everywhere on earth at this moment, within the very core of the new spiritual atmosphere created by the appearance of the idea of evolution, there are floating, in a state of extreme mutual sensitivization, love for God and faith in the world: the two essential components of the ultra-human. These two components are everywhere "in the air," but neither is generally strong

enough to combine with the other in one and the same person. In me, by pure chance (temperament, education, milieu . . .), the proportion of both components was favorable, their fusion came about spontaneously, although it is still too feeble to be propagated explosively—but still sufficient—in order to establish that a reaction is possible, and that one day, the links in the chain will connect. A new proof that it is enough for truth to appear once in one mind for nothing ever again to prevent it from pervading and enflaming everything.

The same text could apply to Lebret if we formulate the dual polarity in this way: love for God and an expert technician's love for men and consequent service for human development.

Looking Beyond the Pioneers

With this description of Lebret, have we reached the real source of the development movement? The question is ambiguous, like that asked by explorers tracing the source of a river. Where is the source? Where does it begin? Just at the point we think we have found it, we have to acknowledge its underground sources or at least the thousands of little streams of water saturating the soil, without which the spring would not have burst forth.

All this leads us to a more basic question: why has development reached the first level of the Christian conscience at this particular moment in history?

We could answer by mentioning the motives for development that will be clarified later in Chapter 8. Within the historical perspective of this present chapter we must say that Christian charity has suffered from a dissociation from human realities, because of excessive legalism and abstractness. Too often charity was diffused in mystical bursts of energy that quickly burned themselves out, in escapist activities, in trifles that were ill-adapted, ineffective, and often ridiculous and which ended by discrediting the word charity itself. This vacuum, this failure, this collective sin continues to trouble the Christian conscience.

The question the development movement is still working on to resolve in the Church today comes at the junction of two increasingly clear historical facts. One is man's accelerated evolution in a growing solidarity, and the other is the ineffectiveness of what in recent centuries has been conveniently called "Christian morality." The subsequent marginal character of so many with good Catholic consciences furnished them with good intentions which often allowed the most relentless kinds of determinism to bring about enormous calamities. And they did nothing to oppose these calamities except with weak words and palliatives. This scandal provoked a conversion of faith which is at the very root of the Church's development movement. In contradistinction to a river which has no definite point of origin, since it has to be traced variously to the moisture in the earth, to the rains, to the clouds, and to the evaporation that formed them; the development movement can identify its transcendent source: the Holy Spirit.

Here again it is important to enlarge our perspective beyond the frontiers of the Church, since the development movement extends much further, and the Spirit breathes where he will. Well, we can do so only with the utmost discretion out of respect for the consciences of others, but also because it is difficult to follow the movement of the Spirit: No one knows "whence it comes or whither it goes" (John 3:8).

Part Two

The Question

Being Examined

THE WORD "DEVELOPMENT"

3

Before going any further we must come to an understanding about the words that express the problem treated in this book. Or put another way, does development have any relation to man's salvation?

"Salvation" has a clear meaning in theology. Salvation is the achievement of the destiny of men in God: an achievement that is brought about in the temporal and remains for eternity. Like so many other words in the Christian vocabulary, the word has lost some of its strength through usage and because the personalism of salvation has become degraded in individualistic terms; this grace has been more or less parodied as a consumer product that one can procure commercially. This is one of the reasons that the word "salvation" is somewhat out of favor today. It is, however, a basic word in the Christian vocabulary, appearing frequently in the Bible and more especially in the New Testament. In a way, it is a reserved word which one day will burst from its source.

"Development" poses more delicate problems. Etymologically development is the opposite of envelopment. Both words are of French origin, coming from a root meaning "wrap up" (one "unwraps" a folded or rolled map; Fr. *développer*). On this level the word can be a synonym of "unfolding," or "unrolling." In the area of living things it can signify the growth of a plant (the "unfolding" of its buds), of an animal as it grows organically and in size, or also of a thought which "unfolds" its potentialities. The word is charged with dynamic energy. It means a normal and spontaneous impetus, a potential, a growth, but also an organic differentiation—an advancement.

Early Usage of the Term

The current socioeconomic definition of the word is recent. Can we give it a date?

"The concept of development dates from 1945," Lebret notes in his *Dynamique concrète* (1967 ed., p. 38). This is an authoritative, if laconic, opinion. Undoubtedly he is making reference to the San Francisco conference at which the UN was founded in 1945. It was there that this term was first widely used among Western nations.

But it is very difficult to date the new acceptation of a word. If with Western nations the operational concept of development was launched right after World War II as they became aware of under-development and the new possibilities for remedying the situation economically or culturally, it would seem quite astonishing if we could not find some antecedents, even sporadic ones—and particularly in Marxist writings.

DEVELOPMENT'S MARXIST ANTECEDENTS

In capitalist quarters, it is often forgotten that the word development (*Entwicklung*) is frequently used by Marx[1] in an economic and social sense with various meanings, particularly in the *Communist Manifesto* (1848), in the *Critique of Political Economics* (1859) and in *Das Kapital* (1867). This is due to his dynamic perspective as a reaction against the classical economies whose conceptions were static, except, of course, that the growth economy theories of David Ricardo and Adam Smith (end of the eighteenth century) exerted a positive and suggestive influence on him.

Most often, Marx applied this concept to isolated elements of the economic situation: "The development of productive forces"[2] of "machinism" (*Manifesto*, pp. 31, 35), of "industry" (pp. 32, 34, 43), and more especially of "major industry" (pp. 41, 58), or of the "family" (p. 48). Or in other writings, he speaks of "property,"[3] or even of money.[4] Again in the *Manifesto*, Marx says that this material development gives rise to a correlative development which is antagonistic to the bourgeoisie (p. 49; *cf.* p. 48), to the proletariat (pp. 39, 57, 67, 70), and to the class struggle (p. 69).

Class antagonism goes hand in hand with the development of major industry, he claims (*ibid.*, p. 68). And, with more precision:

> At a certain level of their development, the forces of mater-
> ial production take issue with the production yields in force or,
> to express the same thing juridically, with property returns with-
> in which context they had up to now been developing.

He is reaching global perspectives when in a letter, he mentions "historical development";[5] and again when he says:

> The whole of development, embracing both the genesis of
> the salaried person and that of the capitalist, has as its point of
> departure the servitude of the workers; the advancement it ac-
> complishes consists in changing the form of bondage, the meta-
> morphosis of feudal exploitation into capitalist exploitation.[6]

He reaches a kind of universal humanism when he speaks of the "development of civilization" (*Manifesto,* pp. 58, 79), and especially at
the end of a passage where in conclusion he blueprints the stages of
revolutionary change (p. 55):

> For the old bourgeois society, with its classes and its class
> antagonisms, will be substituted a partnership in which the free
> development of each man will be the condition of the free de-
> velopment of all.

He specifies the sense of this free development in *Das Kapital* where
he describes the revolution as the time when the historical necessity of
an alienating opposition will be destroyed and where all that will remain will be the "natural necessity" of "needs" and of the "work"
which is the only thing that can satisfy needs. Then, Marx continues
in *Das Kapital,* the exchanges will be effected

> with the minimum expenditure of power and under conditions
> which are most appropriate to their human nature. . . . But a
> domain of necessity remains. Beyond this begins the development
> of man's powers which have no other aim than themselves: the
> genuine domain of freedom; but this cannot prosper except with
> this domain of necessity as its basis. The shortening of the work
> day is the fundamental condition.[7]

We should have to explore Russian and Chinese economic literature
in order to specify how and to what extent the concept of the pre-

revolutionary forces of development gave way, in socialist society born in 1917, to an operational concept of development for the building of socialist society or even of international communism. In this way we could know for sure whether the Marxist concept actually did suggest or inspire the idea set down in 1945 at San Francisco.

In any case, there is a Marxist theory and a praxis of development with its own literature (Henri Chambre, *Union soviétique et développement économique,* Paris: Aubier-Montagne, 1967; Mieczyslaw Falkowski, *Les problèmes de la croissance du Tiers-monde,* Paris: Payot, 1968; *cf.* Paul A. Baran, *Economie politique de la croissance,* Paris: F. Maspero, 1967: an explanation of the Marxist point of view by an American writer). In this literature, Siberian Kazakhstan is given as an example of success in this area. As for Marx's source, it is Jean Jacques Rousseau, *De l'inégalité (Of Inequality among Men)* as rethought by Hegel; see Roger Garaudy's *Pour un modèle français du socialisme* (Paris: Gallimard, 1968) pp. 47, 59, 66, 234, 243–52.

The Term in the Dictionaries

The new acceptation of the word is not fully established outside of technical circles, except in the expressions "underdeveloped," or "developing" peoples, which have become part of our current vocabulary.

The French encyclopedic dictionaries (such as the 1966 and 1967 editions of *Robert* do not mention it. They merely note a vague, and outmoded economic acceptation of the word: "The development of trade, industry . . . of a business deal, of an enterprise."

The meaning here is still a material one. It is limited, as is confirmed by the synonyms given: progress, expansion. Among the uses cited in *Robert,* the one closest to our subject is implied by the expression: "the development of the sciences." This, evidently, refers to an organic growth which at the same time implies progress differentiation, and structural changes in the sciences and in man evolving them; it also involves a change of direction: all of which are traits characterizing the subject of our study, socioeconomic development.

Specialized dictionaries in various degrees underline the fluctuating and imprecise character of the word.

Le Vocabulaire des sciences sociales of Alain Birou (Paris: Editions ouvrières, 1966) stresses the positive and dynamic value of the word (p. 85):

In the biological and moral sense, to develop is to foster the growth of a being or a faculty. Examples: the sun develops a plant, a man develops his memory.

Applied to the realm of economics, the term development is used in a very general and at times imprecise way to signify a harmonized organic growth and therefore an economic progress inscribing itself within the general progress of society. For there to be development in a country, economic progress is indispensable, but it must be in the service of social and human progress.

Birou then points out the differences between simple (quantitative) growth and development which supposes a whole network of structures and institutions, a blueprint, and an adaptation of behavior and mentality. He concludes:

The stages of development do not correspond exactly to the stages of growth. In particular, they require a coherent effort in all the aspects of the life of society, a supervision and a mastery over economic activities (deliberate, studied, and harmonized economy). Economic planning is ordinarily necessary to bring about development.

The *Dictionnaire économique et social* of Thomas Suavet (Paris: Éditions ouvrières, 3rd ed., 1962) simply explains the word in relation to the term "underdevelopment" (pp. 136–38):

The word "development" is still of too recent usage for its meaning to be absolutely fixed. It first appeared in the expression "underdevelopment," used right after World War II in the international documents to characterize the condition of countries in which the low standard of living was considered abnormal by peoples with a high standard of living and also felt to be abnormal by the governments of the peoples in question. . . . The lagging behind of technology seems to be the basic characteristic of underdevelopment.

That underdevelopment is prior to development is clearly and deliberately contested by Father Lebret, but without any elaboration, as we have seen. What we have to keep in mind is that the term underdevelopment became part of our general vocabulary quicker than many new terms because of one of the most significant aspects of the postwar awakening, the awareness of the abiding scandal—peoples starving and dying en masse at a time of plenty. The inadequate growth of the "young nations" is a pathological phenomenon and is due to established causes which must urgently be corrected.

In this respect underdevelopment is something new. England, the first country where industrially-oriented economic development was born, in the eighteenth and nineteenth centuries, has never been an underdeveloped country. Nothing actually shackled or paralyzed its development from the outside. England became rich and built herself up from her own resources and without having to depend on another power. She was not hamstrung by a structure that involved *a developed metropolis with an underdeveloped countryside*. She was simply a country that was *not yet developed*. There was nothing deprived about her situation. The word underdevelopment has been coined to express a scandalous fact: that under present structures, the developed countries are shackling the development of the rest and condemning them to revolve around their superior economies, whether from the point of view of investment capital, equipment, technicians, or through the consumer-goods market with which the underdeveloped countries are inundated from the outside. The expression materializes this violent situation in which riches tend ever increasingly to be concentrated in the industrialized metropolises, while outlying areas become impoverished. And that tends to unleash the mechanism of alienation according to which the rich become richer while the poor irreversibly become poorer.[8]

The word development, then, has a normative value. It signifies an ideal to be achieved. In this regard, Raymond Barre in 1958 gave a very meaningful definition which is particularly forceful and concise (*Cahier ISEA,* Series 7 on development levels and growth politics, no. 11, April 1958, p. 81):

> Development is an evolutionary process for transforming economic, social, political, and mental structures which cannot be accomplished in a brief space of time. It presupposes that in an economy on the way to development the demand for development will be led by a courageous social and political elite which would assign for itself as a rule of action the formation of productive capital. It implies that in developed economies the commercial notions of international economic relations must be abandoned.

In this same sense, Lebret says (*Dynamique concrète,* pp. 38-39):

> It is a question of a harmony resulting from the nature of a being in development. Development is the explanation of values a being already possesses within, the evolution of its potentialities toward the state where they become a reality. Development is the projection toward the optimum. It has come to term once the optimum has been reached.

Lebret tended to make development the new name of a properly understood economy (*ibid.*, p. 28):

> According to us, development is the very object of human economy in the meaning given to it by the group "Economie et Humanisme." This is the discipline of the transition (for a given population and for the subpopulations making it up) from a less human to a more human phase, in the quickest possible rhythm, at the least possible cost, taking into account the solidarity between subpopulations and populations.

And he concluded: "From this analysis it follows that the very concept of development is much less simple than it might seem at first" (p. 39).

The Magisterium

We are not surprised then to find a certain groping even on the level of the magisterium, which has not been exempt from man's common difficulty of finding his way along the paths of history, since the time when the first ecumenical councils said both that Christ had "two natures" and, with Saint Cyril of Alexandria, that he had but "One nature of the Incarnate Word . . ." (*Denzinger-Schönmetzer*, 1963, nos. 429 & 505).

With reference to this particularly exaggerated example, we are by contrast astounded at the coherence with which Paul VI uses the new acceptation of the word development in the original French text of *Populorum progressio*.

But fluctuation is quite evident in the Latin translation which constitutes the official text, and in what preceded it.

In *Pacem in terris* (no. 124) of John XXIII, the word "development" (*sviluppo*), taken from the Italian text of a 1941 Christmas message[9] of Pius XII, is translated by the phrase *rei oeconomicae incrementum*.[10] And the word "growth" is faithful to the image of organic growth signified by the word "development." The Council's constitution *Gaudium et spes*, which uses this solution in one instance (no. 65, par. 2), preferred the expression *progressio oeconomica* (economic progress, nos. 63, par. 5, and 65, par. 1). By doing this, the Council substituted for the biological image of growth the image of a forward step, like the Hebrews' advance through the desert. What dictated this choice was not the attraction of the image but the value attached today to the root of the word "progress" used in order to qualify economic growth within the full dimension of human progress. The translator of *Populorum progressio* deliberately adopted this solution (nos. 1, 14, 20, 35, 38, 41, 44, 47, 48, 51, 52, 57, 73, 75, 77, 81, 84, 87) and, curiously, uses the word *incrementum,* which responds to the same image as development, when he wants to signify a simple quantitative growth, and this precisely in contradistinction to development considered as progress (no. 14): "Development" (*progressio de qua loquimur*) "does not come down to simple economic growth" (*incrementum*).

In this instance the translation gives *incrementum* the value of a simple material growth, but the word ordinarily says more, since it is derived from *incresco,* which means internal growth, the growth that comes about in life itself: *"Jaculis increvit acutis,"* we read in Virgil ("the crop grew with spiny stalks").

Further on in the Latin edition of *Populorum progressio,* "development" is translated by *profectus* (nos. 42, 76, 77; *cf.* no. 15). But this word also serves as a translation of two other terms: "promotion" (70; *cf.* no. 14) and "progress" (no. 50). *Promouvoir l'homme* ("promote man's advancement") is translated *hominis profectus consulere.* "Progress" is also rendered by *progressus* (no. 35), as in *Pacem in terris* (no. 123).

The translator's difficulty is shown further in the variety of terms used in *Populorum progressio* to designate the underdeveloped nations:

Ad progressionem nitentes (those "striving for progress," nos. 41, 55, 81);

Cultu minus provectae (those "whose culture is less advanced," no. 48);

Inferiores opibus ("less affluent," no. 57);

In rebus oeconomicis paulum progressi (peoples "which have made little economic progress," no, 64);

Minus progressae ("less developed," no. 70);

Qui ad provectum civilem nituntur ("those striving to promote the advancement of civilization," no. 76).

The translator did not use the expression employed in *Pacem in terris;* instead he wrote:

Civitates quarum oeconomicae progressiones essent in cursu ("nations whose economic progressions are in course" no. 122).

To this series should be added the expressions in *Populorum progressio* such as:

Perexiguam populorum progressionem ("the feeble progress of peoples," no. 75), which translates the abstract expression "under-development."

And also the expressions used to designate the developed countries:

Gentes progressae ("developed nations," no. 48; quoting *Gaudium et spes,* no. 86).

Quae in operosis artificiis profecerunt (those "which have developed technologically," or "industrially," in accordance with the original French text of the encyclical, no. 58);

Quae in rebus oeconomicis profecerunt (those "which have progressed economically," no. 60).

The Four Levels of Vocabulary

In current usage, the term "development," in its application to social realities, similarly assumes various meanings: from simple economic growth to the organic differentiation of a whole set of human values, and to integral humanism, considered from the point of view of mankind as a whole or also in relation to man's relationship with God. Let us attempt to bring a little order to these four levels of vocabulary:

1. According to "mechanistic" notions, and in line with a usage current in capitalist economies, development often merely designates a quantitative phenomenon: the increase of production indices or of the average per capita income. Here development is the opposite of stagnation and signifies expansion—economic advance considered solely in the light of global material growth. In dealing with this first sense, the encyclical's Latin text prefers the word *incrementum* (nos. 14, 16, 35, 50), or *provectus* (no. 34) as a sort of rhyming echo of *profectus* (progress, promotion).

2. According to the organic notion, which is prevalent today and which is what has made the term "development" so popular, it does not designate a purely quantitative phenomenon, extension or amplification, enlargement or magnification, but rather a qualitative phenomenon: organic growth and the differentiation characterizing it. It is a question therefore of a homogeneous and ordered structural change. A country which is developing passes from a stage of inferior equilibrium to a superior stage as an embryo develops into a child and then into a man. On this second level, we are concerned with con-

trolling not only the speed but also the equilibrium of development.

The structured differentiation that characterizes this organic change may be divided into the following categories:

Technological—with the growing specialization brought about by progress in this area.

Economic—the birth and evolution of the primary, secondary, and tertiary levels: production, trade, and administration.

Social—here we focus on the phenomena of industrialization and urbanization with all the consequences of class division, the state of the family, and the like.

Other categories stress the political structures and tend to define development as an evolution toward democracy considered as an ideal. But this perspective is already suggested by the third stage.

3. This third level introduces human finality, or at least some sort of global blueprint for man. Development is looked upon as balanced and successful achievement—the progress of mankind. The principles involved in this stage are the following:

On the one hand, man's true development is to be found on the level of "being" and not in "having." Hence Lebret's axiom, taken over by *Populorum progressio*, "Have more in order to be more" (no. 6). This distinction between "having" and "being" was stressed by the philosopher Gabriel Marcel in a 1933 lecture entitled: "Being and Having." The word "being" here is taken in its existential, and therefore human sense. The subordination of "having" to "being" is the fundamental idea of the Council, and especially of *Populorum progressio*.

On the other hand, if having and being, in other words economic and human progress, are, for better or worse, inseparable, this is due to the fact that man builds himself up by building up the world itself. By harnessing the energies of the earth, he furthers his own progress. Hence the formula[11] of François Perroux. "Development is the transformation of man by man in an order of things that *can be* entered into the books."

Or again:[12] "It is the conquest of a human living standard."

On that level, development is a process that stabilizes human existence on an individual and community basis, including spiritual values. Such development implies relationships of justice and friendship which result from men's participation and cooperation. It is the reason for the choice of the word *progressio* to translate development, as we have seen.

When Paul VI speaks of development without qualification, it is this plenary human development that he means:

"Development" (*progressio de qua loquimur*) "does not come down to simple economic growth" (*incrementum rei oeconomicae*). "For it to be authentic it must be integral, that is, it must promote the whole man and every man" (*cujuslibet hominis ac totius hominis profectui consulere*). "We do not agree to a separation between the economic and the human" (no. 14).

"To say 'development' (*progressio*) "is . . . to be concerned as much with social progress" (*profectum*) "as with economic growth" (*provectum rerum oeconomicarum*) (no. 34).

4. Those human relationships are definitively brought about through the love that God gives: his own love, in other words, charity (*agape* [Gr. for "love" and in the plural, "love feast"], in Latin: *caritas*). *Agape*, love freely given, differs from *eros* which above all is *desire*. *Agape* (in New Testament usage) is a love that takes the first step, thereby awakening the object loved to its own goodness. Unfortunately this word, to which the New Testament has given maximum meaning by connecting it with the fullness of revelation, has been devalued through the wrong human and even subhuman usage made of it—by equating charity with alms given from on high and without involving human fellowship. One asks, is not "charity" understood as the good done by the mighty for the weak, and thus an image of God's "bending down" to his creatures? It is, but God did not merely bend toward us, he fell, if we may use the expression, into the depth of human misery. Through the Incarnation, he inserted himself in our humanity in order to save it from within. Moreover, he was already present in a certain sense since it is from within his own interiority that he had created the human race, and from within that he awakens man to his freedom, to his capacity to love—to the image and likeness of God. Now he is awakening man to divine sonship, which establishes as a consequence that all men are brothers and sons of the same Father.

It is for this reason that we can comprehend that human development is the fulfillment of love of God in the human community. As the antiphon says, "Where charity and love are, there is God" (*ubi caritas et amor, Deus ibi est*). And Christ himself has told us: "For where two or three are gathered in my name, there am I in the midst of them" (Matthew 18:20).

Christ resides in interpersonal relationships, and he is, definitively, the principal object of every act of love done for man who is made in his image: "As you did it to one of the least of these my brethren, you did it to me" (Matthew 25:40, 45). This is why the pope, who wants development for man, and understands it as humanism, specifies that it does not involve a closed humanism but one that is "open to the absolute," or put another way, open to God for "man reaches fulfillment only in going beyond himself" (no. 42).

These four levels of development certainly belong together. They ought normally to coincide in men's existence. But since current vocabulary confuses them, going from one level to the other capriciously, and often in a misleading way, it is useful to distinguish these levels, each of which could be designated by special terms:

1. Expansion, progress, material accretion: a quantitative phenomenon.
2. Economic growth, characterized by structural differentiation: a qualitative phenomenon.
3. Man's progress or advancement through role transformation: the behavior, mentality, human relations resulting in the enhancement of the person and the community.
4. The integral development of man, including his divinization in Jesus Christ.

But it is especially important to unite the four levels of meaning which are divided between two poles: the technological and the prophetic. During the course of this study we shall acquire a better grasp of this polarity and what is implied by it.

The Limitations of a Word

Before concluding this lexicographical study, we must make one observation. The word "development" is a term chosen to designate a complex phenomenon. This phenomenon is denoted by means of an image taken from life, and more especially plant life. Thus it calls to mind a process that is slow, gradual, and harmonious. And its connotation tends to impose evolutionary patterns, excluding the revolutionary.

Other choices would have been possible which would have stressed the contrasting aspects of development, and the breaks with the past it implies. Actually, development is not only growth; it is also a qualitative change which does not come about without crisis. It might have been characterized as a "creative destruction" from the fact that it implies a break with coherence. It questions morals and modes of thought, and therefore implies tension and struggle. On the level of the spirit, it calls for a collective conversion which in many respects can be hazardous. This dialectical aspect inspired the Marxist view of development. If this sense is stressed too unilaterally, do we not find ourselves, in the Church, too much inclined to disregard this dimension? Is this the result of authentic doctrine? Of ecclesiastical conservation? Or of a kind of excessive anticommunism? We shall have to return to this point. Ecclesiastical circles are still often dominated by a concern for evolving only when there is no question of confrontations. And when clashes occur accidentally, some ecclesiastics wish to hide them under the carpet like some shameful excretion. However, the Church has not always spared herself confrontation, particularly when historic change was taking place. As far back as the time of Paul, we have the instance of his taking Peter to task because the latter's complacency favored the conservatism of the Judaizers. And there is the case of Saint Bernard speaking to Pope Eugene III (1145-53) in terms that go far beyond the language of our present-day contenders.[13]

It is true that the theories of harmonious and harmonized development represent an ideal that is constantly being challenged, contradicted, and postponed by the realities of our situation. Like Saint Paul's notion of Christian life, development often means a battle even for those who are committed to this ideal in a most resolutely peaceful way. We shall return to this point in Chapter 11, section 2.

From the viewpoint of this study in vocabulary, let us say only that these aspects of struggle and contradiction can be integrated within the image of development-growth if we remember its full scope, and do not forget the parable of the seed that dies, or that in relation to nonliving matter life is a revolution and on the level of the spirit it often means a conversion. Such integration was realized in the definition given at the Louvain symposium (December 2, 1968; TM, GB, MB 493, p. 1).

> [Development may be described as] the process tending to transform each man in such a way that he becomes responsible for his own unfolding growth within a community that is the autonomous agent of its own becoming. This implies liberation from the constraints
>> of the natural order
>> of the cultural order (ignorance, magic forms of religiosity, incapacity for understanding one's own situation or that of others, incapacity to assume one's own destiny on one's own)

of the social, economic, and political order, both on the national and international planes (different forms of domination and alienation). . . .

The industrial activity . . . typical of developed societies . . . is . . . a privileged means of development. But it is also ambiguous, since it can become a means of domination and endanger freedom. . . .

The type of domination bound up with the social and economic system of capitalism implies a radical re-examination of this system and the need to face up to the possibility of a break with it. The history of development does not bear out the prolongation of the past, but . . . a procedure set up on new ground.

This definition might be completed by another one which would look at the phenomenon, not on the level of fundamental groups—however important they may be—but on that of mankind as a whole, the real subject of development. Actually, in the change that it is experiencing today mankind is finding its own unity in intensified differentiation and communication. There is no true development that is not universally applicable on this scale. Indeed, the "isolated" development of particular groups or peoples today, from the point of view of mankind as a whole, is a pathological phenomenon like the irregular growth of a goiter or a cancer. This leads us to propose the following definition:

Development is the joint organic change of mankind which must bring about its growth for the benefit of "all men and the whole man." This progress cannot be brought about without tensions, which are signs of life and health. But it is necessary to bring about order in these tensions. This ordering will of necessity be manifold, as it is in the life of higher organisms (in the human body the brain, the sympathetic and para-sympathetic nervous systems, the pituitary gland). It must involve stimulation, unanimity, and synergism for its basic units, and reflexive coordination of the whole. Participation in this human phenomenon is owed in justice to all mankind.

Conclusion to the Word Study

By giving the word its full acceptation as a development of "all men and the whole man," in line with an "integral humanism," Paul VI is following the direction taken by language itself, since the new acceptation of the word has become normative in the light of the awareness of human solidarity, the anomaly of underdevelopment, and the need to remedy it. If the pope's choice of definition is correct it is because he is following the direction indicated by history itself.

The choice he made is not without operational import. It tends to rally the aspirations and endeavors of all men to the service of a quest that concerns them all. Actually, harmonious development is a requisite of justice, of brotherhood, and of the salvation of men. It cannot be looked upon merely as a means to an end, even by religion. It is an end which coincides with the vocation and the salvation of men. This is why we entitled this book *Salvation and Development* originally. It goes without saying that salvation implies freedom and that development presupposes a liberation from systems in which any development is impossible.

IS THERE
A THEOLOGY
OF DEVELOPMENT?

4

The essential aspect of the problem posed by the title of this book: *Liberation, Development, and Salvation,* brings us to a thorny question: Can we even speak of a "theology of development"?

Etymologically, theology is a *logos*; that is, a word, a discourse, a science, which has God for its object. If we then speak of a "theology of development," are we not indulging in the popular misuse of this word as evident today in phrases like a "theology of war," a "theology of revolution," a "theology of violence," and so on?

That there is a theology of God is quite clear. That there is a theology of man considered in his inseparable relationship with God the creator and redeemer, and more specifically in his divinization through grace, is also clear. But should we still speak of theology when we are dealing with optional activities in a technical or political order? Even if a Christian plan of action identifies such choices, or if such options are in some way referred back to God and therefore to theology is that sufficient reason for us to speak of a *theology* of those options, those means, that policy? We wonder, for here we are no longer dealing with the object of divine revelation, but with the order of human involvements: war and revolution are not the objects of theology but rather of ethical judgment, since they are "accidental," caused effects in relation to the essence of God's message. Furthermore, there is a choice not only between a plurality of means but also between various human commitments, according to the principle that a moral action, in contradistinction to truth or a work of art, is not determined once and for all. All this raises serious questions: Is development a specifically theological object at all? Or does development somehow merely happen to relate, intrinsically or extrinsically, to theology?

Still, a scrupulously careful theologian like Joseph Comblin wrote a little book entitled: *Teologia do desenvolvimento*, and similarly, Father V. Cosmao programmed the July 1968 Tignes session under the title: *Toward a Theology of Development*. But in the latter case the preposition *toward* indicates an unanswered question. "I should rather speak today of 'theological reflections on development,'" he had already told me in May 1968.[1]

The question is still open; the key to the problem is this: there can be a theology of development to the extent that development affects salvation in Jesus Christ intrinsically. Here two choices are possible which it is important to identify from the beginning. Actually, whether we want it or not, we are in different degrees committed to one or the other: an eschatology of continuity or discontinuity.

Eschatology of Continuity

The first is a Teilhardian option according to which salvation is achieved in the very fabric of the world, in line with what men, even agnostics, used to call and still do call "progress": economic, scientific, cultural, and the like. Ultimately, eschatology would be the simple fulfillment of this plan which of itself tends toward the *omega* point, Jesus Christ.

This first option stresses continuity in all respects:

1. *Continuity between temporal development and eternal fulfillment.* Eternity—which may at times actually lose its importance or even its significance in this view—is perceived ultimately as the harvest of a ripe fruit from the tree of knowledge.

2. *Continuity between nature and grace.* Let us not be too quick to say that this is a kind of naturalism, a denial of the order of grace and redemption. The most serious upholders of this option rely upon authorities of considerable weight. Saint Thomas Aquinas, unlike most of his predecessors and successors, acknowledges the proper consistency and the importance of the natural order which the supernatural order does not distort, but rather fulfills. More radically, this

view is rooted in the cosmic theology of Saint Paul (Colossians 1:15-20), which is surely very poorly known in the West, as André Feuillet has ably demonstrated.[2] The "continuity" advocates rightly emphasize the following truths: redemption does not create another world but restores the one that was created; it does not burst nature asunder, but brings its potentialities to fruition. Again, they have no intention of denying the gratuitousness of God's gift nor that God calls man to go beyond himself, but they do not understand this gratuitousness as an addition to or an extrinsic complement to nature. Man was indeed created by God, but not in a purely natural state. This is merely an abstraction, an hypothesis, that originated in the need to counteract the teachings of Baius, and care must be taken not to objectify it. Man was created according to a dynamic law. Within him is the seminal power to go beyond himself intrinsically—and that power is planted in him by God. There is a vital unity between nature and supernature. The two must therefore not be dissociated. Henri de Lubac in *Mystère du surnaturel* (Paris: Aubier, 1965) gave a convincing demonstration of this point.

From this perspective, we must reject what is sometimes called the supernaturalist heresy, which tends to oppose super-nature to nature as a value-added-from-without to a non-value. Economic-cultural development would be valueless, since salvation is thus reduced to the supernatural, to the religious self, struggling against nature.

The perspective of continuity, quite to the contrary, makes capital out of revelation: Grace heals nature, and restores it, like the Samaritan, a figure of Christ, who tended to the injured man on the road to Jericho; grace perfects nature within nature's own context and satisfies the aspirations inscribed in man's heart. And man's vocation is to go beyond himself, as Paul VI reminds us in *Populorum progressio,* quoting Pascal's excellent phrase in the *Pensées*: "man infinitely surpasses man" (Paris: Éditions Brunswicg, no. 434).

In other words, man is an equivocal creature, open to the infinite through his reason, his freedom, his self-awareness, through the "eternally-willing-living-loving" in which he was created.

This view stresses the mystery of the Incarnation and human authenticity. But this humanizing seems to betray the validity of the sacrament. According to classical theology, the Real Presence ceases when the species of bread and wine deteriorate, and the consecration would be null if the wine had already turned to vinegar. Correspondingly, development-continuity advocates hold that man and the Faith are mutually debased by superstitious forms of religiosity.

Pushed to its limits this view enables us to have a theology of development, for man's fulfillment comes through total human development, rooted in the material and temporal, both economic and cultural. Man fulfills himself through structures which intrinsically affect his relationship with God and his salvation in the full sense of that word.

Harvey Cox arrives at the same conclusion in *The Secular City* although through different and more radical ways. He believes that in this age man's politics replace metaphysics as the language of theology (New York: Macmillan, 1965, pp. 105–10).

In this view, the whole task is to "make the life of men in the world human." Development, this action, this policy, is *the* theology, both the expressive and the efficacious sign of the human fellowship in love in which we find the essential note of Christianity (Matthew 18:20; 25: 31–46).

This would even be the only theology possible, because in this hypothesis, there is no object of revelation to be contemplated in itself, but a precept of charity to be realized among men on the level of the existential relationships where Christ manifests himself exclusively. It is in the practice of love that the mysterious and implicit presence of Christ is actualized among men.

The Perspective of Discontinuity

In contradistinction to the Teilhardian idea which views human progress as a curve ascending to the *omega* point, other theologians think of human history as unfolding horizontally. They situate salvation in a vertical dimension, and as in another order than that affected by technical, scientific, or cultural progress. For them, salvation transcends human history bogged down in a morass of daily vicissitudes. Is not salvation, definitively, the uprooting of man from history through death, and of the whole world through the *parousia*?

This is the Pascalian view in which the order of grace shares no common ground with the order of the mind. Unlike Teilhard, whose mysticism developed within the heart of his scientific work, Pascal abandoned the sciences for mysticism. For him, it was necessary to make a choice.

According to this Pascalian perspective, eschatology is dramatic and discontinuous. The world is not called to fulfillment through a full flowering of life and at the apogee of its earthly realities. Rather it is called upon to receive its salvation in the very depths of failure, scandal, and death, following the example of the dead and risen Christ. This is a drama eschatology, and not an eschatology of fulfillment; one of discontinuity, not of continuity; of redemption as contradistinguished from one of incarnation. It implies a descent into hell and the destruction of the world by fire (2 Peter 3:12).

Schema of the Two Concepts of Eschatology

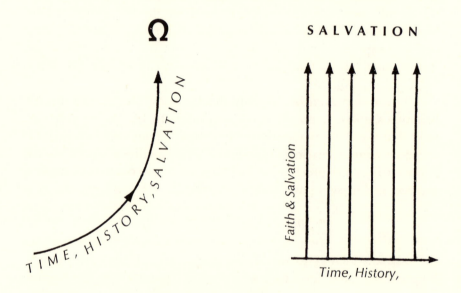

Idea of Man's Seeking of God

Teilhardian Continuity   **Pascalian Discontinuity**

The supporters of discontinuity have a good point when they say that material riches do not contribute to man's full growth in God, that prosperity numbs man's sense of the supernatural. On the contrary, poverty and grief awaken it, for they bring man face to face with his limitations, his helplessness, the truth of his lowliness, and at the same time they confront him with God and the hope founded in him. It is from the depths of his misery that man understands the crucified Christ: "You have wounded me. I allowed myself to be so injured in order to show you by my suffering how absolute my love is. But to understand this you must suffer as I did."

This view is also developed in many biblical themes:

1. God cursing the rich (Luke 6:24; *cf.* 1:53; 16:19; 18:23–25; Isaiah 5:8–25; Matthew 19:23–24; James 2:6; 5:1), and blessing the poor (Luke 4:18; 6:20; 7:22; 14:13; James 2:5–6).

2. Peace and prosperity never worked out in Israel. The case is typical, since even in our own day "the good times" in our developed countries are no more lasting. Our prosperous times are characterized by materialism, selfishness, and immorality.

3. Faith is a "stumbling block to Jews and folly to gentiles" (1 Corinthians 1:23) because it proposes that life is to be found on the tree of death which is the cross of Christ.

Conclusion

We shall have to weigh the meaning of these ideas. What riches and poverty are meant? What scandal and what folly? To what extent is the disaffection accompanying prosperity a vice inherent in riches? Would this not be due to the fact that we have nurtured alienating and inferior forms of religiousness which in turn disappear because of that very alienation? Does this factor not explain at least in part two complementary phenomena?

Some people rush to shrines because they have lost all hope in human resources. They expect everything from God, from a miracle, but they are ignorant of the power of their properly directed actions. Religious hope understood in such a way confirms them in their bad habits.

People who have sought God in that way, solely through being resigned to their misery and their wounds, reject him along with their misery once the exercise of their responsibilities has got them out of their state of wretchedness, once they have begun to do something instead of merely crying to heaven about their plight. Bishop Fragoso stresses in his teaching that men must rid themselves of alienating and passive religion by developing an active and community-oriented Christianity. "Is it God's job to dig wells, build roads, and change society?" he asks, exposing social conditions that are unacceptable in God's eyes. And it is very clear that the answer is no.

We are thus led to a complementary question which will be treated in Chapter 8: "Is religion favorable or contrary to development? The answer can evoke profound differences, depending on whether we are thinking of religions in general, of Christianity, or of Catholicism. Between the first and second terms, there is an intervening question: To what extent is Christianity a religion?

To sum up the state of the question as posed above:

In the Teilhardian view of continuity, and more generally in the secular views that stress the theological import of involvement in the world, we can speak of a theology of development.

In the Pascalian view of discontinuity, this expression would be out of place. Development appears as a more or less commendable human option, with merely an extrinsic relationship to salvation.

It may be that a study of the data of revelation will help us to bridge the gap between these two opposite views.

Part Three

Sources for

Answering the Question

SCRIPTURAL
EVIDENCE

5

Does revelation have anything to say about development? This question is important from the point of view we have adopted: that of perspectives of the Faith. Actually, theology is not laborious, private scholarship but rather the public elucidation of revelation. Here, however, the first evidence the exegete has is negative. We must honestly admit this.

The Negative Evidence

Scripture is alien to the modern notion of development as we have defined it.

Furthermore, the word *progressio* which is used from the outset in the official Latin text of the encyclical *Populorum progressio* is not used by the Vulgate. The word that comes closest is *progressior* but in a form that does not signify progress but rather decline: "I am now old and well advanced in years" (*progressioris aetatis*); (Joshua 23:2). The progression here is the advancement toward decline and death.

As for the verb *progredior*, the Vulgate uses it six times in a material sense, except in the Song of Solomon (6:10) where the forward movement has a symbolic meaning. "Who is this that looks forth" (*progreditur*) "like the dawn?"

A more positive examination of the words *profectio, profectus,* and *proficere* do not give us anything explicit to go on. But at least the verb *proficio* gives evidence of the Bible's concern with human growth, life, and fecundity. Christ's desire is that men "have life abundantly" (John 10:10). However, in the context of the New Testament, what is envisioned is essentially the growth and development of the kingdom. This kingdom is, of course, a human community. But the Gospel keeps its distance in regard to material goods (Matthew 6:26–29; *cf.* Luke 12:24–29):

> Look at the birds of the air: they neither sow nor reap nor gather into barns, and yet your heavenly Father feeds them. Are you not of more value than they? . . . And why are you anxious about clothing? Consider the lilies of the field . . . they neither toil nor spin; yet I tell you, even Solomon in all his glory was not arrayed like one of these.

This evangelical norm is alien, if not contrary, to the perspective of a development program, except that it says—and this is perhaps the real meaning—that man ought not to hoard things for himself. And here we come up against that road block met by the development movement when small groups of people corner the land or some other commodity.

Temporal Prosperity & Eschatology

The negative remarks we have just made call for some distinctions and compensations.

First of all, the Latin text of the Vulgate which we are using as a point of comparison with the official Latin text of *Populorum progressio* weakens the dynamic nature of the original vocabulary of the Old Testament. Hebrew is a less static, more vital language than Latin.

Consequently, and especially, if the Bible says little about progress—although there is the significant figure of the progression toward the Promised Land—it has a great deal to say about fecundity in the sense that, to a rather large extent, it takes on the meaning of the word "development" since in a parallel way it also involves vital expansion. In fact, in certain respects, the word "fecundity" says more—reproduction in conformity with what we are. (See Genesis 1:11, 21, 24 etc., where *myn* must be translated as "likeness" rather than "species" or "race," as H. Cazelles has shown.)

The root *brk* or "bless," which is so essential to the Old Testament, seems originally to have meant fecundity. The blessing of Abraham, which did not yet contain the promise of eternal life, guarantees for him a progeny that will be his continuance on earth, a progeny great and as numerous as the stars in the sky (Genesis 12:2, 7; 15:5). God's blessing is also for the fecundity of flocks and possessions. Similarly, the word "property" (*mqnh*) comes from a root meaning procreation—the possessions of a patriarch form one body with him, they are the vital extension of his very person. When Job is afflicted in his body after having lost his possessions and his posterity, it is merely a further step in the ordeal which affects him organically. The problem of salvation, in the Old Testament, is to avoid catastrophe in growth, threatened as it is by war, sickness, famine, and other calamities. Salvation (*yeshah*) is first conceived of as a dynamic power to produce a people and its civilization. The God who speaks to this people is not an "idea" as with Plato, but a principle of fecundity. Thus biblical revelation eliminates the alienating mythology of gods who breed in the midst of similarly breeding men. God, situated at a different level, awakens and liberates human dynamism.

Yet the ideal of prosperity immediately brings up a problem. In the light of God's promises, the prosperity of the wicked was a scandal to the poor of the Old Testament (Job 8 and 21; Psalm 37; Ecclesiastes 7:15; Jeremiah 12; Malachi 3:15).

This problem was resolved for the first time in Psalm 73. Starting from the point of this scandal, the psalmist reveals the retributions that will come about beyond the grave: he is not prospering, unlike his enemies whose "bodies are sound and sleek" (73:4) and "swell out with fatness" (73:7). But he is always with God; this is his possession. Yahweh holds him by the hand (73:23) and will *"receive"* him [on the last day]. The verb is used in the eschatological sense it had for Enoch (Genesis 5, 24; Sirach 44:16; 49:14) and Elijah (2 Kings 2:3, 5, 9, 10; Sirach 48:9), who were "taken" by God on their last day, the day that means downfall for the wicked. But this eternal outcome specifically de-emphasizes temporal prosperity and the world itself "And there is nothing upon earth that I desire besides thee," the psalmist exclaims (73:25).

This de-emphasis is accentuated in the New Testament, which reinforces the eschatological perspective. Thus the primitive Jerusalem community, however exemplary its integral communism, ended up in complete failure from the viewpoint of what we today call development. The members of this community remained eternity-focused underdeveloped people, and collections constantly had to be taken up for their support. The purpose of these collections was not even to set up "economic development" among them. The collections were merely an "assistance program."

To restore the purely temporal perspective of the Old Testament might be a temptation. It was such for the Church even on the religious plane, and came after the phase of eschatological expectation in which she lived without any earthly home, and thought only of the "temple built of living stones" (1 Peter 2:4–6; Ephesians 2:19–21) by the Holy Spirit—that is, the Christian community. During the Constantinian era she acquired temporal possessions that at times were quite considerable. Undoubtedly it was difficult to escape this, but it was very risky. Temporal possessions may yield service, but they also entail servitude. The greatest danger is to become used to them. No doubt buildings and administrations can manifest the Gospel, but as Deuteronomy warned (8:13–19), they can also be its tomb. Hence the attempts today to return to a Church of the poor which would really be the Church of the Gospel, a Church built of living stones.

Does what harmed the Church better befit the world? In one sense it does, since secular realities are of the temporal order, and material means are essential for it. However, the teaching of the Old and New Testaments invites us to go beyond this perspective. God exalts the poor and lays low the rich. And it is a fact that excessive wealth degrades man, and a certain kind of poverty stimulates him. What then? Temporal prosperity remains a "good," but a relative one. It is valuable within certain limits and must always be subordinated to the human values of justice, charity, and fellowship among men. To seek riches for riches' sake involves a phenomenon of regression and alienation. "Where your treasure is, there will your heart be also" (Luke 12:34), Jesus said. And the "treasure" that counts is one "where neither moth nor rust consumes" (Matthew 6:20), and which neither thieves nor death can take from us.

A THEOLOGY OF TECHNOLOGY

Does the Bible give us any elements that could be used for a theology of technology? The pericope of Genesis 4:17–23 on the invention of metals, the lyre, and the reed pipe is hardly of interest for our purpose; it is merely a statement. We might even stress the fact that all this blossomed with the descendants of Cain, the first city-builder. These verses show the interest of the Bible's authors in human progress, but without any explanation. It was to the extent that technology was involved in the building of the Temple that it interested the sacred authors (Exodus 37:1; 2 Chronicles 1–9). And if the poet (Job 28:9–11) admired man's handiwork, his demiurgic power to build, this had nothing to do with human development.

If there is any trail-breaking in this area, it is manifest on a different level.

First of all, there is the integration of technological activity within the domain of wisdom, in which the Bible will ultimately recognize the hypostasis of God (Proverbs 8:22–31; Sirach 24:1–29; Wisdom 7:22, 8:1), an hypostasis that plays a technological role in the creation of the world (Proverbs 8:27, 30). Wisdom is "the fashioner of all things" (Wisdom 7:22). In the New Testament it is "the Word . . . through whom all things were made" (John 1:3; Colossians 1:16; Hebrews 1:2).

The promotion of these values took place within an ascending process: Israel took over the human wisdom of the Egyptians, a wisdom concerned with life, work, human relationships, and the use of the goods of the earth. It would seem that the Church today, in the throes of what has been called the "crisis of secularism," is taking a similar step: taking over in a secular area which she feels is of concern to God and will lead to God in the long run. The earliest evidences of Egyptian wisdom preserved in the Bible are assuredly as nonreligious and as radically secular as the phenomenon of socioeconomic development. In a different context, we shall again find this wisdom theme identified with Christ, the first-born of all creatures (Colossians 1:15).

THE VALUE OF WORK

We shall also find a theme allied with that of technological activity; the value of human work,[1] and therefore of "culture" in all senses of the word, since in the Bible work is typically the cultivation of the earth (agri*culture*) as in Genesis 2:15 for example. We can also integrate within this context the agricultural dimension of the Jewish liturgy: unleavened bread, the barley harvest festival; Pentecost, the wheat harvest festival; and Tabernacles, the fruit harvest. But it is less a question of work festivals than of rest holidays. They celebrate the blessing of God, the fruit of his creative work. It would even seem that man's work profanes the earth. Thus the Law commands that it be allowed to rest every seven years. It is a homage to God who gives the earth and its fruit. Yet it is the years of work that God makes fertile and not the fallow years (Leviticus 25:20–21). God's blessings extend over man's work, and we shall discover its meaning further on when we consider the theme of creation.

Actually, it is on a more radical level that we must look for the biblical themes that shed light on today's problem of development.

Biblical Anthropology Integrates the Body

The first theme, of the basic value of the body, derives from biblical anthropology. Salvation as taught by Christ is not purely spiritual and reduced to the soul; the body is intrinsically and inseparably involved. Salvation involves the whole man, conceived as a material-spiritual and physical-existential unit.

The body is not despised or condemned as it is in Manichaeism. It is not belittled as in Platonism, where it is something to be escaped. The Old Testament does not rob the body of its worth nor does it oppose it to the soul. It does not separate the two.

The New Testament points up two important facts:

1. *The Incarnation:* "The Word became flesh," he was born into the human race and family. He willed to assume that portion of the world that is the body of a man, with all the cosmic and human bonds that that implies. This was not unworthy of him; the body also was to be saved.

2. *The resurrection of the body:* Saint Paul teaches this second point with much insistence, against the concepts of Greek philosophy. Despite bitter setbacks (Acts 17:32), he in no way weakened this basic teaching. On the contrary, against stiff opposition he emphasized it: "He who raised Christ Jesus from the dead will give life to your mortal bodies also through his Spirit which dwells in you" (Romans 8:11).

This theology implies a very forceful statement of incorporation in Christ (Romans 1:5–6) and that is why Saint Paul is not unconcerned about the needs of the saints in Jerusalem (Romans 12:13; 15:26–27). He provides for them with great difficulty, even if he does so in the context of simple aid, outside any perspective of development. In short, according to the Bible, the body is an integral part of the man it constitutes. It is in no way alien to salvation. Most un-Christian and contrary to Christianity was the later resurgence of a kind of Platonism in which the body seemed to be the prison of the soul from which the soul had to escape, an old shoe that had to be discarded. Until fairly recently we merely counted souls, "a parish of ten thousand souls," as if the body were not an integral part of salvation. This was more than a problem with words. It was easy to have a "good conscience," because *one loved souls*—even while social injustice was degrading or *destroying men* on the level of their corporal-spiritual existence. The Bible attests to the integral reality of man which is fulfilled in a body that is called to eternal life. Bodily realities are integral parts of salvation. This is important for the theme *salvation and development*.

The God Who is Good, Creator of a Good World

Biblical anthropology is rooted in a theology of a God-man-world relationship.

The importance of this biblical teaching is revealed through contrast. Aristotle's God, like Plato's Idea of the Good, is abstract transcendence. Similarly, the supreme God witnessed in African religions is cut off from the world. He is unconcerned with it; he is inaccessible. Another layer of invisible beings is in contact with man: the genies or his ancestors, but these powers are more malevolent than benevolent. Man is not free in the custody of powers which harry and maltreat him. Unsure of what their whims may bring, he feels threatened and alienated.

The milieu in which the biblical revelation appeared was one in which man believed in a plurality of antagonistic gods. The world was born from their conflict, in accordance with an elementary dialectic. In the Bible, on the contrary, God is the author and absolute master of creation, and has man participate in his work.

The Bible is opposed still more radically to the Manichean view in which the world would be the work of a wicked god whom people should wish to be annihilated.

According to biblical revelation there is only one God. He is good. He created all things (Acts 17:24). In creating, he saw "that it was good" (Genesis 1:25, 31). Thus "he loved the world" (John 3:16), and more especially man since he made him in the image of his own sovereign goodness (Genesis 1:26–27; 5:1; Wisdom 2:23; Sirach 17:3; *cf.* 2 Corinthians 3:18 and Colossians 3:10). He set him up harmoniously in a choice place in creation. Therefore, human prosperity, both in possessions and progeny, is a blessing from God.

The transcendent God of biblical revelation is not represented as a remote being situated in another world. He is present in the world and, more expressly, he is present to man. Obviously, the Bible makes use of the image of heaven, but this is a heaven that is part of the cosmos, and God is not exterior to earth. He intervenes at man's level. He strolls in the garden in the cool of the evening (Genesis 3:8). He comes to eat at Abraham's table (Genesis 18:8). He is in the burning bush at ground level (Exodus 3:2). He is in the gentle breeze that blows before Elijah's cave (1 Kings 19:12). Yahweh is not the God of some other time, some other space, he is a God among men, like them, yet so different, immanent yet transcendent.

Finally, the Bible attests to the unity of the world and of the human race which forms one family descended from one couple created in God's image (Genesis 1:26–28 and 2:7–23; Acts 17:26).

THE WORLD HAS A DIVINE HISTORY

Here we have another very important idea—ours is a world that has a history which comes from God and goes toward God. Time is linear. It is a progression toward salvation. This idea of time-as-progress is not universal. For the Greeks, as we know, time was cyclical; and this archetype was resurrected with extraordinary intensity by Nietzsche. Contrariwise, the Christian vision of the world and the kingdom is a vision of development, analogous to that of a seed with the promise of unlimited multiplication. This is the preferred theme in the parables of the kingdom.

Nevertheless, this salvational development, defined in terms of an intimate gift of God and in the moral order, cannot be identified with human economic development. What we are able to say is that this linear concept of time-as-progress seems to have done much to inspire the modern myth of progress, both in the order of development and in other matters.

THE WORLD AS A MIRROR OF GOD

Put succinctly, the Bible esteems earthly values. It celebrates the blooming of life in a world well made. The God-man-world relationship is shown to be just, coherent, organic, and harmonious. Everything comes from God and returns to God. The world is good. It is for man and man is for God. We shall see that sin did not destroy this basic relationship.

These are its two primary themes: anthropology integrating the body; and the theology of creation. More than a framework, they furnish us with a basis, a light, a milieu divine and human for living and thinking development. They urge us to a harmonious advance-ment of the corporal order in which the spiritual flowers, even though, according to the Bible, the development of the visible creature pro-ceeds from the spiritual order. The principle of life in this world according to the Old Testament is the *ruah*: it is both spirit and atmosphere, a life force, connected with the God of Abraham (Genesis 6:2–4).

Other themes derive their importance in relation to these basic ideas. They establish, enlighten, necessitate, or demand more formally and dynamically a development blueprint in these new times in which we live.

Man Completes Creation

Man's mission in the world as shown in the Bible comes still closer to our object. The foundation of this concept is found in Genesis 1:28:

> Be fruitful and multiply, and fill the earth and subdue it; and have dominion over the fish of the sea and over the birds of the air and over every living thing that moves upon the earth.

That verse as quoted in *Populorum progressio* (no. 19), contains two important themes: (1) Human expansion through generation, or growth of the race, which in its way is a development; (2) man's do-minion over the universe: he has dominion over the earth, including animals (originally in a vegetarian context, moreover, as is shown by a comparison between Genesis 1:29–30 and the later account in 9:2–4, but that is another matter).

What is important is that this mission situates man as an exten-sion of the Creator who worked at the creation of the world for six days and rested on the seventh. He is invited to take over God's work and complete it, complying with the septenary rhythm of work and rest for which God gave the model (Genesis 2:2–3; Exodus 20:9–11). He is called to extend God's labor in the image of God.

Indeed, if man has been established as the master of the world, it is undoubtedly through a gift of God, but not one fortuitously given. This function of dominion follows from his very nature, re-lated as it is to God's nature. Man was created "in the image of God." The call to "have dominion over the earth," to reign over it, flows from this basic theme which precedes and founds the mission given to man. Genesis 1:28, which we considered earlier, is preceded (1:26) by this basic teaching: "Then God said, 'Let us make man in our image, after our likeness,' " which is why he concludes: 'and let them have dominion over the fish of the sea, and over the birds of the air, and over the cattle, and over all the earth, and over every creeping thing that creeps upon the earth.' "

Then the basic theme is recapitulated and stressed (Genesis 1:27): "So God created man in his own image, in the image of God he created him; male and female he created them."

And it is only then that God gives man his kingship and dominion, which are due specifically to his nature as an image of God.

The two ideas are similarily joined in Psalm 8:4–6: "What is man that thou art mindful of him, and the son of man that thou dost care for him? Yet thou hast made him little less than God, and dost crown him with glory and honor. Thou hast given him dominion over the works of thy hands; thou hast put all things under his feet." (This text is also quoted in Hebrews 2:3–9, with a messianic interpretation that is connected with the image of God theme; *cf.* Psalm 115:16).

The connection is still better attested in Sirach 17:1–4, which echoes Genesis (1:26–27; 9:2–3): "The Lord created man out of the earth . . . and made them in his own image. He placed the fear of them in all living beings, and granted them dominion over beasts and birds."

Wisdom makes man's dominion explicit in terms of ruling and passing judgment (9:2–3): "O God of my fathers . . . by thy wisdom thou hast formed man to have dominion over the creatures thou hast made, and rule the world in holiness and righteousness, and pronounce judgment in uprightness of soul, give me the wisdom that sits by thy throne."

The doctrine of Genesis 1:26–28 which belongs to the "P" document (middle of sixth century B.C.), is already outlined in the "J" document (tenth century B.C.), in Genesis 2:15, in a more imaginative form: "The Lord God took the man and put him in the garden of Eden to till it and keep it."

Here man does not appear as the king and lord of creation, but rather as God's farmer and gardener. However, the relationship is analogous, for here God himself is pictured as a builder: God "planted" (*wayitah*) a garden in Eden (Genesis 2:8); he fashioned man from dust (2:7) and "built" (*wayiben*) the rib he had taken from the man into a woman. On the level of this imagery, man is still more in the image of God if we may say so, since the anthropomorphism of God is more pronounced. What is important is that the sense is the same: man extends the work of the Creator upon the earth which is entrusted to him. This is what comes out of the preceding verse (Genesis 2:5). Before the creation of man: "When no plant of the field was yet in the earth and no herb of the field had yet sprung up—for the Lord God had not caused it to rain upon the earth, and there was no man to till the ground."

Creation as it comes from the hands of God is rudimentary. It is man's task to complete it through *tilling*. This is a theme filled with meaning. Man completes creation through work, a bodily act that involves his freedom, his creativity, and his capacity to fulfill himself through it. The irksome character of work was not there in the beginning. According to Genesis 3:17 it is the consequence of sin. Human work and rest are in the image of God.

Similarly, in Genesis 2:18–20, Yahweh makes all the animals pass before Adam so that he might name them. He has him perform an act of ownership. To give a name is to have control over some created thing, to have it in one's service. Symbolically, it is to give expression to dominion through knowledge and language: it is therefore a symbol of abstract knowledge and thereby of control and ownership on behalf of men.

This duty of working for the community is by no means abolished in the New Testament, even in the period of the most fervent first-century eschatological mysticism. In fact, it was precisely to the Thessalonians, for whom the expectation of the *parousia* was serving as a pretext for idleness and irresponsibility, that Saint Paul recalled emphatically the rule he had preached in his sermons to them and had impressed through his own example: "If anyone is unwilling to work, then neither should he eat" (2 Thessalonians 3:6–12; 1 Thessalonians 5:14). These are, it is true, the only formal New Testament texts on the duty to work "so as not to be a burden," but they are very significant. Even though they are focused on the life of the Christian community, they go far beyond it. Let us recall that Saint Paul, in the name of God himself, required Christians to submit to the civil power (Romans 13:1–7; *cf.* 1 Timothy 2:1–2; Titus 3:1–3; and this in accord with the teaching of Christ himself in Matthew 22:21; *cf.* 1 Peter 2:13–17; *cf.* Proverbs 24:21).

In short, man, an earthly creature, has an earthly mission. His work, like his rest, are in the image of God. They have a sacred value attested to by the rites of the Law—particularly the Sabbath rest and the sacrifices offered to God of the fruit of human labor.

Redemption Restores Creation

Is the biblical theology of creation destroyed by the theology of the redemption? Some people are tempted to hold that opinion, with this syllogistic figure as a point of departure: the world, created good, has become bad through sin. The redemption frees us from this wicked world which we must flee or spurn.

The biblical perspective is something quite different: Redemption restores a creation functionally disoriented by sin. And this "universal restoration" (Acts 3:21; *cf. Gaudium et spes,* no. 48) proceeds from the redemption.

To the extent that the restoration perspective is presented as the eschatological expectation of "a new heaven and a new earth" emanating from a free gift of God after a cataclysm (2 Peter 3:13; Revelations 21:1–5), it is of little use to our considerations. The millenarianism of Revelation (20:6–7) does show a hesitation between the continuity and discontinuity eschatology mentioned in the previous chapter.

What is relevant to our subject are the texts that affirm the unity of the cosmos, its recapitulation in Christ (Colossians 1:15–20; and Ephesians 4:12–13, cited in *Populorum progressio,* notes 32, 67). According to Colossians 1:15–20, there is an organic connection between Christ and creation; he is its first-born as well as its agent:

> He is the image of the invisible God, the first-born of all creation; for in him all things were created, in heaven and on earth . . . all things were created through him and for him . . . in him all things hold together. . . . For in him all the fulness of God was pleased to dwell, and through him to reconcile to himself all things, whether on earth or in heaven, making peace by the blood of his cross.

This cosmic perspective we find already mentioned by Saint Paul (1 Corinthians 15:28):

> When all things are subjected to him, then the Son himself will also be subjected to him who put all things under him, that God may be everything to every one.

We have here a whole theology of the creation and of the re-creation by Christ, closely connected with the theme of man as "image of God" according to Genesis 1:27; Colossians 1:15; *cf.* 1 Corinthians 8:6; 2 Corinthians 4:4; Ephesians 4:13. This cosmic theology of Saint Paul is important as a source for Teilhard de Chardin and for the conciliar constitution *Gaudium et spes,* and it has been the subject of a noteworthy study by André Feuillet, *Le Christ, sagesse de Dieu* (Paris: J. Gabalda, 1966, especially pp. 361-485) and by Stanislas Lyonnet in various articles.[2]

In this view, all creation, under man's dominion, is involved in the organicity of the world, in the evolution of the redemption, and even in the hope which is its springboard (Romans 8:19-21):

> For the creation waits with eager longing for the revealing of the sons of God; for the creation was subjected to futility, not of its own will but by the will of him* who subjected it in hope; because the creation itself will be set free from its bondage to decay and obtain the glorious liberty of the children of God.

The underlying idea is that man is bound up with creation hierarchically: he is its apex. Therefore he dragged all creation down in his own degradation. But Christ, God made man, who recapitulates all creation, in his regenerating raises it up by setting in motion the redemption. And so everything is to be restored in man, redeemed in body and soul, including the whole creation which suffers its birth pangs, while man who "possesses the first fruits of the Spirit" is also in travail in the expectation of the "redemption *of the body*" (Romans 8:22-23), for the body is included in a redemption which is universal and cosmic.

The forcefulness of the Pauline text is such that the Council toned down its realism when it cited it in *Gaudium et spes* (no. 39).[3]

The service of humanity through development is an integrating part of the movement because it is a factor for justice and friendship among men and, more profoundly, because salvation occurs at the very heart of such human activity.

The way is paved for the theology of recapitulation in Christ by the doctrine of *wisdom* in the Old Testament, especially as introduced by Sirach (24). That text is also the source of John 1. Wisdom had been identified with the Mosaic law, at times as an intermediary in creation and in salvation, at times as something divine and involved

---

*Man, undoubtedly. R.L.

in creation in a vital and somehow organic way. This all became intelligible in the person of Christ, the first-born of all creation and at the same time the Creator and Redeemer of the very world in which he incarnated himself. Sirach's words already point toward the Incarnation. The concept of Wisdom, hypostasis of God, takes root among the chosen people. It is its inspiration. And certainly this development influences human affairs—at least at the Old Testament level— in their skillfulness in crafts and in their administration of civil government. Such activity is considered by Sirach to be both worship and liturgy. Wisdom, personified as a woman (Sirach 24:10–12) fulfills a priestly ministry: "In the holy tabernacle I ministered before him, and so I was established in Zion . . . So I took root in an honored people."

This sacrifice is bound up with a development of the people who are both a political and liturgical community. And the implications are greater, perhaps, than we might think. We shall return to the matter in the last chapter when we consider the connection between liturgy and development.

The Essential Commandment

The basic theme relevant to development is the precept of love as formulated in the Gospel of Judgment according to Matthew (25:34–36; 41–42) and cited in *Populorum progressio,* (no. 74, n. 61):

> Come, O blessed of my Father, inherit the kingdom prepared for you . . . for I was hungry and you gave me food, I was thirsty and you gave me drink, I was a stranger and you welcomed me, I was naked and you clothed me, I was sick and you visited me, I was in prison and you came to me.

And then the negative counterpart: "Depart from me, you cursed, into the eternal fire . . . for I was hungry and you gave me no food."

We must first see this scriptural passage in context: it is the end of the great eschatological discourse that concludes all of Christ's teaching as related by Saint Matthew. The important thing is not the day and the hour, which "no one knows, not even the Son" (Matthew 24:36; *cf.* 44:50; 25:13), but the way that intervening time is to be spent: that *"long* time" mentioned in Matthew 25:19 before the return of Christ.

That is the essential point of the pericope on the judgment. The pericope itself follows the parable of the talents (Matthew 25:14–30). And the significance is identical—in both passages it is a question of what the Lord expects from Christians until his return, as in the new commandment (John 13:34–35). These convergent texts turn on the same axis central to Christ's teaching. What is explicitly stated in the judgment pericope is symbolically expressed in the pericope of the talents. This parable is pertinent because it stresses the industriousness of the charity that should occupy the Christian before the Lord comes. It is clear today that concerned charity must be performed through those structures in which justice and brotherhood among men can be made a reality. Today charity's talents must be committed to the service of development.

In this perspective, Christ's summations which disclose the significance of the two parables take on incalculable importance.

1. Christ proposes service of one's neighbor in the most concrete and basic fashion:

The words "love" and "to love" do not even figure in his discourse. This does not lessen its import, but rather reinforces it. Indeed, love is not a question of a word, an abstraction conceived in the mind, for these can be illusory, but of quite real actions (1 John 3:18): "Little children, let us not love in word or speech but in deed and in truth."

In that discourse, in which Christ intends to express the very essentials of salvation, he does not speak of doing something "supernatural" for one's neighbor. He speaks first of all of material service, beginning with "hunger" and "thirst." The beatitude on "those who hunger" (Luke 6:21) is no conscience soother for us who are aware of the plight of the needy. Finding a remedy is imperative.

Other texts stress the concrete and corporal character of charity, as for example in 1 John 3:17 and in PP 23, n. 21: "But if any one has the world's goods and sees his brother in need, yet closes his heart against him, how does God's love abide in him?"

This verse clarifies one aspect of the other. A love of God that does not reach out to the men and to the universe made in God's image is a false love, an illusion of love. A person who claims to love without so involving himself is deluding himself; he is lying, as the apostle specifies (1 John 4:20): "If anyone says, 'I love God,' and hates his brother, he is a liar; for he who does not love his brother whom he has seen, cannot love God whom he has not seen."

In other words, a person "who claims to love without rendering

such material aid" in reality does not love at all. He has only an illusion of love, and what is more, he is guilty of a lie. John insists upon
this point by specifying that the lying Christian makes God a liar (1
John 2:4, 22). This is true, in accordance with the identification that
exists between Christians and Christ, by means of idiomatic communication, and more concretely, on the level of the witness that Christians
are to give in this regard. We know to what extent the counter-witness
of too many Christians has disfigured God in the eyes of the poor, as
the Council taught clearly (GS, 18, par. 2).

It is important to specify the nature of the typical duties Christ
considered primary. The first two involve the essential needs of the
body: food and drink. The four others bear on factors that can exclude men from the Christian community—that "marginalize" them,
in contemporary language. Certainly the duty of clothing the naked
and visiting the sick is in some way connected with the corporal order,
but clothing has, and in the past had, an even more essential social
significance for man's social integration. Even today, a man will look
in vain for work if he is dressed in rags. One who is well-dressed
can lay claim to a respectable job. In short, if bodily needs are the first
object of charity, the second and complementary one is integration
into the community.

Today, the command to give material aid to benefit society involves a whole sequence of means which, historically, vary according
to the needs of the poor. In our time, the range of these needs and the
worldwide scale of the problem necessarily involve technological, economic, and even political options, which cannot be scanted lest sterility result. Contemporary charity works through structures. In order
to feed the hungry and reintegrate those living a marginal existence,
we must promote the balanced development which will assure food
and clothing and a social and communal life in accordance with honorable, free, just, and brotherly human relations.

The horizon is still widening. At a time when the world is working toward moral and technical unity and when, therefore, it is giving
substance to the universal inspiration of the Gospel, a sustained effort
to attain coherent development on a world scale is the only way we can
avoid absurdity.

2. Christ himself gave *universal import* to the precept that had
been taught since Old Testament times among the chosen people. Yet
we might ask ourselves about the limits of this universalism. In the
sense that it is not limited to family, friends, fellow countrymen it has

no frontiers; Christ has given it worldwide scope (Matthew 25: 32–34). But should such universalism not be limited to one's co-religionists, since Christ continues: "As you did it to one of the least of *these my brethren*, you did it to me"? Is it not merely a question of members of the Christian community? We might be tempted to reconcile this limitation with what Christ says on the road to Damascus: "Saul, Saul, why do you persecute me. . . . I am Jesus whom you are persecuting" (Acts 9:4). But the context advises against such a restriction, and the mention of "my brethren" which might seem to suggest it disappears (Matthew 25: 45): "As you did not do it to one of the least of these, you did it not to me."

The text focuses on salvation on an "all nations" scale (Matthew 25:32); it must therefore be understood for all men without reservation. The theologian can only call attention to the levels and shades of meaning in the duty enunciated for us by Christ—toward the baptized who belong to the visible Church and toward those who belong to it invisibly. And his duty allows of no discrimination since all men are called, without exception, to join the brotherhood of the first-born of all creatures (Colossians 1:15; *cf.* 1:18 and Romans 8:29).

To sum up, the Gospel invites us to serve the "least" of men, that is, every man, and especially those who have the least title to our recognition, in other words, the poor.

In this frame of reference, the precept is also a formulation of the law of nature, that profound law of the vocation and the destiny of man as he was actually created. Such at least is the opinion of Saint Paul (Romans 2:14–16) and the tradition of the Fathers. And it is because man was created for this universal love that so many non-Christians, like Proudhon, easily acknowledge the primordial character of this golden rule even though it was formulated by Christ. Lyonnet concludes[4] that for this reason the Constitution on the Church in the Modern World (GS 77, par. 1) is able to declare "that the Gospel message . . . is in harmony with the loftier strivings of the human race."

3. Christ not only gave the precept its explicit formulation, its central place in ethics, and the grace which permits us to fulfill it, but he also gave it new inspiration. The Old Testament urged us to "love" our neighbor *as ourselves*. He said: "Love one another; even as I have loved you" (John 13: 34; 15:12; *cf.* 15:9). His love went to the ultimate point—death. People do not die for themselves. In this sense then, we have a further surpassing of the Old Testament. Love of

neighbor becomes a love that must go all the way, a divine love (John 13:9).

4. If this love is divine because of its model, it is also divine because of its end, for Christ established an equivalence, even more an identity, between himself and the poor whom we must love. Material aid and social services thus acquire a basic religious value. It is in this way that we do or do not establish a relationship with Christ. What one does for another in the flesh on the level of human fellowship, is done for Christ himself. God is concerned with everything we do to men who are created in his image.

This is a substantial religious change, although the prophets had paved the way for it (Isaiah 58: 6-7; *cf.* Amos 5:21, and the key footnote in the Jerusalem Bible, page 1235, 58a). "Religion" as man conceived it on his own, was a relationship with another world, an indivisible world. And its ideal could be symbolized by the practice of the *Corban* as stressed by certain doctors of the law (Mark 7:11): "What you [the old parents] would have gained from me is 'Corban' (that is, [already] given to God)."

Religion so understood took away from men what it gave to the invisible God. Christ, however, established a fundamental bond between man and God on the human level, horizontally, by means of humble service to one's neighbor. He did not hold to the vertical concept. If he still symbolically situates God "on high," he nevertheless teaches us that we encounter him essentially at the level of human relationships. It is there that we do (or do not) establish communion with him. The Word, image of the invisible God, invites us to find him in other men, formed as they are in God's likeness, and, more especially, in the poor. Mysteriously, it is in them that essentially this image and likeness are to be found. Certainly, the tradition of the Church teaches us that we can reach Christ through other signs—pictorial and sculptural representations, sacramental signs that make present what they signify, but the basic sign, the sign in which earthly communion is achieved, is the clothing, the visiting, and the feeding of the very poor.

Charity is the condition of our communion with God. More than that, such a communion is established even with those who have not acknowledged Christ in serving their neighbor; those who say "Lord, when did we see you hungry and thirsty . . . When did we give you to eat?"

It is of little importance that love for Christ here was implicit or anonymous. By taking on humanity in the world in whose heart God acts and by taking upon himself a kinship with every visible creature, Christ manifests the divine dimension of every act of assistance to one's neighbor.

5. Thus material aid and social service are, according to this teaching, the very criterion of judgment. Man will be judged on this and solely on this, it seems from a reading of the text.

Whatever we may say about this last overtone, God attaches sovereign importance to it. Saint Paul confirms this (Romans 13:8) when he says: "He who loves his neighbor has fulfilled the law."

And he stresses that for him there are not two precepts, love of God and love of neighbor, as it might seem from Matthew 22: 35–39, but one precept that includes everything (Galatians 5:14): "For the whole law is fulfilled in one word, 'You shall love your neighbor as yourself.' "

Once again, this love operates through the contemporary structures of development.

We must stress here the two forms of this precept: "You shall love your neighbor as yourself" (Leviticus 19:18; Matthew 19:19; Mark 12:28–31; Luke 10:25–28; *cf.* Romans 13:9; Galatians 5:14); and "Love one another as I have loved you" (John 13:34).

The second formula reveals the divine dimension of love: a love similar to that of God made man, a love from "on high," given by grace, a love until death. All this is most important, it is the ultimate formula, the fullest and most mystical form of the commandment.

But the first formula remains the basic one on many counts. It is not only an ecumenical formula commensurate with Judaic values but, very broadly, with those of all men of good will who accept it in the light of a right conscience. That acceptance is a universal aspect of the contemporary conscience. A basic formula, it is filled with meaning and is exacting, because it imposes a test which touches us to the quick; no one of us forgets himself or could forget himself. More precisely, for development, this formula is very important because it gives to the commandment of love the exacting form of a commandment of equity. It is normal to treat others as we should like to be treated, even though the law of selfishness and violence in evolving, unfolding life makes us forget this. In its Christological plenitude—to love like Christ, until death—the commandment would risk relativizing the sufferings of men, of aiming too high and too far, and of short-circuiting the whole natural order, under the pretext of making on a far-off day the supreme offering made by Christ.

In the very humble form it has in Leviticus, repeated in the Gospel, the commandment imposes an awareness of daily realities and of the urgency of elementary needs. Do not put or leave others in a condition of hunger, thirst, destitution, oppression, illiteracy, or substandard culture, nor under the thumb of an abstract and tyrannical material "progress" which you would not want at any price for yourself. This commandment imposes the duty of development under its most concrete, most immediate, and most specifically compelling form.

Moreover, for the Christian, the very notion of commandment has been left behind. It is a call, a life, a communicated stimulus. The love of God is "poured into hearts through the Holy Spirit" (Romans 5:5). And the charismata of this same Spirit are a source of discovery perpetually renewed.

THE RIGHTS
OF THE POOR

6

Charity is so inseparable from justice that it can be considered a form of justice if it is true that for God as for men there is no love for others[1] without love of one's self, any more than there can be knowing, however objective, without the personal existence of the subject. Love like knowledge supposes a subject that exists. And this is why revelation gives as the primary and basic frame of reference for love of neighbor, what every man out of vital necessity has for himself— self-love.

This does not prevent charity from transcending justice, or from revolutionizing relationships between persons by means of unlimited generosity, such as that of the God who died for us. Still more profoundly, the love of which God is the exemplar, even though he is the supreme being, is a love of the most poor—of the "least" (Matthew 25: 40–46). But he loves without lowering; on the contrary, he elevates the lowliest. If Christ goes so far as to empty himself mysteriously of himself in order to give himself (Philippians 2:7), it is to replenish all with universal abundance.

The importance of the *agape* of Christ, of this "folly" in which God lowers or elevates himself, as we might say, must not make us forget that charity is grounded in justice or on the basic rights to which each man and every human group can lay claim. This must be stressed for it is of prime importance in development.

The rights of the poor—the subject of the present chapter—call for all the more careful an examination since this doctrine has been obscured over the centuries.

What are these rights according to Scripture? How have they been lost and rediscovered in the course of history? Do they still go unnoticed? These are the essential questions asked in this new chapter.

The Poor in the Old Testament

The rights of the poor belong to a collective whole from which emerge three key points:

1. Poverty is an evil: "The poverty of the poor" (Hebrew: *resam*; Greek: *penia*) "is their ruin" (Hebrew: *dallim*; Greek: *asebôn*) Proverbs 10: 15b. "All the days of the afflicted" (Hebrew: *hâni*) "are evil" Proverbs 15:15.

Similarly Sirach observed, "The life of the poor man (*ptôchoû*) weighs down his heart," according to the Septuagint only (Ecclesiasticus 38:19b).

The apocryphal books speak in a similar fashion: "I ate a bitter apple and swallowed aloes, but I found nothing more bitter than indigence and poverty." Wisdom of Ahiqar (Arm.) 2:69; "I drank gall and it is not more bitter than poverty" (Ecclesiasticus 31:24; Proverbs 31:7; Ecclesiastes 4: 1–2).

The last text gives the idea that death is more desirable than the life of a destitute man, which had great force in a time when people did not believe in retribution beyond the grave. The theme is not isolated: "It is better to die than to beg" (Sirach 40:28; *cf.* 41:2 and Ahiqar 26:10b).

That is why to wish poverty on one's adversary is a dreadful curse (Psalm 109: 10a, 12; 2 Samuel 3:29).

And why Jeremiah curses his lot: "Cursed be the day on which I was born! The day when my mother bore me, let it not be blessed!" (20:14; *cf.* 15:10 and Job 3:1–26).

The Bible describes the plight of the poor in terms that have not grown old. They are:

Loss of freedom which goes even to the point of being reduced to slavery (2 Kings 4:1; Amos 2:6; 8:6).

Unjust treatment of all sorts (Isaiah 32:7; Micah 3:3; Ezekiel 22:29; *cf.* 18: 12, 18).

The poor man has no rights in this world (Sirach 13:3).

"He is despised and rejected" (Ecclesiastes 9:15–16; Sirach 13:21–22). "The poor man's wisdom is despised, and his words are not heeded" (Ecclesiastes 9:16). "If a rich man . . . speaks unseemly words . . . they justify him. If a humble man . . . speaks sensibly, he receives no attention" (Sirach 13:22; *cf.* 10:30–31).

Hence, the text of Ahiqar (Armenian text 2:68 and 70): "If you are poor . . . do not reveal it for fear that you may be despised . . . that people may not listen to you."

The poor man is abandoned. His friends go so far as even to hate him (Proverbs 14:20): "The poor (*ras*) is disliked even by his neighbor, but the rich man has many friends." And Proverbs 19:7, "All a poor man's (*ras*; Septuagint *tapeinos*) brothers hate him . . . He goes in search of words, but there are none to be had."

This thought is frequent in Sirach, who wrote at the beginning of the second century before Christ (12:9; 6:8–9): "In his adversity even his friend will separate from him . . . For there is a friend who is such at his own convenience, but will not stand by you in your day of trouble. And there is a friend who changes into an enemy."

If God loves the poor, he does not love the evil of poverty—just as loving a sick man does not mean loving his illness but rather combatting it. Thus God loves sinners in order to draw them away from sin, and the poor in order to bring them out of their destitution.

2. From this, we have the ideal expressed in Deuteronomy; in the people of God "there will be no poor (*ebyon*) among you" (15:4).

This precept aimed at continuing in the promised land the nomadic relationship in which no gulf existed between rich and poor since brotherly solidarity in this wandering hazardous life favored the positive realization of a common destination and relative equality. But the determinisms of property were stronger. Two series of precepts therefore are directed toward remedying the condition of the poor, since there actually are poor among the people of God.

3. The Old Testament urges those who have to give freely to the poor: "You shall open wide your hand to your brother, to the needy and the poor, in the land" (Deuteronomy 15:11; *cf.* 15: 7–9).

This theme recurs emphatically. It has been exhaustively treated by Cornelis van Leeuwen in *Le développement du sens social en Israël* (Assen: Van Gorcum, 1954; particularly pp. 181–184 on the exaltation of charity).

This duty was limited to the "brothers," that is to the members of the people of God. It did not extend to foreigners; compare for example Deuteronomy 15:1–3 and 6. Christ who "broke down the dividing wall of hostility" between Jew and pagan, by "making both one" people (Ephesians 2:14), suppressed those boundaries as we saw in the preceding chapter. We must now concentrate upon the proper object of this chapter—the rights of the poor.

The law of Israel protects the poor. It gives them rights to counter the power of those accumulating riches and the inequality that different possessions generate. What are these rights?

1. Every seven years, the law of Israel commanded the remission of all debts, and every fiftieth or jubilee year the freeing of all slaves as well—and every seventh year in the case where a poor man had sold himself to a rich man (Leviticus 25:1–17; Deuteronomy 15:1–13; Jeremiah 34:8–17).

Since this law went against the grain, the legislator insists (Deuteronomy 15: 9–10): "Take heed lest there be a base thought in your heart, and you say, 'The seventh year, the year of release is near,' and your eye be hostile to your poor brother, and you give him nothing. . . . You shall give to him freely . . . because for this the Lord your God will bless you."

This debt remission in the sabbatical year goes infinitely further than the protective legislation for the poor in the Code of Hammurabi or even in the Maxims of Amenemope (Egyptian, col. 16, 297): "If a debt weighs too heavily on the poor man . . . reduce it by two-thirds." Actually, this praiseworthy legislation seems never to have been enforced, economic determinism being what it is in a system of private property. And it was an exceptional action when Nehemiah (5: 6–11) effected the return to the poor of their fields, their vines, their olive trees, and their houses, as well as the money, wheat, and new wine which had been exacted as interest. But the oath that Nehemiah required the officials to take for the future in this regard seems not to have been kept. Connected with the same principle is the one concerning the restoration of all lands to their original owners after forty-nine years—during the jubilee year. This law was intended to protect the familial patrimony in the strictest way.

2. The law regulated loans with great concern for protecting the poor.

In Israelite society a loan functioned as a relief measure and not as an investment; *the law prohibited lending at interest*: "If you lend money to any of my people with you who is poor (*âni*), you shall not

be to him as a creditor, and you shall not exact interest from him."
(Exodus 22:25). "You shall not lend upon interest to your brother,
interest on money, interest on victuals, interest on anything that is
lent for interest. To a foreigner (*nokri*) you may lend upon interest,
but to your brother you may not lend upon interest" (Leviticus
25:36; repeated in Deuteronomy 23: 19–20).

The law also limited pawning. If, for example, the pawned
object was a coat,[2] the broker had to return it to the poor man on
cold nights until morning came (Exodus 22:26–27; Deuteronomy 24,
10–13). Deuteronomy also forbids taking as security articles that are
necessary for survival. It especially protects widows whose clothing
may not be taken as security (24:17). In short, God humanizes and
contravenes the law of money and profit.

The law did not provide for the imprisonment of an insolvent
debtor. On the contrary, it prescribes death for anyone who tries to
take an Israelite prisoner by force, either in order to make him his own
servant or to sell him as a slave (Exodus 21:16; Deuteronomy 24:7).
This point contrasts with Babylonian and Roman law, which provided for imprisonment for unpaid debts and even offered the creditor the possibility of demanding the death of the debtor if all else
failed. (See Van Leeuwen, *op. cit.*).

Finally, the law urged men not to refuse the poor man who
wishes to borrow and to lend generously (Deuteronomy 15:7–8;
Psalm 37:26; Sirach 29:2, 8–9, "Lend to your neighbor in his time of
need."

However, the Bible knows what lenders have to put up with.
Sirach speaks of their tribulations in terms that are still applicable
(29:5–6): "A man will kiss another's hands until he gets a loan, and
will lower his voice in speaking of his neighbor's money; but at the
time for repayment he will delay. . . . If the lender exerts pressure, he
will hardly get back half, and will regard that as a windfall. If he does
not, the borrower has robbed him of his money, and he has needlessly
made him his enemy; he [the borrower] will repay him with curses
and reproaches."

3. The law protected the poor man from lifetime servitude (Deuteronomy 15; Jeremiah 34:8–9; Van Leeuwen, *op. cit.*, pp. 58–68;
cf. Deuteronomy 5:14). It also protected the fugitive slave. (Deuteronomy 23:15–16).

4. It protected the poor man from losing his family lands (Van
Leeuwen, *op. cit.*, pp. 68–81: Isaiah 5:8), and against the accumulation

of possessions by the rich (Micah 2:1–2; Deuteronomy 19:14; Leviticus 25:10b, 13b). The land was not to be sold in perpetuity, for it belonged to Yahweh (Leviticus 25:23; Van Leeuwen, *op. cit.,* p. 76).

5. The law protected the poor from being exploited by the rich (Exodus 22:22-23; Deuteronomy 24:14-15; Leviticus, 19:13; Amos 2: 6–7; 5:11; 8:4–6; Jeremiah 22:13–17; Ezekiel 18:7–8; 45; 9–10; Sirach 34:22; 31:8–9; Tobit 4:6–12; 15–18).

6. The law insisted that the poor man be able to obtain justice against the rich man (Exodus 23:3; Deuteronomy 27: 19, 25; *cf.* Job 34:19; 2 Chronicles 19:7; Isaiah 1:23; 10:1–2; 11:4; Micah 3:9b, 11; Van Leeuwen *op. cit.,* pp. 103–116).

7. Finally, the Old Testament was concerned with assuring subsistence to the poor by reserving certain privileges for them:

The right to pick grapes and standing grain by hand in the fields (Deuteronomy 23:25); a custom practiced by the disciples of Jesus (Matthew 12:1; Luke 6:1).

The right to a corner of the field which the owner may not harvest.

The right to the gleanings and the sheaves left behind in the field. This right is limited to the orphan (*ger*) and the widow in Deuteronomy 24:19; but it is more generalized in Leviticus, for all the poor (*hâni*).

The right to whatever grows spontaneously in the fallow fields during the seventh year (Exodus 23:10–11).

The right of the poor to the tithe once every three years (Deuteronomy 14:28–29; 26:12).

The Meaning & Import of Laws for the Poor

Do these laws have any meaning for us? We might be tempted to answer in the negative:

1. They are the laws of a time, a society, and a civilization long gone.

2. They were little capable of fostering trade and development.

3. As the Bible itself lets us learn, they were hardly ever applied effectively because of their impracticality.

Yet we cannot dismiss so quickly the Old Law which Christ came not to abolish but to fulfill (Matthew 5:17). He fulfilled it in two ways:

At times, this fulfillment involved a broadening and a deepening of the Old Law. Indeed, the positive aspect of the precepts are not modified; there is no retrenchment. This is the case, as we saw, for the precept of charity which Jesus extended universally to all men.

Sometimes the fulfillment implies a substantial change, connected with a change in cultural patterns and social forms. The forms themselves no longer exist, but the basic intent remains. Under new conditions fulfillment demands different but analogous realization.

Such is the case with the rights of the poor in the Old Testament. If contemporary circumstances are different, the structural analogies are striking enough to require one's attention.

The situation of the poor in Israel was hardly different from that of the poor today. Practical oppression and contempt were and are the same. The accumulation of riches, against which the Law and the prophets struggled, still goes on today just as it did yesterday, and according to the same economic law of concentration. Efforts under the Old Law to maintain and restore that class of Israelite petty farmers threatened by the development of the great landed estates (the *latifundia*) correspond very strikingly to those aimed at the agrarian problem current in most Latin American countries. Finally, there are structural analogies between the condition of the poor in Israel and that of all poor peoples in relation to the rich. Interest loans wipe out the poor; foreign industrial plants mar and pollute their land by depleting the natural resources for the profit of an alien system. Terms of exchange deteriorate and the poor are brought closer and closer to economic and political enslavement. They need to be protected, as the poor were protected by God under the Old Covenant. Indeed, God condemns such exploitation.

The law of the Old Testament here has value as a type. Through those forms peculiar to Israel and no longer literally applicable, it still gives witness to the same plan of God and to the same need for legal means to resolve these problems.

This law still possesses a typical value therefore, just as its figures retain a reality and its myths a meaning. Today we have to look beyond the outdated forms for God's intention, which must be updated through new forms.

The formal intention appears still to prevail: God condemns the economic processes of pauperization and defends the poor who are victimized by it.

The most striking contemporary analogy is that the processes of pauperization tend to be accentuated and accelerated like everything else affecting people on a worldwide scale.

The Bible, therefore, is favorable to laws protecting the poor. And this is an important area of concern, even today. In certain countries a new type of legislation protects the poor man: with a guaranteed minimum wage, social security, allowances for large families, and compensation for the unemployed. And it is not always the most developed countries that have the most evolved legislation. What is called "social security" in the United States does not even provide for sickness. The victims of grave illness are in a grievous predicament; and their families may at times face a tragic choice, either death for a family member or financial ruin from a costly operation. To remedy this the legislative process remains important at a national level and ought to be utilized on an international level—with a view to world unity. This is one of the ways which will make it possible to give reality in today's world to the divine intention.

LESSON IN REALISM

But here we are taught a lesson in realism, a lesson emerging from the Bible itself. The laws were hardly ever enforced; riches accumulated in the hands of those who "joined house to house," added "field to field" until there was "no more room" for the poor and the rich were the sole inhabitants of the country (Isaiah 5:8). Such obvious ineffectiveness shows that however good a law may be it is not sufficient by itself to solve the problem. Economic determinism is often stronger, and the law has no magic effect. When it is a question of protecting the poor, an unrealistic law remains a dead letter. Either it is never actually enforced, or else it works against the poor through some unforeseen twist. For example, certain laws favoring tenants have provoked housing shortages. And in certain Latin American countries, some praiseworthy social laws are too far ahead of current economic and social development to be enforceable. They remain a fine program without application to real life.

Biblical law opposed economic determinism to an unrealistic point. More exactly, it was geared to the maintenance of tribal solidarity and a nomadic, precarious life. But that was incompatible with any accumulation of riches occurring in the sedentary and stable life represented in a further evolutionary stage and governed by other laws and other structures.

To achieve its ends, workable law must therefore:

Be grounded in suitable methods.

Relate to the existing structures or else create new structures in which the laws will be viable.

Be animated by a spirit capable of energizing those great movements by which man, periodically, overturns the established order.

In this respect, the lessons from the Bible are not solely lessons in failure.

1. In Israel, the law protecting the poor was based in part on ancient taboos, as A. Causse points out in *Du groupe ethnique à la communauté religieuse* (Paris: F. Alcan, 1937, p. 141; *cf.* Van Leeuwen, *op. cit.,* pp. 176–181). Recourse to such usage assured some degree of effectiveness, however inadequate.

2. The law depended upon widespread notions which in part were successful: for instance, the sacredness attributed to the number seven helped establish the seventh day as a day of rest.

3. The most exacting laws were applied in the degree that the prophets were able to create the right atmosphere. In such a context Nehemiah had slaves freed and their fields and houses restored to them without delay. Note that Nehemiah's prophetic action relied on a "great outcry" that arose among the people (5:1–5).

Some said: "We have to [force our sons and daughters to be slaves in order to] get grain that we may eat and keep alive."

And others said: "We are mortgaging our fields, our vineyards, and our houses to get grain because of the famine."

And still others cried out: "We have borrowed money for the king's tax upon our fields and our vineyards. Now our flesh is as the flesh of our brethren, our children are as their children; yet we are forcing our sons and daughters to be slaves; and some of our daughters have already been enslaved; but it is not in our power to help it, for other men have our fields and our vineyards."

Nehemiah's action was based on that demand en masse by the people for justice (5:6–13).

Let us see, then, what spirit and what social dynamics inspired, and to a certain extent sustained, the rights of the poor.

First of all it is a mystique of freedom, for Yahweh is the liberator. Moreover, the history of his people begins with a liberation which is one of the three great stages in salvation between Abraham and Christ. The work of Moses began at this point. He brought an end to an oppression which in many respects recalls that of all oppressed peoples, for destitution may change form and structure but it always achieves the same result. The slaughter of the Hebrew children reminds us of the infant mortality rate in the underdeveloped countries—a different system, but the same result. As for exploitation, the Bible speaks very concretely and in a way that is still reminiscent today, of the manner in which the Hebrews were exploited in Egypt: in brickmaking (Exodus 1:14), in beatings (2:11), through the harsh conditions imposed by the gang foreman (1:11), and by increasingly unreasonable working conditions (5:7):

> You shall no longer give the people straw to make bricks, as heretofore; let them go and gather straw for themselves. But the number of bricks which they made heretofore you shall lay upon them, you shall by no means lessen it; for they are idle; therefore they cry, 'Let us go and offer sacrifice to our God.' Let heavier work be laid upon the men that they may labor at it and pay no regard to lying words.

From this fact, we can understand the ideal that prevailed throughout the exodus and which the Law and the prophets sought always to maintain. It was a question of defending, in the private lives of a people, the liberty that was all but destroyed by the economic oppression of the rich and famous. This was the essential concern later of Isaiah (58:6–8 [text of the liturgy for the Friday after Ash Wednesday]; *cf.* 1:10–17 and Zechariah 7:5–11):

> Fasting like yours this day will not make your voice to be heard on high. Is not this the fast that I choose: to loose the bonds of wickedness, to undo the thongs of the yoke, to let the oppressed go free, and to break every yoke? It is not to share your bread with the hungry, and bring the homeless poor into your house; when you see the naked to cover him?

This is a theme running through the pages of the Bible; it is part of a whole. God loves the poor; he is on their side. He is their defender; he destroys the yokes of bondage (Isaiah 2:15; 10:27; 14:25; 47:6; Jeremiah 28:2, 4, 11, 14; Ezekiel 34:27). The worship and fasting pleasing to him are justice, especially toward the poor who are symbolized by the widow and the orphan (Isaiah 1:17; Zechariah 7:8–10). And the New Testament is no less forceful, since we read there (James 5:1–5):

> Come now, you rich, weep and howl for the miseries that are coming upon you. Your riches have rotted and your garments are

moth-eaten. Your gold and silver have rusted, and their rust will be evidence against you and will eat your flesh like fire. You have laid up treasure for the last days. Behold, the wages of the laborers who mowed your fields, which you kept back by fraud, cry out; and the cries of the harvesters have reached the ears of the Lord of hosts.

That is always the same divine intent; the same ideal of justice, equity, and human fellowship. (*Cf.* Exodus 22:21–27; Leviticus 19:13–15; Deuteronomy 24:14.)

THE PROMISE

Not static and legalistic, this ideal is inscribed in a history. It materialized in a project and in a hope: in the country God gave certain men to conquer, to live in, and to organize. It was, in principle, a development program. The prospect of a promised land has inspired, sustained, and supported this chosen people throughout their history. And exodus and conquest was reborn as an ideal when as an enslaved people they were again converted to God and again marched out of exile in exodus.[3] They were promised land by Deutero-Isaiah (40–41; 43:16–21) and the other prophets. And this promise was capable and still is capable today of creating a nation and promoting a development program to accomplish the impossible—as the same land bears witness in our time. If this is a myth, its strength is that it coincides with a physical element—the reality of a land that has to be lived on and cultivated in common.

That myth and that reality are of utmost value and interest to human beings in the predicament of today's huge populations who are alienated and frustrated because they are dispossessed. So dispossessed, they can no longer establish authentic social relations with their fellow men, nor with God himself. The Latin American bishops perceive that their continent is coming to life again in such an exodus. This is the theme of the prophetic text that introduces their conclusions at Medellín (no. 4):

We are on the threshold of a new epoch in the history of our continent. It appears to be a time full of zeal for full emancipation, of liberation from every form of servitude, of personal maturity, and of collective integration. In these signs we perceive the first indications of the painful birth of a new civilization. . . .
Just as Israel of old, the first People (of God), felt the saving

presence of God when he delivered them from the oppression of Egypt by the passage through the sea and led them to the promised land, so we also, the new People of God, cannot cease to feel his saving presence in view of "true development, which is the passage for each and all, from conditions of life that are less human, to those that are more human."

A DOCTRINE OF LAND AND OF PROPERTY

The promise of land is implied in what our contemporaries would willingly call an ideology, but which here is called a theology, a doctrine, founded on the word of God. It is a theology of land, and first of all of a promised land, which implies a doctrine of property.

The major theme, which had to be freed of Chanaanite corruption, is that the Promised Land belongs to God.[4] It is God who gives it (Genesis 12:7; Exodus 3:8; 32:13; Leviticus 20:24; 25:2, 38; Deuteronomy 7:13; I Kings 8:34, 36, 40; 2 Chronicles 20:7–11) and makes it fertile. The theme is broadened to include the whole earth in Deuteronomy 10:14; Isaiah 42:5; Psalm 24:1, repeated by I Corinthians 10:26: "The earth is the Lord's and everything in it" (*cf*. Psalm 50:10–12; 89:11; Isaiah 66:1–2).

Therefore, properly speaking, man does not have ownership of the earth, but merely its use, its management (Genesis 2:8, 15).

Here we touch the very roots of the doctrine that inspired the Law and made it viable so long as any small degree of faith really lived in the hearts and lives of men.

So far as it concerned the Promised Land, God required as a consequence of the Law that the land be divided up fairly (Numbers 26:54 and Joshua 13–19; *cf*. Deuteronomy 32:8).[5] The law maintained this order. It *cursed* those who changed the borders of the fields (Deuteronomy 27:17; *cf*. 19:14; Proverbs 22:28; 23:10–11; Job 24:2; 31:38; Hosea 5:10). It opposed the transfer of family property (1 Kings 21:3); it provided numerous ways in which land could be bought back by a person who had given it up because of need, or by the closest male relative when the property had fallen to the distaff side (Leviticus 25:8–55; Deuteronomy 26:1, 15; *cf*. Ruth 4:1–6; Jeremiah 32:6–15).

The Bible seems here to make a neat distinction between the gift of the land which, strictly speaking, concerns God and its apportionment which concerns men: "I have given the land to you to possess it" (Numbers 33:53; Deuteronomy 19:14).

God gives and man shares out.

Patristic and Later Tradition

In teaching and developing the biblical doctrine on land, the Fathers of the Church were unequivocal. They taught that the land, symbol of all earthly goods, belongs to God who gives it jointly and severally to all men.

Men, they said emphatically, are merely the users of this gift of God. No one may own exclusively what he has received to share. And while they undoubtedly acknowledged the lawfulness of appropriation, the Fathers qualified it severely after exhaustive analysis. Appropriation, they declared, is abusive and culpable if the poor do not have their fair share: "You shall have your brothers share in all your goods, and you shall not call them your property" (Didache 4, 6, 8 [second century] *Patres Apostolici,* Tübingen: Funk, 1887, pp. 16–17: 2nd ed. p. 12).

The writings of the Greek Fathers[6] abound with forthright teaching on property. Saint John Chrysostom wrote: "What God has bestowed upon us is not for individual ownership but for joint possession. This agrees with nature. He gave to us in common so we could learn to share in common" (I ad Tim., C 4, Homil. 13, PG 562–563).

The Latin Fathers[7] taught a comparable doctrine: "The land was given in common to all men. No one should claim for himself more than he needs *(proprium nemo dicat)* of what belongs to the whole community *(quod e communi plusquam sufficeret)."*

Firmly and exactly the medieval theologians and philosophers defined and illustrated the principles underlying their teaching on property and the logical consequences:

1. By natural right all goods are common to all men.[8] This doctrine was not disputed. Some scholars further specified that this community ownership by divine right suits man's original integrity while private property suits his sinful state *(naturae lapsae).* Without any question, they continued, it is now very difficult for men to be as concerned for the common good as they are for their own good. Hence, men's widespread practice of appropriating consumer goods, even in religious orders, where common usage is advocated most vigorously.

2. The common purpose for all goods is prior to appropriation. The right of private property is a secondary, human right, destined to facilitate the proper use of goods.

3. In case of need, common purpose prevails over private property. As a concrete example, a poor man has a right to the necessities of life; he is not stealing when for survival he takes from someone else. He uses by right, by fundamental right.

GROWTH OF MISCONCEPTIONS ABOUT PROPERTY

This doctrine, which had been common up to the sixteenth century, was gradually obscured by the pressure of economic liberalism. Its obfuscation was aided and abetted by a misconception of Cajetan's in the sixteenth century in his commentaries on Saint Thomas Aquinas. Two successive articles in the Summa Theologica II-II (q. 66, aa. 1 and 2) explain the common purpose of goods which is primary and fundamental, and then the individual appropriation which intervenes on a secondary level as a means of guaranteeing the proper management of wealth. Cajetan interpreted as private property what Saint Thomas called common purpose. Thus private property was conceived as primary and of divine right.

This misconception was not universal. In the succeeding centuries some great theologians—men like Suarez, Sylvius, and Billuart—certainly preserved the traditional doctrine.[9] But matters were made worse in the nineteenth century, nevertheless, when the Church overreacted to collectivist doctrines which were diametrically opposed to the abuses of capitalism. That aggressive opposition to modern errors and the non-recognition of the hard-core truth that animated them, as well as the polemical spirit of the times, brought the misconception to its apex. Liberatore, the principal editor of the first schema of *Rerum novarum* is guilty of the same confusion. It is evident in a recent publication documenting the sources used in writing the encyclical: " 'This is the right of property *(Ecco il diritto di proprieta!)*,' Liberatore had noted in commenting on an article in the Summa, while in reality Saint Thomas was still dealing with the issue of common purpose" (G. Antonuzzi, *L'enciclica Rerum Novarum*, Rome: 1957, p. 40).

Given such misinterpretation, the doctrine on private property moved into first place and seemed to be basic, primary, and absolute. It absorbed to its own advantage the characteristic feature of divine right which Saint Thomas had reserved for the common purpose of goods *(jus naturale,* as opposed to *jus positivum,* II-II, q. 57, aa. 2 and 3; q. 66, a. 2).

Because of this false absolute several popes, up to and including John XXIII, felt obliged to defend the private ownership of the means of production against socialism.

REDISCOVERY

Restoration of the obscured message was begun in 1941 by Pius XII in his radio address commemorating the fiftieth anniversary of *Rerum novarum*. He reiterated at length that private property "remains subordinated to the natural end of material goods and could not be made independent of the primary and basic right which concedes its use to all men."

John XXIII echoed him in 1961 in *Mater et Magistra* and formulated the traditional principle in all its force: "The goods of the earth are above all destined for the decent subsistence of all men."

But in this document, as in the preceding one, the normal order of expository thought was not reestablished. The two popes first speak of private property and only then, as if to offset criticism, do they speak of the right which grants to all men the "use of goods." Although called "primary and basic" by Pius XII, that right, still conditioned by the long-standing confusion, only appears in second place, on a secondary plane.

At about the same time, the first schema prepared by the doctrinal commission of Vatican II restated the official modern doctrine, exalting private property as a primary, divine, and in some sense, absolute right.

> Since man enjoys the dignity of a person and surpasses all visible creatures by his free will, and all the more since God solemnly subjected them to him at the beginning of creation (Sirach 17:2), the Council teaches that to man belongs a both natural and divine right to use creatures in accordance with the end to which the Creator himself destined them. Hence it follows that to man belongs a natural, exclusive, and permanent right to private property in temporal goods, not only in consumption but also in production. If man makes good use of them, he can better provide for his own subsistence and that of his descendants, he enjoys the independence due him in both his personal and family life. . . . This right is connected with the dignity of the human person to the extent that it protects the freedom he needs to obtain perfection.
>
> We see that this right was defended by God himself in the law which he wrote, both in hearts of flesh and on tablets of stone:

these laws clearly separate the welfare of others and property:
"You shall not steal" (Exodus 20:15). (*De ordine sociali* CT 9/61:
24, cap. 4, no. 20, p. 15, lines 1–20).

After thus laying the foundation stone for private property, the draft
schema then considered the social aspect secondarily. The conclusion
returned to the starting point, and the chapter ended on this lyrical
note:

> The Church defends the right of private property in order
> that this right, in accordance with the decrees of sacred Scripture,
> may be the principle of the social order (*exordium ordinis
> socialis*), the defense of freedom, the protection of the unity of the
> family, the stimulus for work, the origin of public prosperity, and
> the defense and dignity of the human person.

At this stage, the memorandum[10] which I filed on September 22, 1961,
and which is repeated in substance here, appeared to be without prece-
dent and hard to incorporate explicitly into the text, even though
many sympathetic people were in fundamental agreement with it.

This idea did make its way into Schema 13; yet, as presented to
the Council in the revision of November 1965 everything on the
rights of the poor now in the text of Number 69 of *Gaudium et spes*
had disappeared. At the same time the concept of the theology of the
common purpose of goods was again blurred. The two doctrines are
interrelated causally, of course, as history itself verifies. I remember
spending the entire night after the distribution of this document in
drafting a four-point memorandum on this essential point. (The pace
of those last days of the Council meant that one had to work extremely rapidly.) Restoration of that ancient text, which had already
been promulgated and approved, was demanded and obtained.

Certainly, we should not exaggerate the difference between the
doctrine held before the Council and that affirmed by the Council itself. The thesis of the common purpose of goods was not unknown to
Leo XIII, nor to those who drafted the conciliar schema of 1961; but it
was not *where it should have been*. It was no longer proposed as a
primary and basic norm of divine right, but, by minimizing objections
to appropriation, it simply became an invitation to owners to use private property well. The common purpose doctrine passed from the
first to the second rank, and then into the background: and in that
way it was devaluated, minimized, and distorted.

The conciliar text restored the normal order for these two principles: first, common purpose of goods, then private ownership. And this restoration is important for a good many reasons:

1. This teaching brought the meaning of private property into proper focus as only one among many ways of realizing the common purpose of goods which is of divine right.

2. The doctrinal restoration is very useful in our day when common distribution is regaining its importance irresistibly through that socialization—or recognition of fellowship—and that interdependence which increasingly gain ascendancy on a worldwide scale in a society that is at once so differentiated and so unified. The doctrine calls for a restoration of community values at all levels. If it was lawful for Naboth to refuse to give his vineyard to King Ahab (I Kings 21), or for the "Carefree Miller" of the fable to avail himself of his property rights against the whims of the monarch Frederick II, it would be flagrantly wrong for an individual to be able to divert a highway or block an urbanization plan in the name of his absolute right to private property. The pastoral constitution goes on to state the lawfulness of expropriation explicitly and favorably. Finally, it notes that the economies of the young nations call for renewed fiscal support of the common purpose of goods especially in the strenuous getting-off-the-ground phase.

3. This doctrine articulates the many ramifications of the two principles—common purpose of goods by divine right and private appropriation of goods. In so doing it transcends the communist and capitalist systems. It allows for a plurality of economic methods. Thus the Church no longer appears intimately allied with capitalism nor unilaterally tied to the defense of its class interests. The restoration of the traditional doctrine enables the Church to affect a reconciliation with men of many conditions and classes.

4. This doctrine is not something purely speculative. It gives a foundation to those rights of the poor which constitute a specific datum of Christian morality: in case of necessity, man has the right to appeal to the right of the common purpose of goods which outweighs the right of private property. Hence the adage current in the Middle Ages: He who takes what is necessary does not commit theft, but takes possession of what is his own *(Non committit furtum, sed suum accipit.)*.

That is the thesis universally accepted in the Middle Ages, which was progressively obscured from the seventeenth to the nineteenth centuries.

Gilles Couvreur was the chief artisan in the restoration of this doctrine, thanks to his thesis, *Les pauvres ont-ils des droits?* (Rome: Gregorian University, 1961). From the beginning of his research he grasped very clearly that today this standard has a new sense and direction, no longer individual but social. The right generally recognized for *individuals* in need in the past must now be looked upon as the right for *peoples* as inequality widens the gulf between the rich and the poor peoples. For every right must evolve and develop in accordance with new realities and with evolving human structures.

The application of this right on the scale of whole peoples[11] is mentioned rather timidly still in *Gaudium et spes* (no. 69, par. 1):

> The Council urges all, both individuals and governments . . . really to share and use their earthly goods, according to the ability of each, especially by supporting individuals or peoples with the aid by which they may be able to help and develop themselves.

The principle is here formulated in terms of an invitation to the rich, not in terms of *rights* which should be acknowledged for the poor. If there is some progress, it is in the sense that what traditional theology said solely of individuals has been extended to peoples: there is also regression so far as courage in affirming the *right* formally recognized by traditional doctrine—a right which had never disappeared entirely from the best manuals of moral theology.

The same criticism of timidity must be made of *Populorum progressio* (no. 49):

> What is superfluous in richer regions must serve the needs of regions in want. The rule according to which in the past those were to be helped who are more closely bound to us now applies to all who are in need throughout the world.

Nevertheless in other respects the encyclical does show progress.

1. The duties of country to country are enunciated more clearly than in the conciliar text, and the abuses are more clearly denounced.

2. Similarly, Paul VI expresses more clearly the relativity of the right of private property (no. 23):

> Private ownership confers on no one a supreme and unconditional right. No one is allowed to set aside solely for his own advantage possessions which exceed his needs when others lack the necessities of life.

In a word, as a consequence of the traditional doctrine,[12] the right of private property must never be exercised to the detriment of common utility. If it should happen that conflict arises "between an acquired private right and the primordial need of the community," it is the duty of the public authorities to commit themselves to resolving the conflict "with the active participation of individuals and social groups" (no. 23).

3. *Populorum progressio* asserts very strongly the primacy of the common purpose of goods and the subordination of the rest (no. 22):

> All other rights, whatever they are, including property rights and the right of free trade must be subordinated to this norm; they must not hinder it, but must rather expedite its application. It must be considered a serious and urgent social obligation to refer these rights to their original purpose.

4. Consequently, where he speaks of expropriation (no. 24), Paul VI does not feel obliged to assert like the Council that equitable compensation is necessary in that case.

The abundance of the material we have skimmed over obliges us to devote a special chapter to development as a duty in justice and as a duty corresponding to a fundamental right. If the duty that originates in charity goes further in certain respects, if it says more, we cannot separate it from this fundamental right from which it is inseparable. We can no more separate justice from charity than we can separate the body from the soul which transcends it or the natural from the supernatural which fulfills it.

This chapter on the rights of the poor recalls a very basic biblical and traditional doctrine which puts human solidarity in first place and appropriation in second place. The latter as a relative means serves the fundamental good of all men.

But there is an admissible objection to this doctrine. Is not its implied ideal of material prosperity surpassed by the eschatological perspective of the New Testament, as by the perspective of material prosperity itself? It is a fact that the ideal of "possessing the earth" is spiritualized to this degree in Matthew 5:5: "Blessed are the meek, for they shall inherit the earth." Both in Matthew's Gospel and earlier in Isaiah (60:21) the earth has an eschatological sense.

However, we must not uproot ourselves from the earth. It is the place where men learn to possess together a heritage which, lived out fraternally among men, is already the sign of the reality of our everlasting heritage.

THE MAGISTERIUM
AND DEVELOPMENT

7

Now that we have considered the contemporary development "movement" and its sources, let us see how its objective, unknown in past centuries, was formally espoused by the magisterium of the last two popes.

An Early Usage of "Development" by Pius XII

Except as anticipated by the Marxists, the humanistic and economic understanding of the term "development" did not become widespread until after World War II. Consequently we shall not find it in the official writings of Leo XIII and Pius XI.[1] Recalling Lebret's statement that the *idea* of development dates only from 1945, the appearance in 1941 of the term and concept in Pius XII's Christmas message is somewhat surprising (AAA, 34, 1942, pp. 17–18 [Dec. 24, 1941]; text published in Italian only):

> In the area of the new order, based on moral principles, one cannot encroach upon the liberty, integrity, or security of other nations, whatever their size or defense capacity. If it is unavoidable that the major powers, both because of their more extensive resources and their power, do open the way to the establishment of economic groups between themselves and the small nations, it is nonetheless indisputable that these small nations have the right

to respect for their political sovereignty

to the safeguard of their neutrality in conflicts between the major powers,

and to the protection of their economic development (*sviluppo economico*), for this is the only way to assure the public good, and the national and spiritual well-being proper to each people.

For its day this text was pointed and forward-looking. But the mention of development was incidental and the concept was in no way analyzed. The stress was on the problems of war and peace which were then so crucial and on the moral principles that must govern the "new order among nations." The dominant point of view is moralistic and static rather than dynamic.

In quoting this text later in *Pacem in terris*, John XXIII clarified and reinforced it. He refocused it on the "right of economic development" and specified that this right is a condition for the "common good of *mankind*." None of these last three terms can be found in Pius XII's text.

"Development" in Mater et Magistra

The encyclical *Mater et Magistra* (AAS, 53, pp. 401–64) is by way of being a significant way station in many respects, if not the point of departure itself. Its concern for development becomes a guiding principle in the renewal of the perspectives which must be brought into focus.

First there is the encyclical's tone and style and goodness. John XXIII inaugurated a practical optimism that broke with the old method of condemning theories current in the modern world. (That had reached its apogee with the publication of the Syllabus.) John's intention was to win over men's minds by stressing the attractiveness of the good rather than the fearfulness of anathemas. He did not speak of the world's widespread evil in order to condemn, but he did speak of the good flowering in the world in order to encourage it.

And with this Johannine about-face, the Church changed the very tone of her teaching. Previously the social encyclicals had been characterized to a certain degree by teaching that came from on high to explain social realities below. For example, Emile Marmy wrote that "the method of the Church's social doctrine is not ascending but descending. It does not start out from the facts, but from the word of

God" (*La communauté humaine selon l'esprit chrétien,* 2nd ed. Paris-Fribourg: Editions St.-Paul, 1949, pp. 13–14).

To be more precise, he might have said: the Church's teaching starts out from her ideas of human nature, for the word of God was not much quoted in the social encyclicals. John XXIII made a quiet transition from that abstract and deductive method to an inductive method which begins with the realities, the aspirations of man for justice, and the facts and institutions which turn these aspirations into reality. He "re-read" them in a Christian fashion. He hardly ever relied on a concept of abstract nature, but instead on the values that evolved from cultures. He acknowledged such values and tried to gain an insight into them.[2]

With an attitude so sensitive to God's work in the world, John XXIII paid close attention to human realities, especially to new phenomena which were appearing: *socialization,* which he considered both a result and a source of progress (nos. 64–73), the structures which aid or hinder justice and charity, and the problems posed by the variations in productivity, by population pressures, and by the inequality of resources among various peoples. Seeing that problems were worsening, John XXIII acknowledged the need to give them priority (AAS, 53, no. 167, p. 440):

> The most important problem of our age is perhaps that of the relations between economically developed (*progressis*) political communities and the developing countries (*quarum oeconomicae progressiones sint in cursu*).

As a solution the pope declared that development must be characterized by balance (*Mater et Magistra,* no. 73, NCWC ed., 1961 and AAS, 53, p. 419):

> Social progress (*rei socialis incrementa*) must always go hand in hand with economic development (*rei oeconomicae incrementa*). The growth of national wealth (*aucta divitiarum copia*) should guarantee the development of all members of society without exception.

Consequently, John XXIII soberly denounced the failures of modern economy and congratulated FAO (United Nations Food and Agriculture Organization) for its contribution to the solution of this problem (no. 156).

He recommended *participation* and gave a positive and constructive sense to the principle of subsidiarity, which had already been acknowledged by Pius XII.[3] Finally, although not without some reservation, he subscribed to the Rights of Man (no. 61) and numbered among them the right to economic initiative. He restored consciousness of a fundamental truism—that vital change and progress more often emanate from society as a whole than from its leaders; from the roots rather than from the treetop, as it were.

He went far beyond the static moralism and individualism which until then had been characteristic of pontifical documents; he gave precedence to *values* over abstract principles. He penetrated to the very core of the social dynamics indispensible to reform, to effectiveness, to existence. It all fitted in with his thinking on life and on progress. John XXIII did not believe in drafting laws whole and complete and from outside a given situation. For him, laws developed in accordance with complex changes and animated by the spirit proper to them.

Pacem in terris and "Development"

Two years later and a month before his death, John XXIII returned to the problem in *Pacem in terris* (AAS 55, 1963, pp. 257–304) where he distinguished four sectors in which there must be peace:
1. Among people in general.
2. Among citizens of the same nation.
3. In relations between nations.
4. In the world community as a specific reality.

In the same spirit, he hails three splendid gains as a sign of the times: improvements for the working classes (no. 40), for women's rights (no. 41) and for liberation of "subject peoples," those colonized by others (no. 42). The second point is surely the most novel, considering his original bias. In a speech given somewhat earlier to the Association of Italian Working Women, John XXIII had showed himself ill-prepared to comprehend that sign. In addressing these women who had organized because they saw work as both valuable in itself and a means for progress, he revived the theme of "mother in the home." And he deplored the unfortunate necessity that compelled them to leave their homes to earn a living. The discourse came as a shock, but not for long. *Pacem in terris* manifests the capacity for renewal that characterized John XXIII, and also his optimism, since women's rights are still far from being a reality. The same lag is evident in improvements for the working classes in India, Brazil, and Portugal, or even in

Spain and Italy. And certain "subject" peoples have emerged from political dependence only to fall back into an economic colonialization that is all the more dangerous since it is hidden, anonymous, and irresponsible.

Yet in *Pacem in terris,* John XXIII furthered the cause of humanity in terms of value judgments and social dynamics (nos. 36–37) along the lines he had already laid down in *Mater et Magistra.*

He made concrete proposals, particularily for setting up a world power (nos. 137–38). That proposal was taken up again by the Council and Paul VI.

He also established two principal distinctions: between *error* and *the erring* (no. 158), and between *doctrine* and *movement* (no. 159). In this way he opened the door to collaboration with non-Christians, including the Marxists, who are referred to transparently in Number 159. His action was most influential in bringing Catholics out of the ghetto isolationism into which they had tended to withdraw until then.

John XXIII urged Christians to take on political responsibilities (no. 146): "Once again, we exhort our children to take an active part in public life."

Yet, development only played a limited role in this encyclical (nos. 121–23). John XXIII expressed the hope "that the poorer countries, in as short a time as possible, will arrive at that degree of economic development (*ita in re oeconomica progrediantur*) which will enable every citizen to live in conditions more in keeping with his human dignity." He added emphatically that the assistance given to these peoples "should be effected with the greatest respect for the liberty of the countries being developed, for these must realize that they are the principal artisans in the promotion of their own economic development and social progress (*progressus*)."

Next, in order to develop his own point, John XXIII cited Pius XII's radio broadcast of Christmas 1941, which had first introduced the theme of development. He clarified and refocused it by extending the meaning of development.

The Council and Development

Vatican II, in the Pastoral Constitution on the Church in the Modern World, examined the whole of economic and social life in the light of development. This key idea became more and more compelling to the writers of Schema 13, and most significant when they reordered priorities for dealing with contemporary problems troubling both the developing countries and the developed nations.[4] It was Lebret who sparked this reordering; and the constitution which grounded it in a theology of commitment and material worth. A theology based on the Bible, it represented an advance in harmony with the empiricism and human wisdom of John XXIII.

From the very beginning, the pastoral constitution takes development as its point of departure, first in the Introductory Statement on the signs of the times, and then in Part One, Chapter 3, on man's activity throughout the world.

As the Council's ideas evolved, development was seen in the context of a theology of creation and of human worth which reconciles men's mundane aspirations with their strong yearning for the divine. The Council discreetly rejects ideologies that foster oppression and domination indirectly. It also effects a transition from legalistic moralism to a kind of theology of values. There is no longer any question of preserving a static order, but of a search in which man can reach fulfillment today—in a new exodus.

The Council praises the conquests made by man's genius and declares that they are in harmony with the divine plan (Genesis 1: 26–27; 9: 2–3; Wisdom 9: 2–3; Psalm 8: 6–9, cited in no. 34, par. 2). It emphasizes Christian responsibilities in such progress (no. 34, par. 3):

> For the greater man's power becomes, the further his individual and community responsibility extends. Hence it is clear that men are not deterred by the Christian message from building up the world, or impelled to neglect the welfare of their fellows, but that they are rather more stringently bound to do these very things.

The blueprint for development inspires and structures the chapter on economic life, especially Numbers 63–64, 69–71. The "principles of justice and equity" which the Church over the course of centuries has clarified "in the light of the Gospel" are considered in the framework of structural reforms and the necessary reorientation of attitudes. The Council then advances formally in its deliberations (no. 63, par. 5): "especially with regard to the requirements of economic development (*progressionis oeconomicae*)."

To this effect, it defines the finality of production as a principle fundamental to a theory of development, since as Aristotle says, the final object is the cause of causes (no. 64):

> The fundamental purpose of this production is not the mere
> increase of products nor profit or control, but rather the service
> of man, and indeed of the whole (*integri*) man. . . . This applies
> to every man whatsoever (*cujuscumque*) and to every group of
> men, of every race and of every part of the world. Consequently,
> economic activity is to be carried on according to its own methods
> and laws within the limits of the moral order, so that God's plan
> for mankind may be realized.

The above statement continues logically to develop from the position
already presented step by step. It puts moral principles in first place
and explicitly presents them as limits (*fines*). That is to say, as limits
they are therefore negative.

Number 65 clarifies most positively what man's control over the
laws of economy must be and how he must orient himself toward
development:

> Economic development must remain under man's deter-
> mination and must not be left to the judgment of a few men or
> groups possessing too much economic power, or of the political
> community, or of certain more powerful nations. It is necessary,
> on the contrary, that at every level the largest possible number of
> people and, when it is a question of international relations, all
> nations have an active share in directing that development. There
> is need as well of the coordination and fitting and harmonious
> combination of the spontaneous efforts of individuals and of free
> groups with the undertakings of public authorities.

With this new emphasis, and in agreement with *Mater et Magistra*,
(no. 63) and with *Pacem in terris* (nos. 72–74), Vatican II here upholds
the ideal of initiative, of maximum participation by men, and "the
principle of subsidiarity." The Council is therefore opposed to deper-
sonalized technocracy. While recognizing the indispensible function
of authority, it regards it as a service for the common good, and acknowledges the fundamental role of ordinary men, in the spirit of the
Gospel.

Populorum progressio and "Development"

Why did Paul VI devote a new encyclical to the theme that the Council
had treated amply, even to including practical applications such as
agrarian reform?

The pope seems to have wanted to emphasize the problem still further—to approach it in language more direct, more dynamic, and more communicative than that in the conciliar text worked out so carefully by a commission of many men anxious to achieve unanimity. Finally, Paul VI seems to have been concerned with stressing plans for the developing countries, while the Council had been involved with the problems familiar to the majority of the coeditors, who were from developed countries. He wanted to denounce injustices more exactly —particularly the excessive "flight" of capital into rich foreign countries (no. 24). Yet, he did not go so far as to speak of the "brain-drain" (from the underdeveloped) to the highly-developed countries.

Finally, it was Paul VI's intention to have his prophetic missions to Bombay (1964) and to New York (October 4, 1965), culminate in an explicit, organic, and conclusive document. This pope, who believes in the virtue of repetition, intended to recall with renewed vigor certain concrete proposals such as the establishment of a "world fund for the underprivileged" deducted from military budgets.[5]

He wanted also to underline the connection between development and peace. It is expressed in the conclusion of the encyclical, *"development* is synonomous with peace *(progressionem idem valere ac pacem)."* Paul VI borrowed the axiom from the pioneers of the development movement. And he had already put it into words several months before issuing the encyclical—in a letter to U Thant (May 26, 1966) and during a Mass celebrated (October 4, 1966) in St. Peter's Square for the first anniversary of his trip to New York.[6]

The encyclical *Populorum progressio* is more incisive, more explicit, more imperative than the conciliar text, and more attentive to the work of discerning and stimulating existent dynamisms.

Should we add that it is also more prophetic? At first I had written that it was, but it is debatable. In this area, it was actually John XXIII who made the prophetic opening, and his encyclicals were so received. Fundamental new themes surfaced. But they were often phrased in terms that were timid and veiled, and as a precaution, linked to statements of the past. But they were also eloquent, winning, suggestive, and vivacious. In that way, in the two encyclicals, John reached out from the depths of his being to touch men of contemporary conscience who had been reached only badly before. That *Pacem in terris* was an inspiration to artists is a fact also. Darius Milhaud, the composer, and more than one sculptor have written with form and with rhythm of the old pontiff holding his young olive branch out to the world. It is to Paul's credit that he refocused everything related to development that had come within the purview of the Council. He also pointed up the urgency of and defined and clarified several aspects of this teaching.

1. As we have already pointed out, Paul's new achievement was in affirming even more clearly the common purpose of all goods and the relativity of private property. In this way the Church begins to move away from economic systems—both capitalistic and socialistic. Yet she still remains intimately enfeoffed in the domain of capitalism in her very principles. In *Mater et Magistra*, John XXIII had believed still that he was obliged to condemn "moderate socialism" severely (no. 34). Moreover, he did not think he could be dispensed from defending the right of private property as the primary means for production (no. 115; *cf.* no. 116). Paul VI does not go over the same ground, nor does he again allude to the duty of giving "a just compensation" where agrarian reform requires the confiscation of the land.

If he no longer criticizes socialism, Paul VI does explicitly criticize the liberal capitalism which concerned Leo XIII: And he does so more vigorously and more specifically than either John XXIII or the Council had done.

However, John remains the man who gave the impulse to matters; he spoke of *socialization* to describe the present evolution. And Paul VI did not use this term again in *Populorum progressio*. In short, here again, John XXIII is more important from a radical point of view, although Paul VI goes further in explanation and coherence.

2. Taking his lead from *Gaudium et spes*, Paul VI tends to go beyond the idea of "aid," and to a certain extent, the duties of the rich, in order to refocus on the blueprint for *joint development*. In terms of universal solidarity[7] he brings into new relief the "fundamental concept of the common good" on a worldwide scale. More generally, he proposes a whole ethic of development.

3. Further on, in Chapter 10, we shall consider whether *Populorum progressio* made any advances relevant to the function of violence and to what extent subsequent steps by Paul VI are a retreat from that new stand.

4. The problem of progress is posed analogously in the matter of demography and birth control.

In *Mater et Magistra* John saw the problem from the most classical of viewpoints (no. 189):

> A course of action is not indeed to be followed whereby, contrary to the moral law laid down by God, the procreative function also is violated. Rather, man should, by the use of his skills

and science of every kind, acquire an intimate knowledge of the forces of nature and control them ever more extensively. Moreover, the advances hitherto made in science and technology give almost limitless promise for the future in this matter.

There is an acknowledgment (no. 190) of the gravity of certain problems in countries that have "insufficient food or sustenance" (*domi habere nequeant unde alantur et sustentur*).

John XXIII's optimism seemed to hold out no other solution for demographical problems than a better exploitation of resources.

Like the Council in *Gaudium et spes,* Paul VI formally acknowledged the seriousness of the problem and the opportuneness of birth regulation. He again takes up in *Populorum progressio* the capital assertion of the Council (no. 37):

> It is finally the right of the parents, having completely examined the case, to make a decision about the number of their children; a responsibility they take upon themselves, keeping in sight their duty to God, themselves, the children already born, and the community to which they belong, following the dictates of their conscience, instructed about the divine law authentically interpreted and strengthened by confidence in God.

He had earlier in the same passage opened the way for intervention by public authorities:

> There is no doubt that the public authorities within the sphere of their competence can intervene in this matter, giving their citizens information on the topic and adopting appropriate measures provided those are in accord with the precepts of the moral law and that the rightful freedom of married people is most completely protected.

The encyclical *Humanae vitae,* despite its formal position against contraception, takes a less severe tone in addressing public authorities. If this encyclical may be looked upon as a restrictive position from the point of view of the Council,[8] it is not so when compared with John XXIII. As paradoxical as it may seem, *Humanae vitae* represents a new proposal in this regard.

5. A more obvious and important step from the ecumenical point of view was that John XXIII spoke as a moralist and a philosopher within the context of reason and the natural law. In *Populorum progressio*—in contrast, moreover, to *Humanae vitae*—Paul VI speaks as a Christian. He quotes Scripture some fourteen times. Ten of the references allude to the problem of development; it is in the name of the

Gospel that Paul VI desires to commit Christians to this movement. In that regard he clarifies and emphasizes the Christian humanism proposed by the Council, a humanism of the Incarnation.

Toward a New Stage for Development

Beyond the stages of development we have surveyed already, do we glimpse others? Undoubtedly, since we are dealing with a problem in the full course of evolution.

Populorum progressio, meant to be an invitation to excellence rather than an authoritative standard, has won over certain Christian groups to new points of view, particularily in Brazil. Grounded in its basically favorable reception and its relatively minor unsatisfactoriness, those new perspectives in the encyclical are:

1. That the encyclical, although preoccupied before all else with the poor, is above all addressed to rich persons and nations; it urges them to solve the problem. In common with Leo XIII's encyclical, *Populorum progressio* reminds the rich (here the rich nations) of their obligations toward the poor, more than it restores to the poor hopes based on their conscious perception of their right and their duty to free themselves. Certainly, Paul VI teaches that the underdeveloped peoples should be "architects of their own destiny" (no. 65), and in accordance with their own genius (no. 41; *cf.* nos. 54, 55, 77, 81). Yet, trading on the principle of solidarity makes it possible to come up with many interpretations advocating salvation of the poor by the poor. And that could be most useful, since the Bogotá discourses stressed the responsibilities of the rich and the nonviolent patience of the poor. Certainly Paul goes well beyond Leo XIII in the way that he thinks about the problem both as it effects people and the whole world; he focuses everything on joint development. But an exhortation to the rich at this level exposes a problem[9] which François Perroux, professor at the Collège de France, has expressed thus:

> Never in the course of the history of the West have we seen a class or a nation give up its own wellbeing for the benefit of a disadvantaged group. Effective altruism—exceptional enough with individuals—is never found in organized groups. Our societies are plutocracies that have to come to terms a little with the masses and with poor people, and they tend to shape technocratic and political power groups to their own interests.

This social structure is reflected in production methods, in consumption patterns, and in aid programs to developing peoples.

It would be culpable optimism to expect a conversion of classes and nations, say one night on the fourth of August.

Today the encyclical *Populorum progressio* should elicit a complementary document. That document should insist on the rights, the powers, and the responsibilities of the poor, and on their ability to be artisans of their own development—with the union, the solidarity, and all the means implicit to the work. Such an encyclical would have to be composed by representatives from underdeveloped countries, in underdeveloped countries by men active in development who are conscious of the still unknown energies dormant in the passivity of the oppressed masses. Certain grass-roots communities, which arose spontaneously in Latin America, tend to be microcosmic manifestations of such development. To set up the process on a larger scale, it would no doubt be necessary to look courageously and closely at the ongoing pilot programs in this area—from Tunisia to Guinea, from Cuba to China—even though these "models" may be alien or even hostile to the Church. There is room to ask ourselves very clearly to what extent this hostility may be due to the position the Church holds in the structures of this world and whether there may not be in those human efforts something to baptize in the twofold sense of the word: not only to liberate from sin or from errors but to welcome the basic worth of those efforts and direct them toward fulfillment.

2. Thus *Populorum progressio* approaches development in terms of ethics. Undoubtedly the encyclical alludes to the laws of marketing, but it does not formally show that development is an object of *science,* and that it is the object of political choices nor whether it presupposes liberation in respect to systems that support underdevelopment.

Those are three key points in present-day thinking; for it is a question of filling up the abyss between principles and accomplishment, between doctrine and praxis, and therefore a question not only of material but also of human efficiency. Such questions are still far from full, critical examination.

And here we come to the last limitation of the encyclical: it chose the word and the peaceful image of development. Certainly this image is dynamic, but in some way it abstracts from the fact that there are struggles, contradictions, crises, and inevitable violence in development's evolution. That is a major problem to which we shall have to return, for it partly explains the persistent, and in some places growing, attraction of Marxist thought which is precisely focused on that aspect of reality.

To single out these problems is in no way to minimize the importance of the encyclical, which is considerable. But, like every document on an evolving problem, it represents an investigative stage which, in the service of its own problem, calls for other investigations.

Part Four

Some Answers

To Development Problems

WHY DEVELOPMENT
RELATES TO
SALVATION

8

In turn we have considered the Christian ideas on development. We have attempted to place the texts in their proper perspectives and,without overstating the case, as historical method demands. So far we have not adopted the method of John XXIII who quotes Pius XII and makes what he says more explicit.[1] Such a dynamic and prophetic method is legitimate on its own grounds. Uncomplicated, it was unquestionably the method used by the biblical writers and by the Fathers of the Church. They took the traditional passages and carefully updated them by explicating the fullness of their content in contemporary terms. Now that is what we have to do. Indeed, it is important to reach a more synthesized understanding of the ideas at work in the present situation and, as far as possible, to go beyond the antinomian options in which the faith-alone advocates seek a solution to the problem. Those are the options we reviewed earlier, in Chapter 4: is there continuity or discontinuity, is there homogeneity or heterogeneity, between man's progress accomplished through earthly development and man's salvation which is his eschatological fulfillment?

By working from the reunified ideas, we will try to elucidate the motives which today commit Christians and even the hierarchy to the service of development. In this way we will gain some understanding of just how the significant options can be reconciled.

First of all, why does the Church see development as an extremely important job for the contemporary Christian?

117

The question has to be asked because we are not dealing with a religious program of actions or even one that is specifically Christian. Its appeal is to all men of good will. *Pacem in terris* and Paul VI's speech at the United Nations keep almost exclusively within this framework. Consequently, some conservatives are afraid that by committing herself to this course of action the Church is turning away from what is essential. They fear that she neglects God in order to aid men, that she is becoming secularized, desacralized, eccentric, that she dissipates her productive energy and is losing her very sense of what is proper to her. They fear that she perverts herself by prostituting herself to the world; in short, that she is betraying her spiritual mission on behalf of material realities.

Secularism is a very real risk. As a matter of fact, seen only in that radical context, Christianity is called to fulfillment by renouncing her specifically religious character. The ideal would be a Christianity without religion. There is indeed a risk there; all the more because this driving force is carried along by a powerful movement like a ground swell which builds up and breaks in the intoxication of fashionable sloganeering—the foam that always rides the crest of the great waves of history.

We might even wonder if whim does not have a share in this infatuation. The atheistic movement that began on the threshold of the nineteenth century thought of itself as religious. It intended to protect the sacred bond among men searching for their destiny. The catchphrase[2] there was "religion without God." The slogan[3] in our own day, according to Bonhoeffer, would be: "God without religion," or "religionless Christianity." This is undoubtedly a healthy reaction against the debasement of the "religious Christian" to a most elementary religiosity—and indeed to a low level of superstition and of purely ritualistic materialization of the sacred. But too often the reaction is unilateral[4] and the "death of God" theologies, which are at the end of that road, are no longer *theo-logia* in the etymological sense of the word. Some of them fall into nihilism.

The following analysis will attempt to explain the authentic activities of the development movement, not historically as in Chapter 1, but in order to thoroughly illuminate its message. We shall thus do justice to the legitimate demands of our time and avoid the risks of secularism.

First of all, the work of balanced human development is imposed by the obligations to justice and charity which are foremost in the Gospel message. (The texts were cited in Chapter 4.)

A New Face for an Old Obligation

Those obligations take on a new dimension in the face of the world's new structures: its specialization, its solidarity, its communication potential, its global unification. The Council and the recent documents issued by the magisterium have stressed this new dimension. Let us try to pinpoint the new terms for dealing with it and the urgency it connotes.

1. The major factor is the evolutionary process which prevails in the contemporary world. The world is progressing toward a growing complexity or interdependence which increases at all levels—of information, of production, of communication. The world is becoming an organic whole. As its elements differentiate, it becomes more and more highly interdependent. There are no more closed economies or closed cultures. In such vast natural and social phenomena individual philanthropy plays an increasingly inadequate and at times absurd role. Sending a few loaves of bread or a few sacks of rice to a place where destitution and hunger are organically produced by the very functioning of established structures and mechanisms is merely a palliative which is at times utterly absurd. Such gestures make one think of a man desperately throwing shovelsful of earth on to a dam that has already broken or collapsed, or of sailors pumping water out of the hold of a ship while a hole widens in the hull. Since the world has become organic, both economically and otherwise, charity functions through its structures. That is an effectual condition for charity if it is not to be either an illusion or a lie.

And that is due to a global phenomenon being experienced on a worldwide scale. Such phenomenal interdependence of the technical and the human, of physical and the ethical, becomes more and more pronounced as the first, the technical factor, reshapes and periodically rebuilds the environment of the second, the human—even in its most intimate relationships. World problems cannot be solved by isolated actions, but only through such a mastery of worldwide organic development that economic progress and human progress can go hand in hand.

2. This obligation increases in scope as world unification increases, and organic unity becomes a universal reality. All men are consciously becoming one community. The assassination of a Martin Luther King or of a John or Robert Kennedy, like a papal trip or a heart transplant in South Africa, is no longer merely local or national news. These events touch all men and are of immediate concern to all. Universal solidarity invites everyone to participate in common human undertakings and to share in common values. The conscience and the responsibilities of each man are in the process of operating on another plane—a world plane.

3. This obligation is becoming more serious, for contemporary development is, in large measure, becoming pathological. "Progress" is so rapidly and so rigidly structured by economic laws that man finds himself left behind. Man has become the passive material of progress rather than its responsible agent, an object more than a subject. He is less its master than its slave. Somehow structures evolving today are unbalancing and dehumanizing man. Development shows symptoms analogous to the progression of cancer—anarchical and organically-hostile proliferation. The spread of this still incurable disease in our affluent societies is undoubtedly more than a coincidence.

These problems are felt acutely by the rising generations. The young are challenging the "consumer civilization" in which man is a slave to the economy and where advertising creates needs for the sake of profit instead of responding to man's basic needs. This was the target of the dissent that burst into flame among the youth of Holland, and then of the United States, and of everywhere else. Today such discord smoulders throughout the world. And where youth do not react through such protest, they become decadent, debased, despairing. Consequently it is urgent that we put the economy at the service of mankind and the deterministic forces of material progress at the service of man's freedom.

The most shocking aspect of this generalized imbalance is underlined in *Populorum progressio*. New forms of oppression and injustice have been born of it. Inequality grows between rich and poor nations. Development in its present state is enriching the rich and impoverishing the poor. In accordance with a merciless mechanical force which we have analyzed elsewhere, such development promotes deterioration in trade exchange, and the concentration of economic and technical assets to the detriment of the countries, regions, or sectors which are satellite economies. As a consequence destitution annually causes more deaths than murderous war and destroys the health of millions of men. Think only of Brazil, where 50 percent of the children die before reaching the age of five, at least in the Northeast Province, where endemic maladies like amoebic dysentery and bilharziasis infect tens of millions of people. The phenomenon of wealth is not even favorable to those supposedly benefitting by it. Think of the problems of overeating and intoxication in rich countries, and the incredible misuse of medicines and the increase of cerebral and coronary disease. The economic law of concentration, which accumulates wealth in certain areas of the globe through the impoverishment of others, destroys the rich and the poor correlatively, although by different means and in unequal degrees.

4. The obligation to pursue true development takes on a special urgency because the present world is governed by a law of accelerated evolution, in contrast to the stable societies of the past, whether biblical or medieval, for example. We are living the adventure of the sorcerer's apprentice. Pathological conditions spread promptly and easily become extreme; but the means to save man also multiply. In the past men were tormented by then-unconquerable calamities: plague, smallpox, and tuberculosis—by and large. Today immense possibilities for their defeat open up at every turn.

In short, enduring obligation changed in scope, has taken on new forms, to cope with new realities. This obligation, which the Old Testament restricted to the chosen people, was revealed by Christ as universal. This universalism which has in some sense remained theoretical and utopian, becomes a palpable reality in a unified world. Each one of us is integral to the body of world opinion mobilizing its forces ceaselessly.

This first point: updating the obligation to justice and charity in the context of present-day realities is fundamental.

The New Name of Peace

More precisely, development is a problem of peace. This has become essential in a time when war could well end in the total destruction of humanity. And now the inequalities resulting from the imbalance in the development process are creating violent and threatening conditions. Such murderous conditions incur the risk of an explosion of violence, as Paul VI has said repeatedly. And so the pope took as his own the maxim thrust like a lance by Cardinal Feltin at Geneva on October 28, 1960: development is the new name of peace.[5]

Here again, efficiency operates through structures. The beatitude of the "peacemakers" (Matthew 5:9) works through development. Later we shall see in what sense and under what conditions.

A Scandal That Must End

This obligation is the more urgent too because of a scandal which affects the Church and her mission most explicitly. By evangelical vocation, the community founded by Jesus Christ is the Church of the poor (Matthew 11:5; Luke 7:22), and to a great extent she has so remained over the ages. But paradoxically she has become more and more the Church of the rich in recent centuries.

This "scandal" began in the eighteenth century in the industrialized countries of Europe. There the Church "lost the working class" which had rediscovered its path to liberation outside of Catholicism and through a break with it. Indeed, the resignation preached by the Church to the poor had actually kept them in servitude. It was by taking up their own struggles and claims that they solved their problems.

Today, the same dialectic is developing between the rich nations which by and large are Christian and the poor nations which are mostly non-Christian. This contradiction raises a question: if Christ is on the side of the poor, where is he today? It is urgent that we put an end to this scandal. Not only is it a condition for validating the authority of the Church, but of her Christian existence. Unquestionably that existence has the promise of everlasting life, but the price is a real solution to the constantly changing problems of existence.

A Remedy for Certain Unhealthy Dissociations

In a word, commitment to development tends to overcome the dissociative actions and attitudes that have compromised the Church's witness and even her life in later centuries. In many respects, in the beginning Christianity transcended "religions" since it had neither clergy, nor temple. Over the course of centuries, however, Christianity developed increasingly and often excessively into a "religion" comparable to other religions, with its priests set apart, distinctively dressed, and living and acting as members of a clerical class, with rites that were isolated from everyday life. Formalism became accentuated, while the influence of worship on man's life (Romans 12:1; 16:17–20; *cf.* 1,9) dropped to second place. Thus the Church found herself in various states of dissociation. Moreover they are correlative and we must now consider them.

1. The most obvious one was undoubtedly the dissociation between the space of the world at large and the space in which the Church tended to enclose herself. Nostalgic for the Middle Ages when everything was hers, when she was everything, when she at least thought she was everything and was able everywhere to command, the Church sought to extend that space. Since that era, she has seemed primarily interested in creating her own space; in her churches, in her institutions, in her schools, in her welfare establishments, in the enclosures of her monasteries. Within this space, she received and protected men without always knowing what to do with them. At least this was so in regard to laymen who lived and worked in the "outside world." Ultimately, it seemed that values were situated within the Church's space, and non-values outside it. What originated in the Church was good; what originated outside seemed evil. And so good Christians were discouraged from dirtying themselves with politics—except when Christian parties existed for the defense of the Church. But they were not urged to commit themselves to the world's major projects for fear of being lost. Hence that aggressiveness toward the world whose quintessence is found in the Syllabus of Errors. It is not accidental that this document concludes with Proposition 80, condemning "those who want to reconcile the Roman pontiff with progress." Many Catholics were formed in that school.

Certainly, we have received the Gospel and the essential values from the Church. But we are ill at ease when we leave her space. Outside we feel like misfits or functional illiterates, or else we are tempted to become assimilated to the world by detaching ourselves from the Church—an evil worse than the first.

2. Paired to this spatial dissociation, another, of duration, is accentuated between the temporal and the eternal. It seemed good to despise the earth and to love only heaven. It is certainly true that the eternal is not proportionate to the temporal. But what is dangerous is to oppose the two, for eternal values are constituted in time. According to the most classical theology, salvation is achieved even in the time

we spend on earth. Once death has come, no one can change anything in his situation, his accomplishments, or his degree of charity, that is, the love for God and for men which he was able to achieve during his earthly existence. And that achievement in time is what will be revealed on the last day as Saint Paul tells us (Colossians 3:3–4; *cf.* 2:12 and Ephesians 2:6–7). In short, it is in time and in the material world that man realizes his participation in the eternal love which does not die. To despise the temporal is to cut off the roots in which eternal life is grounded.

It is to the degree that these roots have been cut that Christians move toward clericalism or secularism. On the one hand, there is the establishment of the clerical world where, moreover, people know well how to erect a temporal ecclesiastical structure often as formidable as it is ugly. And on the other hand, there is the establishment of the other closed world that rejects anything outside secular reality.

Within the framework of this space-time disintegration, there are many other dissociative relationships.

3. There has been a separation between religion and social justice. Religious values were preached in too exclusive a fashion, and the obligations of justice or equity were preached too platonically. We see a resurgence of the *Corban* of the Old Testament legalists (Mark 7:11) who diverted to the temple money they should have devoted to the old age of their parents. To such it seemed better to give directly to God than to men. Thus one no longer owed men what one had given directly to God. This religious deviation had its resurgence, equivocal and complex, especially in the Church of the nineteenth and twentieth centuries. The wealthy were generous to the Church in order to salve consciences burdened with the injustices in which they were entrenched. Others supported and enriched the Church because she guaranteed for them the established social order or disorder. In this way they took advantage of the Church. That was the case with Voltaire, who faithfully practised on his own estate the religious duties that he fought elsewhere, in order to assure the submission of his peasants. Thus clerical structures benefited from the considerable support that reinforced them or rather weighed them down by burdening them with elements either alien to or contrary to the Gospel.

4. Correlatively there was a dissociation between abstract moralism and the meaning of the world's realities, particularly of the world's personal or social realities. Leo XIII's good advice to the rich had scarcely any effect. One exception was the establishment of family al-

lowance funds in France. Thanks to Christian initiative, they were progressively organized. This is not meant as a criticism of Leo XIII. He deserves credit for reversing the trend and restoring certain principles. But time was needed to draw the theoretical and practical consequences of Leo's advice.

5. More profoundly, there was a dissociation or opposition between salvation and earthly values. Often salvation was preached by itself, in an enclosed fashion, independent of the realities of the world or in contradistinction to them, and without any commitment to the world. The most noble earthly values were used purely as means. Hospitals were set up in order that baptisms or the last rites could be administered in them, often improperly.

6. A corresponding dissociation raged between the natural and the supernatural. Consequently too many Christians swung to naturalism or to supernaturalism, for the peculiarity of these dissociations is that they imply a paralysis of the right or of the left. If naturalism is a heresy because it rejects the supernatural order, supernaturalism is also a heresy because it ignores the natural order and thus also destroys man's reciprocal relationships within himself and to all else. This aspect of the problem was excellently treated by Henri de Lubac in his *Mystery of the Supernatural.*[6]

7. There was dissociation between incarnation and redemption. Much mistrust, not to say opposition, greeted a theologian or a priest at work if he spoke of "incarnation." That seemed "dangerous"; the redemption was safe.

Here again, there can be no opposition, since Christ saved mankind by integrating himself within it. He became head of the human race by rooting himself bodily among men. He became the summit of humanity by immersing himself in the depth of human poverty, suffering, and death. So incarnation and redemption are correlative and indissociable. Historically the redemption came out of the plan for the incarnation of the Word in human reality and was realized in the fortuitous and unpredictable interplay of human freedoms, just as fruit comes forth from the tree weathering the changes of the seasons. For Christ it was the tree of the cross; in other places and other times, it would have been the sword, or the guillotine, or starvation. The Council and Paul VI restored the authentic doctrine by proposing a humanism of the God-Man and of divinized man—the humanism of the redemptive Incarnation.

8. Linked to all this was a dissociation between the corporal and

the spiritual as religious language demonstrated. "I have but one soul to save" went the old traditional Christian hymn; "I have a parish of one thousand or ten thousand souls," said priests. People seemed only to count souls, just as in the past the Hebrews only counted men, excluding women and children. The body seemed only an accessory. Here again we must reject such contradistinction. According to the purest Thomistic teaching, body and soul form a substantial unity. The soul is created for the body and begins when the body does. It constitutes it, animates it, is fulfilled in it as the consubstantial organ of which it is the form, the unity, and the dynamism. Therefore our personal relationships with other men are either indissociably corporal and spiritual or they are non-existent. And the Gospel stresses the importance of the corporal for salvation (Matthew 25) as for the Savior himself (John 1:14 and 1 John 1:1).

9. Finally, all those related dissociations implied a dialectic of opposition between God and man; hence the aphorisms current in a certain kind of spirituality from the seventeenth through the nineteenth centuries: "All for God and nothing for men." The creature is nothing, only God counts. Here again, obviously, we must not succumb to the opposite error: God is dead and only man counts. This mistake would be worse than the previous one. Moreover neither should be mocked. People who sought "only God" often found men again in God, in keeping with the mysterious course of action counseled in the Gospel: "But seek first his kingdom and righteousness, and all these things shall be yours as well" (Matthew 6:33). But that did not always happen. Many men and structures were victims of the divorce of God and man. So the restoration of the New Testament teaching is important; and it cannot be done apart from men (1 John 1:6–10; 2:4, 22). He who fed or clothed the least of men has fed and has clothed God himself, and he has saved himself as a consequence. The man who does not do this cannot be saved (Matthew 25:31–46). The man who loves his neighbor fulfills the whole law (Romans 13:8–10; Galatians 5:14).

In a word, all those antagonistic oppositions reproduce and manifest the same structure of antinomian dissociation; hence their correlative nature. They tend to confront men with simplistic choices which lead to contrary errors. For instance, contemporary men make the transition from theologies of God without man to theologies of man without God—or, theologies of the "death of God." "Opposites are in the same species" and "engender one another," the Greek philosophers said quite correctly. Today, then, we have to distinguish in order to unite what has been disunited through opposition. We must rediscover the vital, existential unity that has been dissociated through abstract analysis and rationalization. We must reestablish the vital link, the dynamic continuity, the reciprocity, the indispensible correlation, and also the hierarchy between temporal and eternal, between social justice and religion, between natural and supernatural, between Incarnation and Redemption, between corporal and spiritual. And finally there must be reestablishment between God and man. None of this is easy for it is simpler for limited human reason to live within a system, with the comfort and security provided by oversimplifications.

In this respect, the objective of world development is an overall plan for reestablishing dissociated connections, since man is indeed the "son of his own work" to a great extent. It is in practical action, in the accomplishment of a plan, that man will be able to remake himself in spirit and in truth. Development recommences from forgotten values that the Council has restored, such as the temporal order, social justice, the Incarnation, corporal needs, and man as man. It urges us to humbly rediscover the unity that had been lost in the lowliness of worldly commitments. It is not a question of groveling on this level, but of building man up within the context of realities which make him what he is. It is a question of accomplishing the development of "all men and the whole man," from the viewpoint of a receptive humanism that is fulfilled in God, as the Council and Paul VI teach.

Conclusion: The Reconciliation of Contrary Options

An examination of the Christian motivations for development leads us to reduce the divergence between the antinomian options pointed up in Chapter 4: There is, on the one hand, a tendency to identify the responsible upbuilding of the world with salvation. On the other hand, there is a considerable tendency to the contrary options, which would be heretical if they led to indifference to this task of upbuilding.

Certainly, there is a disproportion, a discontinuity, and in certain respects a heterogeneity, between the temporal upbuilding of the world and its transcendent fulfillment. Two questions clearly show how acute the problem is even within the framework of the temporal.

Does technological "progress" bring moral progress with it? Not obviously; yet moral and spiritual *values* do arise out of scientific and technical progress. The Council acknowledges this, particularly in *Gaudium et spes* in the paragraph on what the Church owes to the world (no. 44). But is this a question of essential moral progress, or is it only the accentuation or clarification of particular values? This is debatable, and to that extent it is difficult to give a firm answer.

Has the advancement of the sciences and of civilizations brought a similar advancement of the Christian faith? It is doubtful. And the contrary has more often been true. The fact is that "progress" submits religion to a purifying but tragic ordeal because substantial changes occur to the structures in which it takes refuge. In the eighteenth century, for instance, scientific progress was largely antireligious.

There is a point, at least, where continuity between temporal life and eternal life is clear. The same love that develops on earth, in the very core of human relationships, will be lived in eternity. If then we neglect the temporal love of visible men to devote ourselves exclusively to the eternal and invisible God, we become "liars" as John tells us in his first Epistle (1:10; 2:4, 22; 4:20; 5:10). We are at once losers on both accounts: the temporal and the eternal, since they are organically connected. In the order of love, we must not oppose what is being done on earth to what will be fulfilled in eternity. It is the same life and the same love that are fulfilled in time and will be revealed beyond the limits of time (Colossians 3:3-4).

If therefore material progress is ambiguous and can be utilized morally for either good or ill, its creativity is a constant appeal to spiritual progress, to the progress of love. Material progress creates new opportunities and new duties. The "light" of God which enlightens every man who comes into this world (John 1:9) illuminates those signs of the times which ought normally to inspire the actualization of the Gospel in every age. Christians should not be the last ones to decipher such contemporary signs. What signs? The signs are the unity of the human community which is forwarded by the interplay of trade, of territorial interdependence, of social communications; and by the search for justice and universal brotherhood in the manner of evangelical universalism's encounters. The signs are in the accelerated cultural evolution of the world, in the insecurity of the unsophisticated, in tragic economic imbalances, in the injustice which is generating oppression and hatred that seek to destroy the world's unity everywhere. Such signs are also the values and new possibilities which are appearing in our world then.

What is important for the solution of this problem is the bond Christ established in his person through his incarnation, between the temporal and the eternal, between the corporal and the spiritual. The Incarnation and the Redemption, as they were lived by Christ, reconcile the opposition between those who believe in worldly values and those who devalue them in favor of eschatology. The Redemption is the fruit of the Incarnation in the sinful world.

THE SIGNIFICANCE OF THE ANTINOMIES

The paired concepts, between which people have oscillated for centuries, must be situated. These structural dichotomies are frequent in philosophy and the sciences. It is the problem of the one and the many, the *continuum* or the *discontinuum*, which has reappeared in our century in the form of dilemmas. For instance, does light consist of waves or particles? Despite the apparent opposition which seems to invite us to choose one *or* the other, *both* must ordinarily be kept in their uncomfortable but stimulating correlation.

This duality seems to stem from a structural condition of the human intellect, from its limitations when faced with the complexity of the world. What is simple from the point of view of the Creator is still ambiguous and complex for the reasoning of creatures. Thus man grasps reality through complementary sides of the same thing, somewhat like a camera which is capable of capturing only two dimensions and must therefore shoot several angles in order to depict the third dimension of a given object. Lautmann, an idealist philosopher, dead prematurely because of the war, was a pupil of Leon Brunschvicg who returned to a kind of realism. He observed how resistant the object is for the human mind because of these antinomies.

The dualism confronting the human intelligence in the philosophical and in the scientific orders is still more perceptible in the theological order where we have to deal with the ontological plenitude of God.

From this we have the pairings of complementary concepts which characterize the major problems:

Nature and grace

Human freedom and divine omnipotence (or omniscience)

The mercy and the justice of God

Service of the world and missionary activity

Finally, all the opposites we have mentioned before, such as the corporal and the spiritual, the temporal and the eternal.

In all these areas, tension between the polarities cannot be resolved by choice, since choice alters the authenticity of Christianity variously—depending on whether one settles for the one or the other of these complementary concepts. Assuredly, the corruption is more serious when one withdraws from the second position—that of transcendence. And yet, when the opposite is done, when one reduces everything to the other extremity, one denatures and betrays. For example, that happens when men seek grace through scorn for nature or when they sink into fatalism in the face of the divine omniscience and omnipotence. In theory as well as in practice, neither pole can be reached authentically except in correlation with the other. There is no question, then, of knowing what choice should be made, in other words, what heresy to opt for (in Greek heresy means *choice*). We must humbly accept the correlation established by God.

If a choice cannot be made, there is still room for various options that can accentuate the one or the other polarity and can more especially capture its light, so long as the other is not eliminated. There are therefore incarnation mystiques and redemption mystiques; there are Christians who are dedicated more explicitly to development and others to evangelization. But it is a fact that every authentic Christian rediscovers *both*. Missionaries are led to serving development and the witness of Christians serving through development has missionary overtones. Here again, let us remember Lebret's example.

We could add here the convergent judgment of historian Dom J. Leclercq. When I asked if the Middle Ages supplied any positive principles for salvation and development, he replied:

> Development was hardly sought as an earthly value in itself, nor as a means for man's salvation. What was sought was the *salvation* of man, and in this sense, his development in all areas, including that of culture. But it happened—and this is where the paradox comes in—that development always followed as a consequence, not as an end, but as a result, a bonus. And this is what actually happens still in all the monasteries of the Third World. Monks go there to give the indigenous peoples the opportunity to live the contemplative life. But once there, since they have charity, detachment, asceticism, a spirit of work, individual poverty, the monks actually become involved in development.
>
> This does not mean that this is the only valid approach. *Populorum progressio* encouraged Christians to commit themselves to a different procedure. Ours is monastic and that is its limitation.

Leclercq states the problem well, and emphasized what is new in the second of the two methods.

One key to the solution is that human existence is inseparable from the supernatural, for the supernatural is not situated in the stratosphere. It is not an extrinsic, juxtaposed element, like a hat on a head.

Thus, where the human is nonexistent or denatured, the supernatural itself is compromised. If the natural ground itself is warped, so also is the supernatural to the same extent. And that can mean total withdrawal, just as the Real Presence disappears as the bread and wine do.

Inversely, where a man fulfills himself in God supernaturally, human development is implicit for him and for others.

The variety of ways and of different spiritualities prevail therefore, not because a person chooses one or the other of the two correlative polarities, but because of the order in which he approaches them. One can make either a goal. This is legitimate so long as their hierarchy is acknowledged: God is worth infinitely more than man, the eternal goes infinitely beyond time, and the spirituality of the soul belongs to a higher order than does the materiality of the body.

But one must take care! God's mysterious reversal of the hierarchical values of this world is at the heart of revelation. The profound law of the Gospel is the *agape*, the gratuitous love of the infinitely superior God for the infinitely inferior man. It is the death of God as God-made-man for the creature, and correlatively the humbling of the mighty and the exalting of the lowly, the confusion of the wise whom God looks upon as fools and the glorifying of fools who follow God in the folly of the cross (1 Corinthians 1: 17-31). It is the glorifying also of the unlearned according to Christ's own words (Matthew 11:25; and Luke 10:21). Because of this, Christ the King lived the lowly life of the poor, of working men, of the condemned. In every way he presented himself as one who serves (Isaiah 53; Matthew 3:17; Luke 4: 17-21; Acts 3:13; 8: 32-33), as one who girds himself to wash the feet of the disciples (John 13:4) and who, mysteriously, will subordinate himself again to those who serve him if they are judged vigilant on the last day (Luke 12:37).

The reason for this paradox which is a "stumbling block to Jews and folly to Gentiles" (1 Corinthians 1:23) is that the law of the divine life and therefore of salvation in God is the law of love. However, love does not take advantage of superiorities. It establishes between partners an equality in which each is willing to serve the other, in which exchange leads to fellowship in God, who is the end for all things and who will ultimately be all to all.

Consequently development, as a human process, is particularly favorable today for the realization of the *agape*. That is to say, the divine love which, in penetrating men and social structures, brings them to God.

"Lord, when did we give you to eat, and to drink, when did we clothe you and visit you?" we will ask on the last day. And he will answer the men of the twentieth century:

"When you changed those structures that generate hunger, thirst, nakedness, and loneliness, when you created or operated structures through which men could finally feed themselves, satisfy their thirst, and clothe themselves in a community of justice and love, it was to me that you did it. And when you abstained, it was to me that you did not do it" (*cf.* Matthew 25: 32-46).

Ultimately fellowship in God would be deceitful without development as a condition of human fellowship. Development is not the only form of Christian commitment, but it is a value that every Christian must recognize and work for here and now according to his lights. No one has the right to censure it, scorn it, or dissociate himself from it.

This is why it is imperative to go beyond the morbid dissociations and the artificial dilemmas that enticed us into choosing God to the detriment of human realities, grace over nature, the eternal over the temporal.

This is the teaching of the Council itself, as we know from the constitution *Gaudium et spes* (no. 39, pars. 2–4):

> The expectation of a new earth must not weaken but rather stimulate our concern for cultivating this one. For here grows the body of a new human family, a body which even now is able to give some kind of foreshadowing of the new age.
>
> Earthly progress must be carefully distinguished from the growth of Christ's kingdom. Nevertheless, to the extent that the former can contribute to the better ordering of human society, it is of vital concern to the kingdom of God.
>
> For after we have obeyed the Lord, and in his Spirit nurtured on earth the values of human dignity, brotherhood and freedom, and indeed all the good fruits of our nature and enterprise, we will find them again, but freed of stain, burnished and transfigured. This will be so when Christ hands over to the Father

a kingdom eternal and universal: "a kingdom of truth and life, of holiness and grace, of justice, love and peace." On this earth that kingdom is already present in mystery. When the Lord returns it will be brought into full flower.

The Council is still more explicit about the problem (no. 43):

> They are mistaken who, knowing that we have here no abiding city but seek one which is to come (Hebrews 13:14), think that they may therefore shirk their earthly responsibilities. For they are forgetting that by the faith itself, they are more than ever obliged to measure up to these duties, each according to his proper vocation (2 Thessalonians 3: 6-13; Ephesians 4:28).

But in warning us of this abuse, the Council does not forget its opposite, secularism. Indeed, the constitution then continues:

> Nor, on the contrary, are they any less wide of the mark who think that religion consists in acts of worship alone and in the discharge of certain moral obligations, and who imagine they can plunge themselves into earthly affairs in such a way as to imply that these are altogether divorced from the religious life. This split between the faith which many profess and their daily lives deserves to be counted among the most serious errors of our age. Long since, the prophets of the Old Testament fought vehemently against this scandal (Isaiah 58: 1-12) and even more so did Jesus Christ in the New Testament threaten it with grave punishments (Matthew 23: 3-23; Mark 7: 10-13).

Not all the world's structures contribute to salvation, and it seems clear that the civilization which developed since the Renaissance was not favorable to the spread of the evangelical ideal. But today there is no salvation without the upbuilding of the world, and still less so if we scorn the task.

THE AMBIGUITIES
OF DEVELOPMENT

9

The service of development, however well established, is not a simple recipe that need only be followed. Christian commitment has to break trail in a virgin forest. Obstacles and hidden barriers are not lacking.

This is normal. In human society, citation of a principle or maxim never suffices to obtain results worthy of the name. Marian devotion, for example, declines when we merely rely on the slogan: "Develop it and the rest will take care of itself . . ."

Similarily, it is not enough to merely pursue development for peace on earth and the kingdom of God for it to become reality. Development is immersed in a world of ambiguities where it is necessary to reconnoiter.

These ambiguities with which we have had to deal all through our study and which were surprising because so numerous result from the ambiguity of life itself, its evolutionary nature, and the fact that we are in an unsettled period of particularly radical change. Ultimately life's ambiguities result from the human freedom exercised in the dialectic of grace and sin.

The encyclical *Populorum progressio* first points out the ambiguity of development, even if it is purely economic, even if it is only a growth in assets (no. 19):

> An ever-growing supply of possessions is not to be so highly valued either by nations or by individuals as to be considered the ultimate goal. For all development has a twofold effect; on the

one hand it is necessary for man so that he develop himself as a human being more and more, on the other it imprisons him as it were if it is sought as the highest good beyond which one is not to look. When this takes place hearts are hardened, minds are closed, men unite not to foster friendship but to gain advantage and as a consequence easily fall into opposition and disunity. Consequently the exclusive quest for economic possessions not only impedes man's development as a human being but also opposes his true greatness. For both nations and men who are infected with the vice of avarice give clearest evidence of moral underdevelopment.

That denunciation of an exclusive pursuit of possessions is a condemnation of consumer civilization. More precisely it is an invitation to men to eliminate the ambiguity of technology in working toward their final goals. Technological progress can serve or enslave, enhance or betray life.

THE AMBIGUITY OF PROGRESS AND GROWTH

The ambiguity of development is connected with the ambiguity of progress then. And all progress is change. Progress therefore implies destroying what is out-of-date while constructing what is timely. It implies the decay of the old forms while the new ones are evolving. This ambiguity derives from the very nature of movement. Every act of generation involves corruption, according to Aristotle. That is inevitable since it is connected with the very essence of change.

To be exact, all growth implies imbalance, for it destroys natural balances. For example, in blithely doing away with so-called "harmful" creatures, we have not only destroyed irreplaceable flora or fauna, but we have also destroyed the agents that prevented the uncontrolled spread of still more harmful parasites. Similarly, by intensively exploiting certain lands, we have definitively ruined them. The problem of birth control comes up in this area of natural balance as well as in the moral order. Human society is not the locus of abstract technological creations, but it is the domain of balanced interdependences. Promoters of development must be aware of these risks and dangers; their major task is to control the balance. Since development is incompatible with static balance, it is a question of effecting balance in movement, balance in the midst of a skid, as it were.

There is another less essential ambiguity when economic progress is purely material and quantitative. Then man is no longer its master but its slave, no longer its beneficiary but its victim—like a technician crushed by the very gears he has constructed. All material progress, however dazzling, is still human progress and therefore a very deficient progress. It is important then to guide progress toward actions commensurate with human finalities.

Of course, this ambiguity is inseparable from another which relates to matters crucial to contemporary disputes about development —evolution (and revolution).

The term development, as we defined it in Chapter 3, corresponds to an option for a slow and peaceful evolution, like that of a plant whose branches are sprouting and blossoms opening. This is the ideal that has been cultivated; but the reality often introduces violence. In fact, if we accept the metaphor of developing life, we must accept everything meant by it. Life has its upsets and violences, its aches and pains. At the beginning of plant life the seed dies, the Gospel reminds us. At the beginning of human life birth implies struggle and pain. Then there are the crises of the young growing up and of the mature growing old. Sexuality implies another element of confrontation and struggle and the renewing of the generations that proceeds from sexual activity implies a dialectic of death and life. Biological life is sown in death: its decay and disappearance are a condition of its renewal.

As we concluded in Chapter 3, development is not merely growth on the spiritual plane. It is substantial change; and change calls for a conversion of mental attitudes. The term conversion evokes the same image as the word revolution—a reversal or about-face in which we reject a past in order to build a future. And like revolution, conversion does not escape all violence; reports by the "converted" bear witness to that. A collective conversion is a revolution. If we want to escape this hard fact of reality at any cost, we risk blocking necessary renewal. Accordingly we cannot avoid consideration of the following questions: To what extent can it be calm and peaceful? To what extent does it go through a phase of contention and violence?

Both scientific analysis and a review of the political options can yield concrete answers to those questions. And they are especially crucial questions in this era of change. We shall return to them in the next chapter, which is devoted to the ambiguity of violence.

THE AMBIGUITY OF WORK AND PROFIT

The encyclical *Populorum progressio* also points out the ambiguity of work, which can liberate or enslave (no. 28):

Work, however has a twofold effect; because it holds out the promise of money, pleasure and power, it incites some to excessive self-love and others to civil discord; but it also causes the development of professional awareness, a sense of duty and love of neighbor. Although work today has been rendered more scientific and is better organized, it can, however, jeopardize the very dignity of man who becomes its slave, so to say, for work is to be called human only when it is based on intelligence and freedom.

This sentence on ambivalence is itself ambivalent and somewhat obscure at first sight. In saying that work which is "more scientific and is better organized . . . can jeopardize the very dignity of man," Paul VI does not mean to deny what he had said previously (no. 26): "the organization of labor (and) industrial progress made a necessary contribution to promote development." What he means is that this growing organization implies the risk of dehumanization: this happens if the organizing is abstract and technocratic, if man does not remain "intelligent and free."

The ambiguity of work is correlative to the ambiguity of material profit. To pursue development is to pursue enrichment. How are we to reconcile this to the principle in divine revelation that God loves the poor and not the rich?

The answer—poverty, like wealth, is ambiguous. We must first distinguish destitution from poverty: destitution is destructive in itself. A distinction must also be made between a properly understood voluntary poverty which liberates and a poverty which, arbitrarily imposed, is frustration, oppression, alienation, and destruction. We must also demystify the deceptive idealizing of all poverty. We should also have to uproot the complacency shown toward poverty by some churchmen, at times from motives that are quite defective. It is a fact that the destitute often constitute a "good people," docile and unargumentative, because they are passive, without incentive or initiative. Certain sorts of leaders in the state, as well as in industry and the Church, are pleased to have at their command such a mass of unskilled laborers, available unconditionally and on demand, easily pleased and grateful for anything that may distract them a moment from their despair. It is a temptation to use people who are so docile. And the Church is subject to this temptation, for such groups of men turn easily to the "supernatural" in all its forms, whether in religion, magic, or superstition. To whatever degree certain pilgrim-shrines owe their prosperity to this, the Church equivocates and justifies the criticism leveled by Feuerbach and the Marxists. The Mexican film *Raíces* is outstanding in depicting such cruel exploitation. For the working classes as for others, it is important to cultivate an authentic Christianity—a Christianity which is not a "cop-out" in the face of human problems that must be resolved. So far as we foster or encourage a religion of alienation then, we delude ourselves and pave the way for rebellion.

Wealth also provokes alienations: wealth enslaves by means of the needs it multiplies artificially. And those needs are an alibi for, and at times, even a destroyer of men. Industrialization can provoke even worse alienation since, while a factor in development, it is not a good in itself. It can become a power center for domination and thus endanger the freedom of the very proletariat it has so often developed.

Accordingly one must distinguish between excessive wealth and necessary resources. But that is a delicate matter, since nobody finds his own wealth excessive. What is important is that the wealth which evolves according to its own law, the law of profit, is condemned by the Gospel itself (Luke 16:9 and 13; *cf.* Matthew 6:24). Wealth must be kept for the service of man. In this regard, it must be available for sharing and not be for hoarding. In short, wealth is a human value only to the degree that it promotes justice, charity, and fellowship among men. And this is far from being the case today.

The ambiguity of wealth and the ambiguity of poverty are correlatives, for the concentrated growth of immense wealth deepens the chasm of poverty. Thus, certain contemporary methods of economic "development" actually "develop" both the alienation of those who have nothing and the alienation of those who are subjected to the law of "unrighteous mammon" (cited above from the Gospels of Saint Luke and Saint Matthew).

PEACE AND CONFLICT

"Development [as] the new name of peace" is so beautiful and, in one sense, so true, but it is no magic formula. Peace is not necessarily development, and development does not always favor peace. It can even foster war. Indeed such problems are much more complex than one might realize. This is brought out in the article on aggression by J. Galtung (*Journal of Peace Research*, Oslo: no. 2). His exposition reveals that belief in quasi-automatic pacification through economic development results from confusing the situation in developed countries, where it is relatively easy to raise the standard of living for the underprivileged, with the situation in poor countries.

> [In the latter] it is impossible to work simultaneously on all fronts of underdevelopment (living standard, working conditions, education, nutrition, health, participation in political life . . .)
> But action taken on one or the other problem, independently from the rest, produces internal imbalances that generate frustrations and extremely violent conflicts . . . For example, set up universities and institute mass education and you make a population rich in education, while it remains poor in all other respects . . . You have created the very conditions for revolutionary upheaval.

The author gives an example: the radio training schools in Colombia touched off a fresh outbreak of guerilla activity and violence since the state was unable to also produce jobs or opportunities for social and political advancement. Here we touch on the problem of inertia that plagues development. Political and economic leaders are well aware that progress in culture and in social awareness stimulates legitimate demands and compromises their position. It explains the exile and persecution suffered by those who, in Brazil for example, had been working effectively to develop literacy and "social awareness." But such ostrich politics, which prolongs inhuman conditions by aggravating them, merely delays the changes that ultimately are irrepressible. This burgeoning self-awareness, which is not being developed constructively through literacy and the development of solidarity, is being realized in ways which lead to a cycle of ever more dangerous violence. For instance, when they have a little money in their pockets, the poor can buy the inexpensive transistor radios one finds all over Latin America. And these radios advertise the consumer society everywhere. The result is that the poor become exasperated by their own indigence, while before they were resigned to their lot out of ignorance. To so arouse the most self-centered and often the most artificial desires causes violence that is much less purposeful, and consequently less well-planned than that in normal cultural development. Here again we recognize the crucial problem of violence which will be discussed in the next chapter.

We also encounter again a very real problem for the Church: to talk of peace and keep apart from all strife can at times be the same thing as resigning from one's duty and committing the crime of not assisting a person or a people in danger of death. We must be on our guard here against a mythology of peace and unrealistic pacifism. Often they end in war. To participate in man's advancement, the Church and Christians must plunge into the very center of the contradictions in the struggle that constitutes the human adventure. The principal objective is not always to put an end to struggle (or to deny it), but to find in it its meaning for man. If we are to be in the human story, must we not know how to accept its contradictions?

Here again we encounter the difficulty of reconciling order and progress, both of which imply the antagonism of stability and change. And here again we must discard simplistic choices which are disastrous, for if improvident and imbalanced flash growth produces serious crises, those that result from immobility and intransigence are even more ruinous. In our world only death is without movement; life causes problems. But who would be cynical enough to say openly that he counts on death as a solution?

THE WORLD'S AMBIGUITY

The Council came to grips with another ambiguity: that of the world.[1] Some Council fathers were troubled at seeing the Church reconciled with the world and participating in it, since Saint John had written, "Do not love the world or the things in the world. If anyone loves the world, love for the Father is not in him" (1 John 2:15; *cf.* 17).

And the counteraction was also mentioned: "The world hates me" (John 7:7; 15:19); "the whole world is in the power of the evil one" (1 John 5, 19; *cf.* John 14, 30; 16:11; 1 Corinthians 1, 20).

Christ was so opposed to the world that he did not even pray for it, said one Council father, referring to Saint John's account (17:9).

In rebuttal, others quoted the words of Christ: "For God so loved the world that he gave his only Son" (John 3:16).

This is the ambiguity of the world considered as *created things* (Acts 17:24) and as *sinning*. Other biblical texts outline the solution. God proves his love for the world precisely by freeing it from sin: "Behold, the lamb of God, who takes away the sin of the world" (John 1:29 & 36); "Keep oneself unstained from the world" (James 1:27); "For the bread of God . . . gives life to the world" (John 6:33; *cf.* 3:17, 19; 9:5; 12:47).

Christ came into the world to ransom it, to heal it, to renew it.

Besides this fundamental ambiguity which is recorded in the Bible itself, there are others.

The world is ambiguous because of the complexity and indeterminateness issuing from its freedoms and its many overlapping and unknown quantities and because of the values that are fashioned and refashioned, formed, extended, and lost within it. The result is that the world is enigmatic. One can love it or one can hate it—depending upon the angle from which it is regarded.

But the real and specific problem is that of the relationship between the Church and the world. The Church established herself in a world that had its own existence. Up to the beginning of the famed Constantinian era, the Church was a "leaven" hidden "in the dough," respectful toward institutions but the yeast of spiritual renewal. Then she took her official place in world affairs. There followed centuries of either violent struggle or latent tension over who would prevail— pope or emperor, Church or world. That was the challenge in the *dictatus papae* of Gregory VII: the pope has the right to depose kings and emperors. It seemed then that the world was good insofar as it was subject to the Church and enveloped in her maternal mantle. But in a third age of the Church, the world asserted its autonomy and assumed independence at all levels. Science developed in harmony with its own laws so that outside intervention was valueless. Society, whether political or economic, also developed according to its innate laws. It became more and more absurd to want to subject a world occupied with discovering itself and establishing new structures, to pre-established abstract principles. Even certain moral principles no longer took effect within that reality. They fell to the scythe. The real problem, then, is the new relationship which recalls the situation in the first three centuries. That was a time when Christians were not a state within a state, still less the whole state. But they were a leaven in which those virtualities developed that orient man toward God.

MAN'S OWN AMBIGUITY

In all of this, we have alluded to man's own ambiguity. Development must serve him, but what is man? In the past he was defined by his nature. Today the tendency is to define him by culture, by the capacity he has to direct himself—his inner-self through his aspirations, his environment through technology.

Man's own ambiguity is related to his freedom. At his birth he is a particularly indeterminate animal, not complete and not self-sufficient. He becomes capable of self-subsistence only after years of training which, over the centuries, have become longer in a world of increasingly complex values. The present accelerated rate of change intensifies man's natural ambiguities in relation to his condition as civilized man. This evolution and the best knowledge available on the diversity of cultures lead us to ask ourselves more and more what human nature is.

The encyclical *Humanae vitae* revived this crucial debate, less and less reducible to a simple choice between nature and artifice. For instance, the transplant of a man's heart (from a dead person to a living one, from a woman to a man, from a white to a black) would have seemed monstrously against nature in the last century. Today it is universally accepted. The transplant even of an animal heart (and the pig is the Number One candidate) has not given rise to objections on principle. It is merely a particularily striking example of the universal and quiet penetration of technical method into human life.

Here as elsewhere, it would be dangerous and absurd to proceed by choosing between alternatives—nature or culture. All "culture" is at the service of nature's realities. At every turn, laymen and technicians have to be reminded of this imperative. The miracle-like interventions by technicians intending to rid the earth of harmful species have often backfired disastrously. That, of course, is the problem of "natural balances," mentioned earlier. And the natural balance of *man* is the most delicate and the most precious of all. We do not tamper there with impunity. Moreover, it is significant that successful technology stimulates powerful back-to-nature movements, however tentative and muddled they may be. We have only to think of the mad rush of city-dwellers to the country on weekends; significant even if it is only to breathe in exhaust fumes during a hasty picnic at roadside tables. And think of the spread of nature and health movements whose still marginal and at times peculiar findings are ultimately more beneficial than the so-called normal ways of doing things. This matter of the nature-artifice equation is fundamental for man's future. Weight and counterweight must balance always. One must acknowledge the crucial issue—that development serves man. But what kind of man? One cannot predict exactly, since man is a creator of values which he establishes unpredictably—values which are decisive factors in his evolution. In part this is due to the extreme complexity of mankind's development plans in which prophetic vision far exceeds known facts. Development is also unpredictable because of an even more tenuous factor—man's free exercise of his own creativity.

Besides, the history of cultures and of their diversity inclines development toward pluralism. The unification of mankind must not reduce all men to one type and all cultures to one pattern. Moreover, world unification demands specialization and functional diversification. Anything else would undoubtedly be a dreadful impoverishment, an imbalance for which we would have to pay dearly.

The Gospel brings to development a most essential value which is capable of giving meaning to all the rest: the love of one for the other. And we should capitalize Other since love of the other is always directed, ultimately, toward God. Such love particularly maximizes those values which increasingly dominate our aspirations for solidarity, dialogue, collaboration, participation, communication, and fellowship. In a way, they are the harmonics of love. So far as the world is concerned, the Gospel remains original because it has revealed the *agape* and situated it at the center and summit of all values. The *agape* is the precept which implies all laws, known or unknown, all teaching, past and future, "any other commandments" we might mention—or invent—or, as Saint Paul wrote: "You shall love your neighbor as yourself" (Romans 13:9).

According to Pauline doctrine, this is the golden rule in the heart of every man, as Lyonnet points out[2] when referring to Romans 2: 14-16: "The law inscribed in the heart" of the "pagans." is the same one that Paul afterwards sums up (Romans 13:9; Galatians 5:14). It originates in the "true light that enlightens every man coming into this world" (John 1:9). What is new in the Gospel is the full revelation of the *agape*, and the grace which makes its realization possible.

Here again the evangelical message reveals its proper function as "leaven in the dough." That is why Christ did not impose dogmatic formulas or set up institutional structures. Where love truly exists, it invents, orients, and fulfills all the other laws governing human life.

RELIGION IS ALSO AMBIGUOUS

One final ambiguity which concerns religion is actually twofold: its impact on development and development's impact on it.

Is religion, which concerns itself with salvation, favorable or unfavorable to development? There are three typical responses to the question:

1. According to Marxism, religion's influence is either nil or negative since it is the influence of an opiate which mesmerizes, alienates, and corrupts the people. These are the material conditions in which development is called for.

2. At the opposite extreme, according to claims made for North American capitalism, and by Adolph Berle notably, economic development in the United States is due to religion. In this, the United States is considered a leader.

3. Max Weber attempted a synthesis[3] of the two preceding views, the materialistic and the idealistic. Development, he thinks, is due to the clash of material and moral factors. Calvinistically influenced groups, particularily the Puritans, were a decisive force in development because of their secularization of salvation. Passionately preoccupied with the soul's salvation and convinced, moreover, that salvation is accomplished through work, the Puritans produced a great deal and consumed little. And that certainly fostered the development of capital. Underneath all this, Weber detects Luther's ideas on *Beruf* and its consequence: "Duty is accomplished in temporal affairs. . . . It constitutes the highest moral activity. . . . This is something absolutely new [Weber emphasizes]. Inevitably, daily activity thus takes on a religious significance . . . common to all Protestant sects."

John U. Nef[4] cites other results of the Protestant Reformation: it suppressed unproductive church properties and eliminated the inactive class of monks, and in that way put into the production process goods and persons previously aloof from it.

Those theories call for a second look and some clarifications. Given the complexity of the conflicting influences, no method seems yet to have entirely mastered them:

A particular religion can mistrust development, speak out against it, or actually foster it. For instance, Wesley looked upon wealth as the source of vice and unbelief. Nevertheless historians credit Methodism with a favorable influence on economic development because Methodist thrift fostered capitalization.

Another religion can encourage one stage of development yet discourage another. As an example, Catholicism stimulated the golden age of Iberian civilization when it held first place in the sixteenth- and seventeenth-century world. On the contrary, the Industrial Revolution saw the decline of Catholic countries and the rise of Protestant nations.

Besides due consideration for the complexity of facts, value judgments require that we be even more wary about these theories. We cannot argue that "fostering development" is a good thing pure and simple, and the opposite of evil. This naive concept would restore us to the bourgeois moralizing of the nineteenth century where the rich were good and the poor were bad, lazy, malcontent, and incompetent. And is it a great honor for Catholicism that it supported Spanish imperialism and its expansionist policy? In any case, Spain's triumph had deadly consequences, and the Church lost a great deal by remaining too long a prisoner of that vainglorious heritage. Similarly, the rise of capitalism and the enslavement of the proletariat are no glory for Protestantism insofar as it was a positive factor in their growth. Now some Christians go so far as to say that capitalism is intrinsically evil.[5] In their view, the construction of a civilization on the bedrock egoism of profit could be the major sin of modern times.

We are now ready to consider what concerns us specifically. How are Christianity and, more precisely, Catholicism favorable or unfavorable to development?

To summarize the several negative factors already examined:

1. First of all there were certain religious prohibitions such as the condemnation of money lending for profit, the guilt associated with great wealth, and the repression, in the name of humility, of the desire for social or economic ascendance. Finally, there was the tendency to depreciate or fault social relationships and activities that developed outside the Church or, more precisely, outside clerical control.

2. There was the collusion of the Church with conservative or reactionary social classes, which played a considerable role in nineteenth-century affairs.

3. A third group of factors unfavorable to development was the cult of resignation and the repression of the will, of learning, and of possessions as widely cultivated in many Catholic circles.

4. Finally, a certain spirituality of fear and conformism fostered an elemental religiosity that was sometimes mixed with superstition. This is no myth. Fairly recent Church documents still bear traces of such spirituality. For example, the answer given to the archbishop of Santiago de Chile by the Holy Office in 1903 permitted[6] the practice of "swallowing small pictures of the Virgin melted in water or made into pills for the recovery of one's health." This sort of religiosity favored alienation and tended to stifle true evangelical desires.

To summarize factors favorable to development we must include:

Secularization or desacralization of the material world favors development. In Christianity, worldly realities do not harbor genies or occult forces. So man can use and change such unmagical matters at will. There are no sacred animals or similar taboos. "The earth was created, the earth is not a divinity, it can be utilized. Hence the possibility of building and knowing, instead of merely enduring," said one of the very committed young men of the May 1968 revolution (*La Rue dans l'Église*, Paris: Épi, 1968, p. 52).

Secularization of the moral world favors development since society and the life of the individual are no longer dominated by uncontrollable forces. Fatalism gives way to responsibility, to a freedom which makes men feel capable of victory over evil.

Salvation is no longer an escape, but an effective love for one's neighbor, according to Saint Matthew (25) and the whole Gospel.

The foregoing positive factors are value factors. So if Protestantism fostered the rise of development in the nineteenth century, it could be because of the stress placed on the first two principles.

Without being rash we must conclude:

That, after all, Christianity and Catholicism particularly were unfavorable to development in certain historical circumstances. This was particularly so when there was a widespread tradition of immobility that assisted the preservation of obsolete structures and systems. For example, one such was the retention by the Church of immense properties in poor countries, in the same places where the Church also opposed formation of the secure governments necessary for the launching of development programs. Nineteenth-century social Christianity cultivated an excessive personalism and inclined toward an individualism which contained elements of anarchy. This may explain the difficulties experienced by Christian democracies trying to promote reforms in depth.[7] These antagonisms do not derive from the essence of Christianity, but from the confusion between living tradition and immobilism or systematic opposition to progress, and from the confusion between personalism and individualism.

That, ultimately, Christianity seems more often than not to have favored development, since the developed nations are for the most part Christian. It is still hard to specify to what extent this is due either to its essence or to historical options. However, the second factor seems to be the more conclusive. Today it is necessary that Christianity foster development not only because of the human urgency of development itself, but in order to manifest, in the contemporary situation, the new virtualities that are now necessary if Christianity is to fulfill its historical vocation.

This point is important, and it is an accomplishment that we have become aware of it. In the age of social Christianity and the encyclicals of Leo XIII, Pius XI, and Pius XII, Catholics reasoned as if they were solving problems by merely stating the traditional moral law. It seemed that there was a Christian social doctrine, that it was good, that all one had to do was apply it, for progress to happen.

As a matter of fact, the encyclicals proposed abstract moral regulation, without any concomitant dynamism. At times such regulation imposed inhibitive restraints also, particularly through the obstacles that Church authority put in the way of political commitments by Christians, whether on the Left or on the Right. In some way, they neglected effective points of departure for development, whether moral, immoral, or amoral. They paid little attention to the spirit of enterprise, to active solidarity, to the existence of secure governments, and to the decisive function of scientific analysis while making plans and projects for which the political options were sometimes agonizing. In short, their weakness lay in being content with commonplace social morality that was neither realistic or workable.

Today Christianity is in a better position; it is facing up to history. It serves human history but does not determine it; it has no magic recipe to propose. It is compatible with development and can foster it but does not do so necessarily. If commitment to development has become decisive today, there still remains, to a large extent, the matter of free and personal commitments which can be expressed in many systems.

Lacking any definitive scientific analyses, we can only give an approximate answer to the question: "What is the influence of religion on development?" We are tempted to conclude that insofar as Christianity has debased itself into a religion "like the rest" and, that insofar as Christianity has succumbed to the conservatism, immobilism, and formalism which waylay all religions, and especially, that insofar as Christianity has, at times, degraded itself through superstition, it is an impediment to development. But, by itself and in the light of its authentic mission, Christianity moves toward development and orients itself toward its full sense and its full value. At this point and time in world history, this is then a decisive factor for Christianity in following its own vocation.

The question of the repressive effects of religion on development gives rise to its counterpart—the influence of development on religion. According to doctrinaire Marxists, development tends to make religion disappear. Nevertheless, Louis Lebret and Paul VI think that today development is the necessary human foundation of true religion.

Here again, we must distinguish between authentic Christianity and religious deviations. Some factors influencing the deviations are readily perceptible.

1. Development tends to inhibit expressive actions and sensibilities as Lebret, Houtart, Carrier, Pin, Fichter, Labbens and Rémy, all demonstrate. Or, in current terms, it tends to diminish religious practice because it secularizes and reduces religion to private life (the *Privatisierung* of the Germans) and to religious individualism. But this is perhaps only an a priori view. Investigations[8] by Boulard and Rémy into religious practice have indicated that the urbanization-development factor does not determine the rate of religious practice. Other factors, linked to the evolution of regional cultures and independent of city-country differentiation and urban vastness, are causing this evolution. One conclusion of the Boulard-Rémy work is that understanding the pastoral role ought to help overcome largely chimerical fears:

> The large size of the cities, sudden growth of populations, advances in technology, urbanization as a break from the rural world, the increasing proportion of working people . . . all these factors seemed to us, one after another, without any marked influence on the overall level of religious practice in the city. This does not mean that the preaching of the Christian message does not meet specific problems in this area; but rather that it can meet them without feverishness or, for that matter, defeatism.

2. According to Pitirim Sorokin, development acts in the direction of "de-idealization"; it dulls interest in transcendence by developing concern for the immediate and the tangible. But T. Parsons observes that religion can work in another way: it can be the leaven in the dough, it can vitalize the world order.[9] In this case, a lack of concern for transcendence as such does not imply religion's progressive decline, but rather a substantial change in its field of action.

We must therefore be wary of facile slogans. Ultimately, everything depends on the direction in which religion applies its forces and on concrete historical commitments.

Uncertainty over this is connected with the very problem of "religion," which satisfies something deep in the heart of every man. What is this something? If he is a theist, it is man's bond with the totality which he calls God; if he is a pantheist, it is with the universe; if he is a humanist, it is with mankind. In its fullness, genuine religion is a bond with God in all men and with all men in God. This deep-seated yearning responds to our sense of human destiny. But it takes on many forms and many directions; and again there is ambiguity.

In popular terms, religion means chiefly the materiality of the rites that serve as an expression of those bonds, and which sometimes becomes self-serving and degenerates into superstition. It accounts for a very critical attitude toward religion and the question so often asked: "Is Christianity a religion?" Is it not rather a faith that transcends "religiousness" in the narrow sense of the term? Certainly that is the underlying problem.

This chapter on ambiguity may seem depressing to people who like clear-cut, incisive situations. It is unavoidable, for we must accept realities for what they are; indeed it is not depressing but stimulating for those who face up to them sincerely. It is not a matter of drowning in ambiguities, nor even of delighting in them, but of swimming with a straight and steady stroke in the ocean of ambiguity. In other words, we have to accept the fact that a search is necessary for man and more especially for man today. Blunders, obstacles, and sometimes struggles accompany this search. And these problems direct us to the theme of the next chapter, the ambiguity of violence.

VIOLENCE AS
A CONTEMPORARY
PROBLEM

10

Everything comes about in the universe through violence.
VAUVENARGUES, *Réflexions et Maximes*, 187

We are considering a final ambiguity separately, because it, violence, has taken on considerable importance today, as a means of exorcising underdevelopment.

The Reality of Violence Today

Actually, an about-face has occurred in recent years. Concerned Christians who, right up to the eve of World War II were pacifists and advocates of nonviolence, today speak only of violence. The word is fashionable; it figures in the title of an increasing number of books and articles,[1] even if violence is not their essential focus,[2] and even if it is *violence des pacifiques,* diary[3] of the peacemaking prior of Taizé.

The matter is treated on an ecumenical scale. The Abidjan[4] Conference which brought together the Christian Churches of Africa at the end of March 1968, the Uppsala[5] Assembly of July 4-19, 1968), the Lambeth[6] Conference and others, all[7] broached this subject. And at Uppsala, the concluding note[8] of the conference was "In countries where the ruling groups are oppressors, indifferent to the aspirations of the people . . . revolutionary changes may have to take a violent form."

And Catholics are no less involved in such considerations. In recent years they have sponsored many studies, manifestoes, and appeals, even amongst people who had remained nonviolent[9] for a long time. And the nineteenth Semaine des intellectuels catholiques was given over to this theme[10] in February 1968.

Emmanuel Mounier originated this about-face. He announced the theme which gave the problem new focus—the distinction between *institutional violence* and *insurrectional violence,* between established disorder and actions meant to reestablish order. So, revolutionary violence is the issue today, in the sense that revolution is opposed to evolution and signifies, not merely adaptations, but structural changes. Such changes imply a break which does not come about without physical or moral violence. In 1932 Mounier[11] said, "we are doubly revolutionaries, but in the name of the spirit."

He explained his usage[12] from the Christian point of view:

> The first stage of our revolutionary soul catches fire from the law of perfection and from the continual violence of the Kingdom of God.
> In the second place . . . our revolt against the world of 1932 implies without reservation the condemnation and overthrow by every means, chiefly by illegal means—that is to say, by efficacious means—of the present capitalist regime. We do not want a happy world, we want a human one. And a world is human only if it is possible to satisfy mankind's essential needs in it.

In 1933 he analyzed the dialectic[13] of the two violences:

> Can those who were told "Blessed are the peacemakers" think of violence, even in a grievous situation? The objection raised is not serious; it results from a too superficial psychology. We must rid ourselves once and for all of our distorted idea of insurrections which is the chief impediment to a clear understanding of the situation today. Moreover people think much too much about acts of violence, which prevents them from seeing that more often there are *states* of violence—as when there are millions of men out of work, and dying and being dehumanized, without visible barricades and within the established order today—and that just as the tyrant is the real subversive, so real violence, in the hateful sense of the word is perpetuated by such a system.

This proposition was strikingly confirmed in the Resistance when violent men were on the side of human values and freedom while the supporters of the established order found themselves the accomplices of a regime of occupation, police repression, and denunciation. Order proved to be ambiguous and subversive.[14]

Latin America is another arena for this resurgence. Student protest was on the rise as early as 1918. The Córdoba[15] movement fought to lower the educational barriers which, under clerical control, had shut out elements considered "undesirable." Three years later, in 1921, the movement of the People's Alliance for Revolution in America broke out in Peru.[16] But the theme of violence is really imposed when we analyze underdevelopment. An implacable determinism concentrates wealth in already rich countries, while capital, raw materials, and trained minds leave the poor countries. This violence is most serious in spite of aid programs which, paradoxically, often aggravated the whole process.[17] It seems increasingly clear that the situation cannot be resolved without a radical change of structures. The situation calls for a complete and open break with them. That such insurrectional violence is preferable to institutional violence is a proposition which gains in credibility despite the drawbacks that Sartre himself underscores in *Situations* (II, p. 309):

> I recognize that violence, in whatever form it is presented, is a set-back, but it is an unavoidable set-back because we are in a world of violence; and if it is true that recourse to violence against violence risks perpetuating it, it is [also] true that it is the only means to put a stop to it.

This opinion, which is becoming the predominant one in the Third World and in intellectual circles (particularly among students), was voiced insistently on the occasion of Paul VI's trip to Latin America. From the time of his Allocution to the Sacred College[18] in December 1967 and up to the days following his trip to Bogotá (of which this[19] was the *leitmotiv*), demonstrations escalated. These demonstrations in behalf of liberative violence were mounted while the pope was stressing the urgent need to guard against violence. The Latin American episcopate attempted a compromise solution. The bishops adopted the thesis of nonviolence, but basing their stand[20] on *Populorum progressio*, they left the door open for the hypothesis[21] of violence.

It is important now to step back out of earshot of such heated discussions, which often seem like a dialogue between the deaf. With that in mind, let us consider the basic data in Christian history and in the Bible.

Historical Variations

History invites us to a certain sense of relativity on the subject of violence since the positions taken by the Church have varied greatly.

During the first Christian centuries, the job of soldier was considered incompatible with Christianity, as was that of judge since a judge also put people to death. We can read as much in the *Apostolic Tradition* of Saint Hippolytus, after a reconstruction[22] by Dom Botte, and in various parallel texts:

> The simple soldier shall kill no one. If he receives the order, he shall not execute it. And he shall not take an oath. If he refuses, he shall be sent away [from the catechumenate]. One who has the power of the sword, or a magistrate of a city who wears the purple, shall cease [his function], or else shall be sent away. The catechumen or believer who wants to become a soldier shall be sent away because he has spurned God.

When the state became Christian, especially when "Christendom" appeared, violence recovered status under various guises—both warlike and repressive.

1. It was made a point of honor to defend Christian society and great religious causes, such as the liberation of the Tomb of Christ. Violent forces internal to Christianity and which ecclesiastical legislation had been unable to reduce by means of the truce of God and the system of chivalry were channelled in this way. That was true of the Crusades, of the holy wars against the Turks, of the liturgical feasts established to celebrate victories over pagans, and finally, of the wars of religion. Eventually the cumulative effect discredited such violence.

However, the mystique persisted to some degree; and it was used for various purposes. During the major modern wars, each country tended to mobilize the values of a holy war to its own advantage: God with us. In my childhood catechism the soldier dead on the field of honor was likened to a martyr because he gave his life for his country. His halo reminds us of the halos bestowed on contemporary guerrilla heroes. The analogy is sustained by the fact that the cause for which the soldier died is considered a sacred cause so that he is really making a sacrifice of his life. In this way it is possible to apply the maxim: "Greater love has no man than this, that a man lay down his life for his friends" (John 15:13). Possible that is, so long as we prescind from the attempt on the life of the enemy, and from the example of Christ himself who shed his own blood, not that of others, as Paul VI emphasized on November 14, 1968 (DC, Dec. 15, 1968, no. 1530, col. 2144).

2. The Church also practised institutional violence. In the beginning she only used sanctions of the moral and sacral order, such as exclusion from the community (1 Corinthians 5:3–8; *cf.* 2 John 1). The Church of the Middle Ages, however, made use of physical coercion and violence in judgments handed down by her Inquisition, but executed by the secular arm. This violence was justified by a multitude of biblical texts taken from the Old Testament and even from the New Testament (John 15:6, particularly). God was seen as the first Inquisitor since he had commanded Israel to exterminate ungodly peoples. And God had struck down Ananias and Sapphira (Acts 5:1–11). Yet, the ecclesiastical judges sometimes had a bad conscience about this violence when they thought of the parable of the weeds that were to be allowed to grow until judgment day (Matthew 13:29), and of the commandment "not to shed blood." They got themselves out of this dilemma by handing over the actual performance of violence to the secular arm. The culprit was delivered up with a juridical formula urging the secular officials to "avoid any shedding of blood or danger of death."

However, the secular arm clearly found itself obliged to put people to death. The clause used by the tribunal "fooled no one. Its purpose was to safeguard the principle: *Ecclesia abhorret a sanguine*" (note by Vacandard, DTC, 7, 2066).

During the modern period, when the era of revolution and violence opened, the magisterium proved to be vigorously opposed, for the revolutionaries were attacking Christian states and even the Papal States. But the popes showed some understanding for those who rose against antireligious states.

It was in that frame of reference that Pius XI considered the subject of insurrection in the apostolic letter[23] addressed to the Mexican episcopate (March 28, 1937).

Yet the pope limited the conditions of insurrection very strictly:

1. This legitimate defense has the character of a means, of a relative end, and not of a last or absolute end.
2. Their character as a means only justifies lawful actions, and not intrinsically evil actions.

3. If the means are to be proportionate to the end, they must only be used to the extent that they are useful in obtaining it or in making it possible in whole or in part, and in such a way that they do not cause harm to the community that is worse than the harm one wishes to repair.
4. The use of these means . . . is in no way one of the tasks of the clergy and of Catholic Action as such, although it is incumbent upon the clergy and Catholic Action to prepare the laity for a proper use of their rights and to defend them by all legitimate means in accordance with the exigencies of the commonweal.

So, one could match up two series of contrary texts, for and against violence, and attempt some synthesis.

The Principles of Violence

The principles of violence are rooted in the treatment in the *Summa* by Saint Thomas. First, there is the point on laws (I-II, q. 93, a. 3 ad 2.):

Human law has the true nature of law only insofar as it corresponds to right reason, and in this respect it is evident that it is derived from the eternal law. Insofar as it falls short of right reason, a law is said to be a wicked law; and so, lacking the true nature of law (*rationem legis*), it is rather a kind of violence (*sed violentiae cujusdam*).

One finds an analogous doctrine in the treatment of sedition (II-III, q. 42, a. 2 ad 3):

The tyrannical regime is not just, because it is not ordered to the commonweal but to the private good of the government, as the philosopher explains (in III *Politics*, chapter 5, and in *Ethics*, chapter 10). For this reason, insurrection against the government does not have the character of sedition, unless that insurrection undertaken against the tyrannical government is so disordered that the consequences of the insurrection do more serious harm for the public than does the government of the tyrant. Still more seditious is the tyrant who encourages discord and sedition among the people subject to him, in order to dominate more securely. This is a tyrannical action since it pursues the good of the one in power to the harm of the public.

Periodically, this doctrine is unearthed to combat antireligious governments. And there is room for thinking that the prospect of Marxist regimes facilitated the recall in *Pacem in terris* (no. 51) of the text by

Saint Thomas on unjust laws. Nevertheless, that encyclical elsewhere does exclude any violence or revolution (no. 162):

> To proceed gradually is the law of life in all its expressions; therefore in human institutions, too, it is not possible to renovate for the better except by working from within them, gradually. Pius XII proclaimed: Salvation and justice are not to be found in revolution, but in evolution through concord. Violence has always achieved only destruction, not construction; the kindling of passions, not their pacification; the accumulation of hate and ruin, not the reconciliation of the contending parties.

At this precise point, *Populorum progressio* (nos. 30–31) opened new vistas. Indeed, Paul VI looked squarely at the problem of oppression "whose injustice cries to heaven" when he made this denunciation:

> When entire populations, deprived of the necessities of life, are so subjected to the domination of others that they are denied any self-initiated activity, responsibility, attainment of higher culture, participation in social and public life, men are easily tempted to remove by force the injustice done to human dignity.

It is true that the pope qualifies these situations as *unjust* and not *violent*. He reserves the name "violence" for insurrection, which he considers a temptation to be rejected, for "it engenders new injustices, introduces new imbalances and provokes new disasters. It would be impossible to combat a real evil at the cost of a greater catastrophe."

Nevertheless Paul VI admits that the exception is provided for by traditional doctrine "in the case of obvious and prolonged tyranny which would seriously endanger the basic rights of the person and dangerously harm the good of the country."

Since this particular phrase was being unilaterally exploited, Paul VI reacted and dismissed bluntly[24] as an "aberration . . . what is called the 'theology of revolution and violence' " on June 24, 1968.

It was this snarled web of discussion that the Medellín assembly tried to untangle by distinguishing between the thesis of nonviolence and the *hypothesis* of violence.[25]

Biblical Principles of Violence

The Bible itself is ambiguous in regard to violence.

If the murderous violence of Cain is "cursed" (Genesis 4:11), God still protects the culprit against the violence of others. For this reason, he marks him with a sign (4:15). If someone were to kill him, Yahweh would seek vengeance "seven times." Cain's posterity continue acts of violence under cover of this protection, hence the saying of his descendant Lamech: "I have slain a man for wounding me, a young man for striking me. If Cain is avenged sevenfold truly Lamech seventy-sevenfold" (Genesis 4:23–24).

But in that instance violence is in the wrong.

We find violence without offense in the story of Moses who, with Abraham, is one of the greatest figures of the Old Testament. To defend his oppressed brothers, Moses kills an Egyptian (Exodus 2:12). But with this deed, he enters on a cycle of violent events. And, as often happens, the oppressed themselves turn against the liberator; they hold Moses responsible for their ill-treatment, which is on the increase (Exodus 5:5–23).

The manner in which the Israelites left Egypt is even more violent since it involves the death of all the firstborn of the oppressor people (Exodus 12:29–33). The Bible attributes this murderous violence directly to God. But we have the right to wonder here if this is not a transfer of the second cause to the first cause, in line with a procedure current in the Bible. Thus, for example, the multiplication of the spotted sheep in Jacob's favor is by turns attributed to the dexterity of that astute patriarch (Genesis 30:37–43), and to the direct action of God (31:5–13). In the Exodus account, the death of the firstborn (12:29), the blood on the doorposts (12:7), the fright of the Egyptians who "were urgent with the people to send them out of the land in haste" lest they all die themselves (12:33), and especially the despoiling of the Egyptians before the departure (12:35–36), are convergent signs of the active violence practised by the people of Israel. The religious memory of the people recoiled from accounts of the raw facts, so the editor seems to have stylized the insurrectional violence by attributing the consequences of the liberating action directly to the primary and transcendent cause. This euphemism is palpable in Exodus 12:35–36:

> The people of Israel . . . had asked of the Egyptians, jewelry of silver and of gold, and clothing: and the Lord had given the people favor in the sight of the Egyptians, so that they let them have what they asked. Thus they despoiled the Egyptians.

The "asking" was obviously not a friendly persuasion, but a peremptory demand engendering fear. It reminds us of the visits of Russian soldiers to German farms in May 1945, when they "asked," machine gun in hand, for the watches, jewelry, and gold pieces hidden away in wool stockings. The expression: "the Lord had given the people *favor* in the sight of the Egyptians" is presented as a hieratic interpretation of the situation created by the Israelites' revolt. Even the fact that the Egyptians "let them have" [borrow] what they wanted is a euphemism. It is quite clear that nothing was returned since the Hebrews went off into the desert without intending to return with the "borrowed" wealth inferred in the word "let." We have even fewer doubts about these softened terms when the naked truth is finally expressed in the stone-hard final words: "Thus they despoiled the Egyptians."

The practice of *herem* (Deuteronomy 7:1-2; Joshua 6:17-21 and see footnote c in the Jerusalem Bible), the law that obliged Israel to put to the sword the men of the conquered peoples, did not benefit from the same stylization. It was considered that the nationalistic wars of Israel were holy, and that religious contagion from other cults was a recurring danger.

Yet there was historical evolution in time. More and more, the wars undertaken by the chosen people miscarried. So the transition was made from holy wars in which the people were champions for God to messianic wars in which God is champion for people of eschatological times (Psalm 110; Joel 3).

CHRIST'S VIOLENCE AND NONVIOLENCE

Christ waged such an eschatological war in a disconcerting way. He did not restore the political kingdom as the apostles had hoped (Acts 1:6); the triumph of Yahweh over his enemies was accomplished by the crucifixion of the Messiah, a victim of violence. It is no longer the battle of man for God nor God for his people. But it is the victory of God conquered in the midst of men by men and for men. The salvation of Christ is built on the successive breakdown of two hopes: that for a holy war, at the time of the exile, and that for temporal messianism, on Golgotha.[26]

The nonviolence of the Christ, crushed by the violence of his enemies, is the underlying theme of the prophets and the persecuted poor. A theme that begins with Jeremiah (11:19): "But I was like a gentle lamb led to the slaughter," and culminates in Isaiah (53):

"He was despised and rejected by men; . . . Surely he has borne our griefs and carried our sorrows, . . . But he was wounded for our transgressions, he was bruised for our iniquities, . . . stricken for the transgressions of my people. . . . Yet it was the will of the Lord to bruise him, . . . he makes himself an offering for sin."

But was Jesus purely and simply nonviolent? It would be hard to sustain this thesis. Certainly his attitudes are generally nonviolent. He either hides or he flees from one place to another (Matthew 4:12; John 7:10; 8:59; 10:39–40; 11:8; 12:36) just as he counsels his disciples to do (Matthew 10:23). He is also the lamb led to the slaughter (John 1:29, 36; Revelation 5, 6, 8, 12; *cf.* Isaiah 53, 7). He does not resist, he wants no help from the twelve legions of angels (Matthew 26:53) nor even from Peter's sword (26:51–52). At this point in time, the *herem* has become unthinkable.

But violence is perceptible in other relationships. There is the verbal violence against the Pharisees whom Jesus attacks as a class and without any of the nuances that historians introduce today among the various categories of Pharisees (Matthew 5:20; 7:29; 16:6, 11; 23:13-29, 36; *cf.* 15, 11–12; John 8:44, 55).

Certainly Pasolini was pushing too hard when he had Christ speak in a uniformly violent tone in the film, *The Gospel according to Saint Matthew;* but that tone does fit more than one text. We might even ask ourselves if Matthew did not make Jesus' words harsher than they actually were. But it is clear, on the other hand, that Luke often softened them, as a comparison with Mark shows. Christ's words were more than once "hard sayings" (John 6:61–66). They "scandalized the Pharisees" (Matthew 15:12).

He did not come specially to smooth out human relationships, like someone writing music specifically to soften moods. Referring to Micah (7:6), Jesus said (Matthew 10:34–36; Luke 12:51–53 & *cf.* 2:14, 34):

> Do not think that I have come to bring peace on earth; I have not come to bring peace, but a sword. For I have come to set a man against his father, and a daughter against her mother, and a daughter-in-law against her mother-in-law; and a man's foes will be those of his own household.

Even physical violence is not absent from the scene when Jesus drives the money-changers out of the Temple. There was one explusion and not two, although John puts at the beginning of the public life (2:13–16) what Matthew and the other synoptics place at the end (21:10–17). Yet, Christ expressed himself forcibly to Peter against the violence of death: "Put your sword back into its place; for all who take the sword will perish by the sword" (Matthew 26:52; *cf.* 10:34 & Luke 22:36, 38).

Jesus did not arm himself with a sword, but only with a cord whip when he chased the vendors and their animals from the Temple (John 2:13). The scene offended Luke's already "ecclesiastical" sensibilities. He eliminated the violent touches; with him, Jesus expelled only "the vendors" and not the "buyers" as with Matthew and Mark. Jesus did not "overturn" the "tables of the money changers and the stalls of the sellers of doves." Luke silently passed over all those shocking facts which were known to him (19:45–46).

Revelation gradually advances to the acceptance of controlled violence: for example, David in defending himself against Saul does not kill him. Moreover revelation goes beyond and transcends that development: in principle, the New Testament is nonviolent. If it does tolerate some violence, it does eschew the shedding of blood, when it comes to affirming the essential claims of the Kingdom, and it does so in a perspective of universal reconciliation. In short, violence is, in one sense, rejected as destructive for the human community and, in various degrees, is acknowledged as necessary for the community and even for the Kingdom. We are touching here on an ambiguity which calls for one last analytical consideration.

The Philosophical Problem of Violence

Violence is inherent in life, for human life is organized intrinsically by constant struggle, not only against the processes of gravity and disintegration, but against concurrent forms of life. This is the "struggle for life" dialectic. The phrase seems to give weight to the reconciliation between life and violence since in Latin, the two words *vita* and *violentia* have the same sound at the beginning. The similarity is still more striking in Greek where life and violence are expressed in the words *bios* and *bia*. But philology does not confirm that rapprochement. *Bios* (life), *bia* (violence) and *vis* (strength) derive from different roots: *gweya*, to live; *gweia*, goodness; *wei*, to be strong, according to etymological dictionaries—that of E. Boisacq for the Greek and that of A. Ernoult for the Latin. Whatever the case linguistically, there is inherence and coincidence between the ideas. Violence in a certain sense is the *élan*, the very energy of life.

And so love, the superior form of life, is violent. Love, like authentic friendship, has nothing sweet about it. It implies a confrontation of existences, and it advances along a path between the cliff of hard knocks and the precipice of hatred. It comes across opposing forces that must be mastered. Moreover, these difficulties raise the level of encounter and broaden fellowship. Certain passive dispositions also exist in love and friendship, or else love and friendship are doomed to a degrading mediocrity. On occasion a normal child asserts himself by being contrary-minded. Such rejection of passivity is a source of enrichment for the family as a community. In this sense Jesus asserted himself considerably when he left home at the age of twelve for his dialogue in the Temple, as related by Luke (2:43–49). It was a dispute upon which Mary had to meditate deeply in order to understand its meaning (Luke 2:50–51).

Even the mystical relationship with God is not purely and simply nonviolent. Jacob's encounter with Yahweh at the ford of Jabbok is a combat (Genesis 32:24–29):

> And Jacob was left alone; and a man wrestled with him until the breaking of the day. When the man saw that he did not prevail against Jacob, he touched the hollow of his thigh; and Jacob's thigh was put out of joint as he wrestled with him. Then he said: "Let me go, for the day is breaking." But Jacob said, "I will not let you go, unless you bless me." And he said to him, "What is your name?" And he said, "Jacob." Then he said, "Your name shall no more be called Jacob, but Israel, for you have striven with God and with men, and have prevailed." . . . And there he blessed him.

If at the political level, there is a casuistry of violence to some degree, there is a *theo*-logy of violence here, since God is directly involved. The mysterious violence of these nights nurtures fellowship.

Such struggles can be considered from God's vantage point or from man's.

1. God seems unable to penetrate the moral hardness of certain men except by a kind of forced entry; he strikes down Saul the persecutor violently. But he does it to make a "chosen instrument" out of one who was persecuting him (Acts 9:15) and an apostle of a true freedom still so much misunderstood.

More generally, God's love is so total and so deep that at times he offers himself to us in a violent way. Indeed, if we take a new look at the Eucharist, prescinding from our habitual attitude toward it—since habit enshrouds everything—we see that that eucharistic memorial in which Christ gives himself as food to those he loves is a violent act. That is why the recriminations of the crowd and the confusion of the disciples burst out (John 6:52, 60): "How can this man give us his flesh to eat? . . . This is a hard saying; who can listen to it?"

2. We are tempted to ask ourselves whether violence is not reciprocal on man's part, whether violence does not enhance one aspect of debate, and, indeed, of the acquistion of absolute love, as we see in Job's arguing with God or even in the dialogues of Abraham and of the prophets: "How long, O Lord?" (Psalm 13: 1–3; 79: 5; 89:46). This is the whole mystery of intercession in the face of the omniscience, the benevolent gratuitousness, and the irreversible will of the Creator.

Indeed, all life is violent, for it is a force (*vis*), a struggle for self-affirmation, growth, self-defence, or at least a struggle to defend and conquer for God and for all men the good and the values which honorable men bear within themselves. Love is violent. It partakes of struggle, of confrontation, and of resistance at the very time it is giving. Those who love themselves, most hurt themselves. The course of true love never runs smooth. And, in a way, even our love for God can take on the look of a conflict.

Certainly, to a large extent conflicts are the product of sin, which divides and opposes and which gives the Redemption the character of a contrasted struggle. We shall come back to this point.

But are these struggles only the result of sin? In some way are they not engraved on the very nature of life, at least of flesh and blood life, the only object of our human experience? It seems that life, subject to the law of growth and choice, cannot escape such tensions and such convulsions. It seems that life cannot make the gift of itself without doing itself violence, and without the loved one, reciprocally, suffering and engaging in some violence. Intrinsically life seems to imply making some violent self-affirmation or personal stand that derives from its very existence. Life is a driving force. In both communication and fellowship one confronts ambiguous forces. In this confrontation, selfishness is cast off, and one's being expands. Even regenerated by the *agape* of God (charity), love does not escape this fundamental law; if it did it would be at least castrated and lifeless. And that is because no authentic love is possible in self-annihilation, even for the benefit of someone else. For love to exist, there is need first of all for the existence of the one who loves, who loves himself in accordance with the fundamental law of all existence. It is in this sense that well-ordered charity begins with itself: it begins by existing. Christ the Savior is an example. He loved himself supremely as God. And this supreme love that he had for himself and which underwent no diminishment, is the source of his love-unto-death for those whom he created.

Forms & Limits of Violence

The problem of violence is unavoidable because it is bound up with life, its driving force, and with love—even the most noble. It is in this way that violence finds a place in the Bible and even in the Gospel: "the kingdom of heaven has suffered violence and men of violence take it by force" (Matthew 11:12). In this context, Christ's life bears marks of the violence which has caused some exegetes to place him in the tradition of the zealots.

There is no project that does not imply violence in the form of structure or of act. And there is permanent tension between the two forms: the institutional and the insurrectional. Life strives to free itself from systems which constrain it, but at the same time it imposes law and structures which evoke other ways of resisting and other struggles. Where structures become inflexible and pathologically hardened, life defends itself. Where disorder is rife, life organizes and uses violence to establish order. Man will always oscillate between violence and nonviolence. He cannot escape from this ambiguity. The demanding nature of violence begets the need for peace in all areas, as the monotony of peace gives rise to violence.

This is a dialectic we cannot escape even though there are moments of blessed harmony. However, violence should not be canonized. It is experienced as an evil; it is a sometimes necessary evil, a means made to be transcended. And there is no authentic transcendence unless the force (*vis*) of violence is channeled in the direction of fellowship and undertaken in peace and for peace.

We must then denounce current simplistic temptations to approve all violence.

1. Drawing-room violence is absurd.

2. Temperamental violence, which used to be considered shameful and culpable, is too often stimulated nowadays by the prestige that

public opinion grants to all violence. But such violence destroys others and itself for it is without freedom or lucidity. It does not lead to fellowship.

3. Violence for violence's sake is a more subtle temptation. How is it even possible? The fact is, means and end are easily confused, and it is hard to keep means in their subordinate position. And then, violence is intoxicating, it exalts itself both in action and word. But violence can only be a means; it must be limited, controlled, mastered, surpassed. It is of value only if it turns into recognition, reconciliation, and fellowship. Thoughtless violence harbors no advantage; it accumulates the disadvantages rightly recalled by Paul VI, and by Jean-Paul Sartre as well: "Blood, hatred, failure."

According to Christian tradition and experience, violence is a dangerous force that can only be utilized within certain limits. Mention of those limits always sounds false, since action proceeds from intimate aspirations and expanding force (*vis*) and not from extrinsic rules. Law making will always tend to suppress violence because violence always seems aggressive, and therefore evil and empty when considered a priori. *True limits,* in fact, come only from the intrinsic quality of love. Public authorities charged with repressing explosive violence by institutional violence will never administer anything but palliatives.

Nonetheless there are just principles for the right use of violence.

1. First of all, violent intervention can only be the last resort, when all nonviolent means are exhausted.

2. Violence should not be a mere impulse. It is legitimate only if it involves a political act that is thought-out, mature, and prepared.

Actually, violence is legitimate only where it succeeds. This maxim, which may appear Machiavellian, seems to govern the practice of the Church herself, which ordinarily recognizes all existing regimes as long as they endure. However, God knows how many originated in violence. Hence the response of Pope Zachary to Pepin the Short in 750: "It is better for the one who wields power to be called king . . . so that order be not disturbed" (PL 104, 374; DTC 15, 3674-75).

In effect, what governs this matter of conscience ultimately is the establishment of the common good.

3. Violence should be minimal. In this, we must distinguish between Helder Camara's "liberating moral pressures" and physical and bloody violence (a distinction made at Beirut, ICI, July 15, 1968, p. 8 C). Serious revolutionaries, those who are possessed by a great con-

structive project and not by hatred or vengeance, know and say that the effectiveness of a guerrilla war or a revolution is not measured by the number of shots fired, nor by the number of dead men, but by the *participation of the people.* Under ideal conditions, the mass participation of a whole country could do away with all material violence.

4. Finally, violence (*bia*) makes no sense unless it is life (*bios*) capable of promoting a better order. That is what the prior of Taizé says in his book *Violence des pacifiques.*[27] Here he opposes creative violence to destructive violence: "It cannot be a question of just any violence. The one that takes possession of the kingdom is creative. It is not stamped with the need for power."

5. His last formula, moreover, touches on an essential point. Here as elsewhere, the principle that the end justifies the means cannot be admitted. The end determines them, orients them, undoubtedly; but the end does not justify the evil—hatred primarily. Whoever uses intrinsically evil means for a good end corrupts or destroys the objective pursued. In this process, the end becomes bogged down in the corrupt means, it is buried in them. Often violence gives birth to a still-born child, killed while being brought into the world. Then everything is lost.

It is of that that Camus[28] speaks in *The Rebel*:

> When revolt discharges its energies in destruction, it is illogical. By claiming the unity of the human condition, revolution is a force for life, not for death. Its profound logic is not that of destruction; it is that of creation.

This is also what Boris Pasternak[29] in *Doctor Zhivago* says in his nostalgic way, reflecting on the revolution; "Revolutions produce men of action, fanatics provided with blinkers, cramped geniuses. In a few hours, a few days, they overthrow the old order of things. The revolutions last weeks, years, then decades and hundreds of years; people adore as something sacred that spirit of mediocrity that created them" (Michel Aucouturier, *Pasternak par lui-même,* Paris: Editions du Seuil, 1963, p. 156).

Again we find the problem of violence and revolution here. Revolution is to the progress of society what conversion is to the progress of each man. The two words mean the same thing: a turning-around, an about-face. In both cases, there is a break with an established situation considered regrettable. And every break is violent.

Surely many changes come about through peaceful growth, through evolution without revolution. But the law of sin, and more radically, the inertia of the establishment, its rigidity and its corruption, from time to time call for the forceful action which keeps life from becoming inflexible and debased.

In what concerns our subject, development, violence[30] seems necessary in order to cross the threshold of the injustice and oppressions that become steadily worse. But violence only makes sense if it is proportionate to its service for mankind's future.

Certainly, with Paul VI, we must uphold the fruitful principle of nonviolence as lived and taught by Christ. But the hypothesis of violence cannot be excluded. And more often than not it is among the hypotheses being considered by contemporary men. Such hypotheses derive, not from basic principles, but from optional methods, from political viewpoints, and from casuistic reasoning. And this happens because man, complex being that he is, accomplishes the improbable and the impossible while using routes that he maps out during his march. Like a conversion, a revolution or a *coup d'état* is always impossible a priori. And yet hope, merely human hope as well as that infused by divine grace, obtains what it seems vain to hope for. That is what is so fitting about the graffiti seen on a Paris wall in May 1968: "Be realistic, ask for the impossible."

THE END
AND
THE MEANS

11

Let us be careful not to sink into the quicksand of the ambiguities we have had to examine so carefully. Indeed we must come to grips with the specific goals and means of development as it is to be promoted.

The Finality of Development

Development is "finalized" by *man*, not by production or wealth as such. This "finality," as expressed by Lebret, was incorporated in the encyclical *Populorum progressio* (no. 6): *"Have more to be more."*

A January 1965 allocution of Paul VI borrowed by the Council (*Gaudium et spes*, no. 35) further clarifies this maxim: "Man is more precious for what he *is* than for what he has."

This being-worth-more is less having-more than it is being-more. The future must be finalized by being. It is a question of developing the whole man: man in his entirety and in accordance with the hierarchy of his potentialities, and all men in accordance with their diversity. This totality of organic finalities culminates in man's vocation to a universal love calling for eternal fulfillment in God.

Here we have to situate the two concepts of development as they are understood internationally.

1. The Anglo-Saxon idea, inspired by the scandal of suffering men, organizes a global strategy for productivity by mobilizing eco-

nomic means, essentially business capital, for feeding the hungry and for eliminating destitution through abundance.

To do this, the developers of aid programs calculate needs, means, and calories. They make full use of computers. They evolve effective projects indigenous to underdeveloped peoples from within the pragmatic framework of a particular industry. For example, in the initial program they attempt to lower the external barriers to development, such as deterioration of the terms of monetary exchange, by maintaining an equitable rate of exchange for raw materials.

2. The Latin idea, considering the human condition globally, aims for the development of the whole man. That in turn implies freedom with its concomitant dynamism and its open-ended potential. From this viewpoint, development is defined as "the process leading to transformation of every man, so that he becomes responsible for his own achievement in a community which is itself the agent of its own 'becoming' " (Symposium of Louvain, November 1968).

The Latin view places more stress on liberation than on the "barriers" to development. Not only does it see the external barriers whose overthrow seems to demand changes, but it also sees the internal barriers, such as class prejudices, outdated agrarian systems, and inept economic, social, or educational structures even. And finally, it sees in the overall scene, the constraints of the natural, cultural, and political orders—and even the religious order where religion is a factor of alienation. This viewpoint is therefore better disposed to violent and revolutionary liberation. Thus, while Paul's standards of conduct are mostly influenced by the Anglo-Saxon perspective, he was unable to avoid introducing the possibilities for insurrection in the encyclical *Populorum progressio*. That document is much committed to the Latin viewpoint on insurrection which later discourses have distorted.

Consequently the Latin viewpoint—which is that of *Populorum progressio*—insists on the cultural factor in development. From this angle, man seems less a final plan to be kept intact than a rough draft to be freely completed through "culture." The word "agricultural" comes into the picture here, since the essence of culture is its improving upon the natural order as in the case of the primitive agrarian civilizations. Culture modifies the natural order in order to release its hidden potential.

In this respect, development, which is initially a problem of liberation, is ultimately a cultural problem, as we shall see more precisely.

Indeed, man is a being who constructs himself freely by constructing the frame of reference, the social environment, and the functional instruments of his life and thought.

A problem arises because culture is at a critical stage of development, at a point where the very word culture appears to be swept away by the technological tidal wave. We speak of "deculturization" because technical ingenuity has triumphed. Cybernetic systems have taken over the function of the intuitive ear of nature, and are deciding complex problems which only life used to know how to resolve. We have therefore to add the correlative ambiguity of culture to those examined in Chapters 9 and 10. Will culture change substantially? To what extent should it remain modestly human or should it aim for the superhuman? It would be pretentious to specify limits at this crucial moment of both free and necessary cultural evolution. That evolution issues from a basic fact of nature and it is also opening out onto a plan that can only be specified through experience. What is certain is that man will always maintain his modest existence as well as his transcendent vocation to an eternal state given by grace.

Prescinding from futuristic complications or eschatological problems and the unknown factors in a future about which we have to speak since it is coming, the cultural problems already pose very real and too often poorly understood questions within our own sphere.

To situate the problems, we should have to try to define culture, less in its essence than as an operational method. We are referring here to concepts prevalent in North American social and cultural anthropology. From this angle, culture is the totality of human production in all the orders which characterize a group. For the purposes of analysis, we can distinguish six levels of interdependence which range from the most material to the most spiritual:

1. Technological capital.
2. Economic systems.
3. Power systems: political theory and political activities.
4. Structures of elementary groups: family and neighborhood.
5. Basic personality: the differentiating make-up of the person and his character type.
6. Values.

All this is organized into a sociocultural model characterizing each group. And it is all interconnected. Development modifies this model, since it is culture in progress.

And yet, however profound the changes may be, they can only occur when there is a certain vital continuity. In this respect, the most far-reaching revolutions logically imply "taking charge." For instance, the French Revolution was very concerned with the cultural heritage of the past. It drew up an inventory of works of art and assembled them in a way that had never been done before. Similarly the Russian Revolution, by another method, assumed many of the cultural values of Czarist times. Revolutions that would want to start with a *tabula rasa* are purely utopian. They are incapable of so doing—and they cannot last.

All of this has serious consequences. First, there is the matter of aid from "developed" countries to the underdeveloped. The former do a dangerous and brutal job if they are content to export their own cultural model. Next and worse yet, it is not even the complete model they are exporting. That would not be possible. Only dissociated elements are exported, such as an industry, a school, a hospital of a certain kind, a particular type of business, or an economic organization. Ivan Illich has shown, less paradoxically than it might seem, how the establishment in Latin America of North American or European school-university systems interfered with normal evolution on this continent which was meant to develop differently. Transferred foreign cultural elements cannot be assimilated and often traumatize those who experience them. The situation is analogous to that of children who are made to live completely like adults and who react more or less neurotically. Or better, for the underdeveloped peoples are not necessarily more childish than others, they react like any men transplanted to a cultural milieu foreign to their own and supplied with its own neuroses.

Development calls for a pluralism which can find values, not only in material resources but also in the human resources indigenous to each land.

Each type of culture calls for a corresponding cooperation and tends to question the prefabricated sort. When such an investigation and adaptation are scanty, one does not set up a development program but rather a colonization program with all the neuroses that that implies. Afterwards, it is easy to complain about the instability of peoples so traumatized, and about their excessive, fiery, and adolescent over-reactions. But development does not deserve the name if it does not have roots in each country. Each movement must be native to that land.

This cultural perspective offers a wide view. From within, it questions the activities of the Church and even of her theology.

1. If authentic and full development is a cultural development, it must, according to the spirit of the Council, respect the values proper to each people. Here, the Church ought to be the first to give the example. After centuries of promoting an unvarying culture and administration for the peoples she converted, she must, from now on, be the first to listen to the voice of the various cultures. Christianity is called to be the leaven not the grave cloths.

As much as and more than a plan for economic development does, the Church's implantation in a given country must take into account the realities of its situation. She must approach each cultural type from the inside: the Asian cultures, more ancient and often more refined than ours; the African cultures, centered on an intuition of the world as an interplay of forces; the Latin American cultures with their genius for hospitality. These last have, in their Mediterranean roots and intermingled Indian blood, what in some way constitutes their deep subconscious. In Chapter 2 we saw the impact on Lebret of this discovery on the bilateral plane of development and of preaching the Gospel.

Therefore, the Church ought less to take charge of development than to allow herself to be taken in charge by development; that is, she should integrate herself with the various cultures in order to animate their evolution from within. And she should trust them, in accordance with the ancient tradition affirmed in them, in accordance with the ancient tradition affirmed in Eusebius' *Ecclesiastical History*, III, 37. According to the fourth-century historian, the messengers of the Church "were content to give the bases of the faith to foreign peoples, install pastors there, and give them the care of those whom they had just brought to belief."

The Church must respect, awaken, and stimulate the life of Christ from within. The more she considers herself superior to and outside of the vicissitudes of history, the more she espouses, and in fact, supports those who escape these vicissitudes—that is to say, those who dominate and who, at times, oppress.

2. As for theology, it is affected by cultural change despite its aspirations to represent the unchangeable and the transcendent. After all, theology is a *logos*, a discourse, a language about God. Like all language, like all thought, it is implicated in a culture. It says what men are able to say about God, within their cultural limitations. Because of that, it experiences, from within, the repercussions of cultural development as a consequence of organic solidarity.

This new perspective suffers from one difficulty. Is not God, the object of theology, *above* all cultures? Does he not transcend them? Yes, in a sense; but insofar as we involve ourselves *unilaterally* in such reasoning, we are led to say *nothing more* than that he is the Totally Other and that we must not say anything other than that about him. We would be hiding behind an "apophatic" theology, one that is implicit and silent. If we want to speak of God, it can only be humbly, as exemplified by Christ. And then, it is better to say with Bonhöffer that God is *in the very depths* of the cultures.

In any hypothesis, theology speaks of God from the starting point of the image of God who is among men and in a system of values. We cannot avoid doing this any more than we can speak without using a given language or without its being either verse or prose. If the absolute of itself is independent of the ups and downs of history, it is in history that man's question about the absolute arises. If Christ had become incarnate in another milieu, he would have spoken a different language and used a different mode of expressing himself, just as Rabindranath Tagore would have been a different poet had he been adopted at birth by a French or a German family. Born elsewhere, Jesus Christ would have borne a different name and been nurtured on another culture. He would certainly have revealed the same God-Agape, but how? This question must be resolved in the inner life of each cultural milieu and at each historical period. For in this sphere, the universal is not abstraction; like Christ, it is incarnation of the most precise, the most particular, and the most deeply-ingrained truths.

This again is full of exacting and fruitful consequences. Actually, interchanges are not unilateral within a sociocultural model; there is total interaction at all levels. If theology is brought into question by the development of culture, it also reacts on the totality of cultural problems proposed by development. And this is its mission and responsibility. Such evolutionary interaction ought to be continually directed toward the most vital problems. An evolution of family, economic, political, or even technological values calls for theological study which ought normally to stimulate the counter-evolution of these values.

This is a very exacting matter; theology may not put its certitude under the protection of a system. It must rid itself of its ethnocentrism and initiate a new type of exegesis. Theology must not only decipher the Bible and the history in which revelation was reflected, it must also decipher the cultural movement taking place today. Indeed, one can read there "the letter written by God on the heart" of men (2 Corinthians 3: 1-3); and it must be deciphered with the same patience, with the same care, with the same openness, as other testimony, even though it may be more tangled and more ambiguous.

Human development, Scripture, and tradition—the three books of life publish one message, whose key words today seem to be:

1. In contemporary cultures, we must be able to read men's aspirations for liberty, reciprocity, communication, dialogue, solidarity, wholeness, responsibility, creativity, temporal commitment, and finality—for all the transsubjective values manifesting themselves both in positive awareness and in concrete action.

2. In Scripture we read the meaning of man and the meaning of the *agape* (charity), revealed by the Gospel as a divine and human exigency.

3. In history and tradition we read of the manner in which the Church, in her life, has surmounted crises and confrontations by subduing abuses and misdeeds, but also by subduing intellectual productivity. And we read how a contrary excess of devitalizing simplifications stifled the necessary conflicts of life at times.

This should lead especially to a rethinking of doctrine in the light of cultural milieus and their unrecognized resources, and to a rethinking of moral theology in the light of the social conditioning in ethics. In short, the cultural change implied by present-day development calls theology to new research in twofold fidelity to the revelation of God and to the problem of mankind. At each stage we have to decipher the meaning of evolution and, therefore, of the paths of salvation as well.

The Criteria of Development

However open the humanistic and cultural perspective is, it must not neglect the strictures of economic factors. It is always necessary to estimate and to plan on an accountable basis, even if something eludes the planning.

The author of this book cannot expand on this subject since it is not his own. Citation of Giorgio Sebregondi's criteria of genuine development will suffice. Sebregondi,[1] a young economist, prematurely deceased, attempted to define them in a 1954 article. (They were later used by Lebret.[2])

Finalization: In order to realize the optimum for human potential,[3] development must be finalized not only by improved well-being or comfort, but also by man's being more and being worth more. That supposes an "arbitration of needs."

This finality which must be consciously pursued ought to be embodied not in a myth of illusion and demagoguery, but in a "great design," as Perroux said. A design that is both realistic—that is, realizable—and capable of instilling conviction. It must be remembered that in the matter of human projects, one should not pronounce the word "impossible" too hastily. Truly new projects always seem impossible beforehand. In development, "impossible" fits the immensity of the tasks, the poverty of means, and the vicious circles of underdevelopment. So it is necessary to test development as it progresses stage by stage.

Coherence: This second criterion concerns the balanced movement that must be realized unfailingly *at each stage* and in any organic growth. The biological, educative, cultural, technical, residential, economic, administrative, and political, ethical, and spiritual aspects of development are interdependent. To activate only a few aspects is to create discontinuities that are difficult or impossible to correct afterwards:[4]

> The same holds for what concerns coherence among the primary, secondary, and tertiary sectors, whether like Colin Clark we define these sectors from the "production" bias as extraction, transformation, and service, or like Economie et Humanisme from the "consumption" bias as subsistence, comfort, and constant improvement.

We must also consider coherence among complementary activities, such as agriculture, stockbreeding, forestry, fishing, and basic and light industries.

Homogeneity: While the criterion of coherence concerns the interdependence of the aspects of development at each phase, homogeneity concerns the harmony of the evolutionary process *in time*. Homogeneous development is one which avoids abrupt stops and starts and which relies on past and present to give birth to the future. In the matter of development, there is no absolute revolution, but rather evolutions such as those occurring in the development of a living being. Crises are not always avoidable, but they ought to be limited, for they are burdensome.

Development must effect a balance in movement, corresponding to the model presented by the material and spiritual growth of each human being from conception to maturity.

Self-propulsion: An evolving structure ought to find the permanence of its impulse in itself. Structures performing servile tasks are deceptive in this respect, and so the finest projects are enfeebled and perverted. Conditions have to be establishd so that creative initiative can develop and endure organically at the grass roots and at all levels. We must here recall that, according to the principle of subsidiarity, the upper echelon must not substitute itself for the lower, but rather must allow the lower responsibility for the tasks that concern it. Self-propulsion always implies what Lebret calls "self-correctivity"; that is, the aptitude to adjust objectives and policies through rapid judgment of facts which call for realignments. Development is symbiosis and continuous creation.

Indivisibility: This last criterion is connected with the two preceding ones. The abstract word "indivisibility" signifies the communitarian character of development which establishes the common good on all levels by realizing optimum conditions for the creation of hierarchic communities. Development is indivisible in the sense that it must call for the conjoined advancement of all the members of the society which it transforms. Development, said Lebret,[5] is "a discipline of a living synthesis, which is irreducible" to particular disciplines, and "which places them all at its service."

We can see that these five criteria interrelate and partially overlap. But the objective here is not to come up with an abstract analysis of adequately distinct notions. It is simply to propose operational concepts. Lebret adds that we must consider this dynamic ideal without pretentiousness:

> It is evident that human development, insofar as it is a concrete process of evolution from the less human to the more human, always falls short of a perfect finalization, a perfect coherence, a perfect homogeneity, a perfect self-correcting self-propulsion, a complete indivisibility. Yet it is necessary to have described it in its perfection so that societies and groups may clearly perceive the totality of its imperatives.
>
> Fully authentic development is undoubtedly a myth, but a myth which leads to the most sound and most effective realism. However scientifically one might wish development to operate, it still remains in the domain of art and it will always need men of exceptional quality to lead it to a successful conclusion.

The practice of development and its evolutionary state lead us to enlarge upon Lebret's reservation and the criticisms which he expressed.
Roland Colin, his successor as the head of the IRFED, wrote this to me
about the subject of Lebret's book:

> A development which is integral, harmonized, self-pro-
> pelling . . . of course. But people have made too much of a myth
> out of it. Those modifiers distinguish the horizon line. The prac-
> titioners who have callouses on their hands and plenty of scars
> and gashes from the concrete reality of everyday living, know
> that harmonized development doesn't exist. What does exist is
> the fight for harmony. As Hirschmann said so well (particularly
> in *La Stratégie du développement économique,* Editions ouvri-
> ères; [originally in English, New Haven: Yale University Press,
> 1958]). Development results from a sequence of imbalances
> oriented toward progress: structuralize–destructuralize; econ-
> omists are beginning to be quite familiar with the process.
>
> In this sense, it seems to me that it is important for us to read
> Marxist thought anew. The Marxist movement has to be given
> great credit for having emphasized—it did not invent—the idea
> of contradiction in movement and therefore in progress, as well
> as the close connection between interpretation and action in the
> praxis. Those are fundamentals we must learn to integrate into
> our analysis of development and from which we should be able to
> make infinitely more of the consequences than can be done in the
> mainstream of traditional Marxist thought.

One can see that accepting those facets of truth which are indispensable
to development is not to adopt the Marxist system wholesale. The
dialectic mentioned in Colin's letter would harmonize better with the
Aristotelian and Thomistic views that all generating implies corruption, that every renovation entails a destruction, and that every birth
has death as the counterpart.

More importantly, we are referred again to the doctrine of salvation itself which is, even according to Scripture, a dialectic of life and
death, of grace and sin, of spiritual combat against the powers of this
world and of darkness (Ephesians 6:12; *cf.* Romans 6:13; 13:12; 2
Corinthians 6:7; 10:4). Materially the cross is a dead tree, spiritually
it is a tree of death from which life sprang forth. These contradictions
and contrast are surely no less radical than those of Marxist thought.
They send us back to face the same realities; they urge us to become
aware of them. They have their echo in the phenomenon of development itself. And the sins of the world are within its purview. Good
grain and weeds are growing in the field of mankind: justice and in-

justice, responsibility and irresponsibility, effectiveness and ineffectiveness, good faith and bad faith, concern for man and exploitation of men, liberation and oppression (Matthew 13:25–40). This all goes on everyday in contemporary life. Its contradictions ought to be explored in interdisciplinary collaboration in which the theologian would immerse and integrate himself in order to help us to make out their meaning.

The Means for Development

It is not our function to go into detail about the means needed for development. That is in the vast domain of the technicians.[6] The theologian must not try to take their place; he must send people to them.

These means are numerous, and varied, for development integrates a quantity of sciences and technologies.

They are viable depending upon material and human resources. And the variety of cases is extreme. Generalities would be futile and tedious.

CRITERIA OF UNDERDEVELOPMENT

It has been suggested that the objectives of development be classified in relation to the criteria of underdevelopment which we must outline. The general criteria[7] usually accepted are the following:
1. Low per-capita national income.
2. Undernourishment of a substantial part of the population, and prevalence of endemic diseases.
3. Primitive, drudgery-ridden, and nonmechanized agricultural systems.
4. Low-density substructures.
5. Scanty industrialization.
6. Illiteracy.
7. Absence or insufficiency of scientific and technical management groups.

At times less convincing special criteria are added. Less convincing because they have doubtful significance, they depend on the preceding criteria, and refer to a value scale tied to a special notion of development; they are:
1. Predominance of an agricultural economy, a rural population, and considerable hidden chronic unemployment.

2. Weak financial potential, unfavorable savings and investment rates, low level of capital.

3. High fertility rate or inadequate restriction of births.

This last criterion raises a particularily thorny problem from many angles, such as respect for freedom, the principle of subsidiarity, the limited right of institutions to condition men on this vital and intimate matter, the problem of means, their effectiveness, and their morality.

Generally speaking, the special criteria are not acceptable because the *signs* of underdevelopment are not necessarily its *impetus;* we must be careful to distinguish cause and effect. It is important then to analyze the key factors which govern the other factors, to establish the relative importance of values, and to set the priorities which call for options.

Rather than invade this vast territory which belongs to the technicians, we borrow a synthesized view from Jean Marie Albertini, *Les Mécanismes du sous-développement* (Paris: Editions ouvrières, 1966, pp. 45–46): "The economy of the countries of the Third World is . . . an economy . . . that is at the one same time disunited and unilaterally dominated. This is the very essence of and the cause of underdevelopment."

Consequently it is necessary to restructure the Third World economies through planning. But for that purpose, they must be freed from internal and external domination:

The former means freedom from unjust land distribution which cries out for agrarian reform and freedom in all spheres of activity from the communication barriers that set up classes or castes.

The latter means freedom from being mere satellites of foreign economies. Nor will there be any solution to the problems of development if the long, dark shadow of capitalism continues to be projected on Latin America and that of socialism on other countries where, moveover, the socialist state functions as state capitalism.

THE WORK OF PLANNING

With so much planning work to be done, there must be an interdisciplinary dialogue here, and an exhaustive list of many different kinds of scientific and technical collaboration is needed. We will limit ourselves to recalling some of the immediate objectives set forth at the 1968 international conferences in New Delhi and Uppsala:

1. To forestall the collapse of fair market prices for the raw materials which are the principal resources of the underdeveloped countries, and to set up manufacturing procedures with increasing yields.
2. To stop the constant decrease in aid to the Third World by the developed countries. To work toward a contribution to the underdeveloped countries that represents 1 percent of each developed country's national budget.
3. To review the *modus operandi* in aid programs. To insist upon multilateral aid which involves less chance for the economic subjection of the underdeveloped countries.
4. To prepare the radical structural changes which are becoming more and more necessary.
5. To work for the development of minimal standards for an international moral code.
6. To establish international control agencies, particularly a court of justice on human rights.

The most fundamental and least controversial tasks are well summarized by François Perroux in his first commentary on *Populorum progressio*. From it he educes what he calls the four commandments[8] of mankind:

Feed men.
Care for men.
Instruct men.
Free enslaved men.

"Those basic good beginnings," as Mouroux points out,

offer men access to the company of peoples and societies for whom life means more than mere subsistence. They allow men to strive for "fulfillment," an idea scientifically studied today by psychology and psychiatry, and one which we also find both in the encyclical *Populorum progressio,* and in the declaration on the rights of man.

It is by such means that "all men . . . will benefit from the minimal conditions[9] that will allow them through self-fulfillment to become complete men."

SOME NORMS
FOR DEVELOPMENT

12

Without becoming involved in the technical work of the economists, we complete this schematic survey by proposing a few significant norms for authentic development. In keeping with the viewpoint proper to this book, we will stress what can be called the "Christian elements," or more precisely, we will stress the manner in which the Gospel and Christianity can become the leaven in the dough. That will be the object of three last criteria particularly. The latter can only be viewed in continuity with the first criteria which are organically connected to and interdependent with them.

Technical Precision

First of all, commitment to the service of development is no dream. It means taking charge of economic and human realities as complex as they are difficult to keep in proper balance. For this, good will and nice feelings are not enough. They can even be a dangerous excuse. Generosity must be combined with competence to set up a development program. More specifically, development involves considerable accumulation of personnel with technical skills and related scientific training who must dialogue with one another to maintain a balance between command and communication structures.

In any technical area, a person who wants to get involved without

180

being qualified and without determining exactly what his service is to be, can only cause problems and disqualify himself. In such a context, information and precision are fundamental, as John XXIII said in *Pacem in terris* (no. 148): "One will not be able to enter these organizations and work effectively from within unless he is scientifically competent, technically capable, and skilled in the practice of his own profession."

Policy

However necessary the scientific analysis of facts may be in this field, that is not enough. The gulf is between the present—however well known—and the future that must be given life; it requires a mediatory policy to integrate abstract technical means into the service of man. Policy is an option, an inventive process, a creative force. It is an intellectual technique for sorting out incompatible possibilities and preparing a plan of action for the future. Ultimately policy is a global blueprint, implying a structured totality of dynamic choices inspired by realities as well as by finalities, by the laws of the economy as well as by the service of man.

Policy is necessary for development, under penalty of its remaining mere words and theories otherwise. It is at this level that an almost imperceptible trigger goes off, or else nothing happens. That was the case with the unknown dynamic force that gave rise to life in the primitive ocean depths when molecular chains of DNA formed into the nuclei of living, proliferating cells. Such vital force is imperative. Invincibly it produces energy that would be most improbable for inorganic matter—the growth of a tree thrusting against the forces of gravity, the recuperation of life in contravention of the law of the dissipation of energy, the differentiation of species from the confusion of genera, organization of life out of chaos, and advancement—even when men and society are wont to shut themselves up in a closed circle of set habits.

Therefore a necessary step today is the discovery of the "political" in the broadest sense of the word. Lebret does not seem to have completed this developmental stage, at least explicitly. He explored the technical domain in depth, including arbitration techniques, and if he was possessed of a prophetical inspiration as evidenced by his humanistic concepts, he had reservations about this intermediary stage which is so necessary today. In a sense, that was one of his limitations. He feared that he was not capable of correct political analyses, nor of integrating the political dimension with the theory and practice of development. With that in mind, Lebret told his followers: "What I was unable to do, must be done after me. You must go faster." His reservations were sustained by still another factor: respect for the competence of others, especially for the competence of political leaders in underdeveloped countries.

He tried to limit his work to the harmonization of development. He concentrated on keeping to matters of technical choice in the service of the political choices to be made by governments. But often, the choices he respected left only a restricted area for the participation he was aiming to establish. After all, "to participate" is to participate in *something*. So participation can be a mere lure in the underdeveloped countries in the absence of a political option that can put the wealth of all in the service of all. Seen at his level, political policy involves options—at times agonizing—between violence and nonviolence, between capitalism and socialism, between the development of certain human or material potentials and the sacrifice of incompatible ones. It is difficult for a political policy to avoid turning into an ideology. And that was at the root of Lebret's mistrust. It is understandable. But commitment in this area seems increasingly inevitable since withdrawal from politics often results, finally, in putting one's self in the service of the established political system, whether it is good or bad. It means being used and adopting the passive attitude that one would reject on principle in any other area.

Here we are touching on a contemporary problem that is a particularly delicate matter in Catholicism. Catholics cultivated being *a*political because the medieval Church—and even more so the post-Tridentine Church—was mistrustful of its members' being involved in political affairs. She tended to see such participation as an abandonment of pure contemplation for the impure domain of earthly commitments, a desertion of the space of the Church for the space of the world. Thus the Church discouraged or even condemned the political parties of the Left or the Right; for example, *Sillon* or *Action francaise* —and especially those of the Left. If the embargo seemed to be lifted for a moment with the advent of Christian Democracy, it was because that was a Christian party whose politics seemed, essentially, to be directed toward the service of the Church. But the clericalization that resulted, to the extent that it did, made the Christian parties sterile, as it did the Christian press, its other news media, and many other Christian projects.

Now we are becoming more and more oriented toward a concept that holds that the duty of charity—or put concretely, the service of men—is accomplished through a plurality of forms whose operational limits are not dictated in detail by Christian doctrine. In this activity every Christian surely commits his whole Christian soul, but without committing the Church as such. The postconciliar hierarchy no longer tries to get Christians out of politics, nor to absorb them within a clerical-political bloc under the pretext of keeping them exclusively together within the Church. The Church seeks the unity of Christians, not on the political level but on the existential level and within a range of choices in which a wide area of self-determination is allowed.

Certainly allowing such latitude in commitment does not mean that political action is exempt from any ethical determination. If the situation seems modified in this respect, it is because ethical consideration is not a deductive moralism which can content itself with the application of ready-made rules. It depends on an inductive process which relies on men's experience in order to discern in them its nascent values and understand its significance in the light of the human condition, enlightened by the Gospel. It is less an *application* of rules to a given situation—rules that do not correspond exactly to the situation, more often than not—than it is an evangelical re-reading of developing human realities.

What is clearest in this evolution is that political policy is necessary in order to make the transition from magical attitude to creative stage. And it is on this precise point that a stubbornly-held illusion in Catholicism is in the process of being uprooted. Catholics had the naive conviction that an idea, simply because it was formulated or promulgated, was going to become a part of life and would even structure it. They forgot that life grows from the roots upwards, that it is structured from within, that it is realized in forces, whether given or received, which are immersed in reality. Such force is both strong and weak: weak from all that a choice must sacrifice. It is a luminous and obscure life force, aware of its own plans and anxiously unaware of the goal it can reach only as time passes. We have here to go beyond a clerical attitude which leaves us at the level of spectators and glib speech makers who try to reconcile everything without having to make any choice. Fine words and fine teachings are not enough, any more than good intentions or good feelings. What is needed is a commitment that compromises; what is not needed are compromises that dispense from commitment.

Prophecy

Abstract scientific competence and the capacity for political commitment are not enough to effect the authentic human development discussed in *Gaudium et spes* and *Populorum progressio*. And this is for very deep-seated reasons.

By themselves, neither technology nor even science can effect human destiny, they are not concerned with it. In a discussion with Father Paul Ricoeur, Claude Lévi-Strauss, a resolute upholder of a perspective of static structuralism, said in substance: "Meaning? That does not concern me. There is no meaning. There are structures."

The order of the finalities of human fellowship, which ought to be the ultimate goal, also goes beyond the pure capacity for commitment which can be made on all kinds of levels and in the context of a very great diversity of ideals.

Perceiving the *meaning* cannot be done except on the level of a symbolic thought. We even have to say on the level of a religious thought, if we define religion in its etymological sense. Deriving from the verb *religare,* the word signifies a binding. The religious consciousness which abides in the human heart is always fulfilled in some way in the fellowship of men in search of their destiny. And that perception of a common destiny is necessary before we can, in the phrase of François Perroux, embark upon a "great design" which will effectively draw men to the realization of authentically human programs. It is here, and not in the order of science that the Gospel lights the way. So we must specify the two main characteristics of this destiny:

1. Human destiny is fulfilled in God, who is its root cause and its actual satisfaction. It is in God that the fellowship of men becomes a reality both in time and forever: in Jesus Christ, God who became man in order to re-establish the bonds with men at the level of his total plan of love.

2. The concrete perception of destiny comes from prophecy. The prophet is one who perceives the sense of history within the perspective of salvation, or better: the one who understands where salvation belongs in history. Thus the movements and changes of direction tak-

ing place in the human ocean have significance in the prophet's eyes for man's temporal and eternal fulfillment in divine and human fellowship. The prophet discovers a new direction taken by the word of God during a new stage in history. And he discovers the possible significance of human life which, so often, progresses blindly into the "absurd," as some existentialists say. Are we saying that such existentialists are resigned to it? Certainly not. They intend to give direction to their human lives, often by means of scientific knowledge and in accordance with serious political choices. In that respect, they esteem prophets as free creators of the future, but they are led to think that such direction is created by mere commitment to freedom. There is some truth to this. The direction and meaning of human destiny which is built upon a virgin future qua future is to a large extent a discovery. It is manifested in the praxis by the execution of the plan in freedom.

This element of unpredictable discovery deserves our attention all the more since it went so long unrecognized. But a disciple of Christ should not forget an essential objective element: the word of God, which appeals to human freedom and *reveals* to man, in the full sense of the term, the clue to the direction he must effectively discover in his time in the midst of contemporary events. This discovery is also a decipherment. Human freedom does not create direction *ex nihilo*.

It would be useless to give a long abstract dissertation on this subject. What counts in prophecy are the prophets. We have already spoken above about Louis Lebret who catalyzed the development movement. He is a prophet who came to technology by way of the very demands of his activities. But we also find scientific men who assent to a prophetic role; that is, they put their knowledge to work in the service of men and to the actual benefit of scientific accuracy as well. Actually, the ideal science is not the most abstract and the least human, like that described by Quesnay in his physiocratic thesis. The human sciences are normally given finality by human destiny. Great scientists are often prophets, not in the sense that they manipulate science or encumber it with extraneous data, but because they articulate major and ambitious questions which have been excessively polarized by the search for direction. The research of such men, which could be lost within an infinite maze of speculative questions, escapes from this maze and focuses on man instead. It traces avenues that go a long way toward solutions precisely because they are directed toward something instead of merely circling aimlessly. And humanism can put new life into the sciences provided it respects their methods and discipline strictly.

Finally, there are the grass-roots prophets: men who bring to fruition great and small projects in the field. One of the greatest was Paulo Freire who wanted to bring literacy to the whole of Brazil in one year. He started with pilot experiments that prove how realistic this apparently utopian ideal is. Other projects are accomplished by a people, in a limited area. They originate from popular prophecy, or else give rise to it. I have given many examples of this elsewhere: Bishop Leonides Proaño Villalba of Riobamba in Ecuador, Father Edgard Beltrán at Girardot in Colombia and Bishop Antonio Bastista Fragoso in his diocese of Crateus, Brazil. These men understood in the field that postconciliar Christian restoration was inseparable from a human project on the scale of "grass-roots communities," such as they exist or cry out for existence (*L'Amérique latine à l'heure de l'enfantement,* Paris: Seuil, 1969).

Participation and Communication

In speaking of development we have touched several times on another main point: the law of development and participation. Actually, a society has to be established where all men can work together for the common weal which would be genuinely theirs—in material goods and in cultural values.

Participation is a demand of today's youth: it is the condition that keeps man from becoming a robot and makes him a subject rather than an object.

Participation is a biblical term, closely connected with the word *communion,* and the dynamic idea of a common destiny.[1] The three ideas appear to be interchangeable in the official Latin translation of the Bible, the Vulgate.

It is a word current in tradition and in the liturgy. It has a privileged place in the *Acta* of the Council, which uses it on all levels to express constructive work in the life of the Church and in society. Such participation is an idea essential to a human destiny which is a social destiny. We find participation, then, as the objective of salvation as well as the means to it. The word designates a dimension of love which is both means and end. It is a question of men sharing together the supreme value, the love of God here and now and forever; it is here on earth that this love grows.

Almighty God did not accomplish salvation autocratically, although no one could challenge his right to do so. Instead, God included all men in the responsibility. He turned over complete control of the Church he had founded to men; and he set no precise rules for it. Nor did he leave precise codes or structures, but only the basic lines of action. He left to man the building of the rest. He placed in each man's hands his own salvation, so that each man enters into participation in the divine life freely and actively. We participate on all levels of consciousness, at all stages of existence, and in all ways. And that ought to be the rule for the Church as well.

"What is of concern to the whole community should be decided by all," is a principle which once governed the life of the Church. The very name [2] means "assembly" in the original languages. But application of the principle declined over the centuries. It seemed to be reduced to a formality that maintained the principle but robbed it of any effectiveness. Formally and officially Christians were consulted before priests were ordained and cardinals were consulted at the end of consistories. But nobody answered the questions asked. That custom was firmly established for centuries and it would have seemed scandalous for anyone to answer.

At the consistory, when the pope pronounces the ritual words: "*'Quid vobis videtur?'* (What is your opinion?), those called on to speak do not say a word. They get up—uncover, and bow as a sign of assent," writes A. Bride (*Catholicisme* 3; s.v. "Consistoire").

He adds clearly: "The pope is regarded as taking the advice of the council of cardinals as he once did."

The Council has returned participation to its rightful place. But there is a long way between the principle and its practice. A whole spirit has to be recreated in the Church. There is a trend toward this, although not without some groping and hesitancy. In this matter, then, the Church not only provides us with clear written evidence but also with the example of revival, albeit somewhat halting.

Actually participation is a complex and difficult matter, in the religious as well as in the secular order.

First, it is not a magical recipe. Participation can be a fraud and an excuse for autocracy—if it is a simple administrative organization, if it is not representative, if it does not make room for initiative and bilateral communication, if it is made up of complacent "advice" behind which an authoritarian leader can hide, if it does not respect the rights of minorities. The problem is to find a middle way between anarchy and excessively harmonized participation. It is not easy, because the relationships are complex.

In the economic order we must distinguish among the kinds of participation, namely:

Participation in the profits which the capitalist system reserves for stockholders and which essentially ought to be for the workers.

Participation in the management of production.

Participation in economic power.

The problem is a thorny one because attempts at organizing co-management meet resistance from both parties.

Employers are suspicious of the workers' tendency to neglect investment reserves which are nonetheless necessary for the future of the enterprise.

As for the working men, they often instinctively prefer to remain in their positions of protest.

If participation, sustained by irresistible aspirations, is progressing rapidly in the universities, it is hardly moving at all in the economic area.

Development and Liturgy

The last theme that we must broach for consideration may seem strange. And yet it is necessary for the cross-checking of convergent data.

As a first basic fact, the Christian liturgy is not self-fulfilling. It is not sealed up in ritual; it is not meant to close off, but rather to open up the whole of life. The prophets of Israel said that most forcefully, almost to the point of making a blanket condemnation of all liturgy: "I hate, I despise your feasts, and I take no delight in your solemn assemblies. Even though you offer me your burnt offerings and cereal offerings, I will not accept them, and the peace offerings of your fatted beasts I will not look upon" (Amos 5:21–23; *cf.* 1 Samuel 15:22; Isaiah 1:10–16; 29:13–14; 58:1–8; Hosea 6:6; Micah 6:5–8; Jeremiah 6:20; Joel 2:12–13; Zechariah 7:4–6; *cf.* Psalm 40:7–9; 50:5–15; 51:18–19).

That denunciation of ritualism and liturgical formalism is so forceful that these prophetic texts could almost be accused of secularism.

The institution of the Eucharist does not diminish but rather re-inforces the positive demands that the texts make. For if the sacrifice of Christ is the source and the summit of the act of worship it is not its limit. His sacrifice is fulfilled and accomplished in his body which is the Church through "sacrifices of praise," offered by each Christian.[3] These sacrifices by the members of Christ are essential and they are irreplaceable because they are the very life and death of the Christian; they are accomplished in his inward consciousness. For Saint Paul this is the proper finality of the priesthood. In the only passage where he considers himself as a priest, or more precisely, as a minister of worship (*leitourgos*), he defines his ministry as an evangelizing whose object is that the Gentiles [through their conversion to the faith] become "an acceptable offering, sanctified by the Holy Spirit" (Romans 15:16). We know the essential role this verse played at the Council in restructuring the theology of the priesthood.[4] What is surprising in this text and in several others is that Saint Paul defines this worship in spirit and in truth (*cf.* John 4:23), without explicitly mentioning liturgy and rites and without saying a word about the Eucharist. This, it seems, is due to his effort to stress its ultimate finality and as a reaction against the formalism already indicted by the prophets. In short, the sacrifice of the Mass which actualizes the paschal sacrifice—despite its fullness—does not dispense Christians from personal obligations. It invites Christians to the actualization of this fullness in their own lives. Its object is the Passover—that is, to arouse each Christian's "passing over" to the Father.

In the past, this bond between the sacrifice of the community and the sacrifice of Christ was not only signified but made reality at the offertory, which involved a double action.

On the one hand, the fruits of the earth and the work of men were offered to the Father as the matter of the sacrifice. That offering was representative of the whole man; it witnessed that God is the source of all man's gifts—the goods of the earth and the free activity of man. It made a restoration to the Creator of everything that comes from him. That is the sacrificial significance of the offertory.

On the other hand, this sacred offering was not reserved strictly to God. The offertory gifts were not totally consumed as a burnt offering in tribute to the divine transcendence alone. They were distributed in several portions, signifying man's partaking of food with God:

1. The bread and wine, offered to God and in their substance

mysteriously transformed into the efficacious sign of the body and blood that Christ offered to the Father, are given as food to the faithful at communion. The whole community thus comes to the meal at which God is one of the participants and the host. That is who Christ was at the Last Supper. He still is symbolically in the person of the celebrant who speaks in his name. And he wished also to be the food (Matthew 26:26) and the server of it at the banquet (John 13:1–15; *cf.* Luke 12:37–38).

2. Another portion was allotted to the poor, who are also a major sacrament of Christ on earth (Matthew 25: 34–46).

3. A third portion was set aside originally for the ministers at the altar, who are normally among the poor, among those who give up earthly means in order to await a hundredfold return from God and who are also the representatives of Christ.

To sum up the twofold action: first, the gifts of the Creator were offered to God so they could be divinized and in order to involve men in the process of divinization. Secondly, those gifts were shared out among men according to their spiritual and material needs. All this both signified and accomplished the fellowship of men and God.

The final celebration at the Council attempted to renew that tradition under new forms. It was designed to be a Schema 13 liturgy, as it were. More precisely that last conciliar liturgy was meant to express council teaching on development. Before returning to their dioceses throughout the world, the Council Fathers tried to include all of humanity in this last communal Mass. That was the meaning of the gifts brought up at the offertory—as encouragement for development in the nations. That was also the intent of the messages addressed to the different classes of people—the intellectuals, the workers, women, and the sick. Finally, that was the message explicit in the communions of the children from five continents. With this final liturgy the Council sought to reassemble the whole world in God and to exorcise the unfortunate dissociation between prayer and commitment to the service of men.[5]

The second basic fact: in the last unfortunate centuries, the liturgy has become cut off from life's realities. In fact, it drifted into formalism and rubricism. We have not yet finished correcting those deep-seated abuses; the connections between worship and life are being re-established with great difficulty. It is as hard to establish as a heart transplant; and we often have the impression that the transplant is not taking. Restored by the Council's constitution on the liturgy, the tradition of the Church encourages a revitalized liturgy which can use all the varied means suitable to its purpose.

A third fact: "religion" conceived as a closed world, a super-structure of ritual formulas guaranteeing the other world but without connection with the world in which we live, is losing ground today. It is another sign of the times. In the past everybody wanted a religion; to day it seems that no one wants one any more.[6] The formulas: "God without religion," "Christianity without religion," have supplanted the "religion without God" formula which was in vogue with nine-teenth-century philosophers—men like Fredrich Forberg and Ludwig Feuerbach, and even Auguste Comte with his religion of humanity.

This radical about-face resulted from a twofold process.

On the one hand, the confused symbiosis of the religious and the secular has come to an end. The world has won autonomy by struc-turing itself in accordance with its own laws, which cannot be rejected or modified from the outside. Only by respecting them can we incor-porate them in a human or Christian plan of action. Thus, in *Gau-dium et spes* the Council recognized "a just autonomy of earthly values" (no. 36, par. 2):

> If by the autonomy of earthly affairs we mean that created things and societies themselves enjoy their own laws and values which must be gradually deciphered, put to use, and regulated by men, then it is entirely right to demand that autonomy. This is not merely required by modern man, but harmonizes also with the will of the Creator. . . . for earthly matters and the concerns of faith derive from the same God. . . . Consequently, we cannot but deplore certain habits of mind, which are sometimes found too among Christians, which do not sufficiently attend to the rightful independence of science and which, from the arguments and controversies they spark, lead many minds to conclude that faith and science are mutually opposed.

On the other hand, religion has lost its prestige because of the abuses into which it allowed itself to slide when its consecrated total power prohibited all challenge. Criticism has taken its revenge. Religion is often identified in men's minds with its corrupting errors rather than with its essence. Religion came to mean support of "establishment" disorder, alliance with injustice, privileged place for the rich, and such an appetite for pomp and magnificence that the hundredfold of the spirit promised by Christ took the graceless and unevangelical form of great landed properties, of direct political power sometimes, and of the honors and splendors with which the princes of the Church surrounded themselves.

Today some Christians overreact to the point of rejecting all properly religious forms and structures. De jure or de facto, they reject the value of rites. For them, action in the world in man's service is liturgy in spirit and in truth. The rest is superfluous and outmoded.

In this hypothesis, radical secularists see the Church—as the liturgical assembly in the original sense of *ecclesia*—fading away and dispersed throughout the world. They see even its boundaries done away with; true Christians are those who work effectively in any service for men, even if they are strangers to the Church or her dogmas.

There is some truth in that view if we again consider that in the Gospel (Matthew 25) the unique criterion of salvation is the effective service of the poor—even when those who serve them are ignorant of Christ's presence. In that sense, we must also keep in mind the parable of the leaven in the dough.

Yet such a disappearance of the institutional structures of the Church, particularly of the sacramental order as the effective means of salvation, does not correspond with Christ's plan, nor with the Church's original real activities, nor with the dialogue desired by the Council. This dialogue supposes that Christians exist, "that they may have life and have it abundantly" (John 10:10), and that this life gives evidence of its vitality through appropriate activities.

Certainly charity becomes real in the context of the real world's hard facts. Charity is the essential. Charity is also the witness which will make Christ known or rather will make recognizable the Christ indelibly written into the profound yearnings of contemporary men (John 13:35; 17:21–23). Indeed it is apparent in the fellowship of love being really practiced in life itself that man today is searching for the key to his destiny. But this love which is a fellowship in the absoluteness of the God of love, is given from above and received through the sacraments in a community of faith and prayer. It is a love that would dissipate if it did not remain in actual communication with its source through the acts of worship whose basic elements Christ himself established at the Last Supper.

THE CONNECTION LITURGY—DEVELOPMENT

At this juncture of these findings it seems urgent to *restore the vital bond between liturgy and action in the world.* That is the supreme means for averting the perils of secularism in contemporary life.

We must rediscover a balance between the two excesses described. In the past people misunderstood the relevance of the liturgy to their worldly commitments. Conversely, we should not fail today to comprehend the ritual dimension of the liturgy. Such a failure would cut the Christian off from his inspiration, his divine source. In certain respects such secularism is a new Arianism. That heresy of the first centuries reduced Christ to the human. Secularism reduces the Church to the human. And the consequences are analogous. In such a movement the devalued Church breaks up, for she loses her divine root, her vertical connection with the salvific power of Jesus Christ.

The very nature of development, as it is understood by Paul VI and the bishops, invites us to overcome this dissociation of the liturgical celebration and secular action. Liturgy and development, after all, have the same vocation—the making of one's way to God which is realized mysteriously through liturgical signs and which is also the goal of development. And it must be accomplished for all men and for the whole man in a shared love which gets at the knowledge of God and is fulfilled in God (Matthew 25).

In this spirit it would be desirable to establish a union and an association between liturgy and development. And, whether we start with development or with liturgy that could be done.

On the development side, we have to rediscover the importance of festivals, of popular celebrations within that collective conversion which is development. Cultural activity is not a mere escape or dream. It has to be the experience of the aspirations of a people, an awareness-in-process. Can we not rediscover that sense of popular feeling which was appropriately represented in the harvest festivals of the Old Testament and in the rites of the early Church? The bishops of Latin America may be well on the way when they present the whole enterprise of development as an Easter, like an exodus analogous to the one discussed in Chapter 1, when the Hebrews crossed over from oppression to the freedom of the Promised Land. The coincidence with the Eucharist which is the Passover, the viaticum of these earthly stages toward eschatology, is striking.

From the viewpoint of the liturgy, it should be a question of restoring the value of signs, of their human and communitarian content, for the liturgy is based on human signs, and our contemporaries no longer comprehend any except those concerned with mankind. Within this framework, the rediscovery of the significance of the offertory, which we tend to minimize today, would be a great good then.

We can surely understand the reasons for the current disaffection, and particularly the reason for the objection that the offertory is a duplicate of the canon which involves oblation. Besides it is not a question of compulsory protection of or reinforcement of the forms of the classic offertory. We ought rather to go back to its origins, whatever the form. In the beginning, in the Jerusalem community, one found something much more radical than the offertory. The Eucharist was the meeting of a community that pooled its resources—using everything in common. Sharing was a preliminary condition and very important to the very existence of the community. The violent episode of the death of Ananias and Sapphira, who had cheated in the distribution, is a brutally frank indication of that (Acts 5:1–5). Similarly this remark in regard to the malapportionment at the agapes of Corinth: "That is why many of you are weak and ill, and some have died" (1 Corinthians 11:30).

The meal was a special moment of this using things in common—the appropriating from the common store what was needed for the eucharistic meal. What we must revalue is that communitarian root of the Eucharist—expression of a love basic to the sharing in which the Lord comes in his fullness. What is fundamental is not that objects be handled but that community really be the raw material of and the preliminary to the Eucharist. It is therefore not necessary for the offertory to be a specialized rite. The real concern must be that the human community as such exists and that the Eucharist be for it an authentic sharing—that is to say, be a matter of commitment and of relevancy and not limited to words, to feelings, and to ceremonial activity.

THE LITURGICAL EXPRESSION OF DEVELOPMENT

Like development, the liturgy provides passageway for redeemed man journeying toward the redeemer God. It is a thrust of the whole community involving action in common. This convergence, this coincidence which transcends present-day dissociations, ought to be expressed in the life and culture of each people. In this way, liturgy would be altogether set free of the boring and the esoteric, and the subsequent alienation.

Something of this kind is expressed in the eucharistic celebrations by certain grass-roots communities committed to working for development. I take the liberty here of quoting from an interview I had with Bishop Fragoso.

> I asked everybody to bring his working tools: a pickaxe, a shovel, a seamstress's needle. At the elevation, they raise up their particular tools. After that I asked while holding the host over the paten:
> "How many hosts are there?"
> "One."
> "No, there are a number of hosts: your one, your work. Each profession, each man has his own host."

This is merely one example generated by a specific reality. There is room for a great deal of inventiveness in this area. In that respect the liturgical reform, which is not yet sufficiently flexible, has to be more liberated from its formalism and from a twofold mistrust of men's creativity and their capacity for expressing themselves authentically in worship. The liturgy demands not only that commissions of liturgists express themselves, however excellent they may be, but also that grass-roots communities do so. It is there that we must look for liturgical expression.

It is a question, then, of restoring the authentic spirit of the liturgy, particularly in its relationship to the whole of life. We must restore the capacity to express contemporary man authentically in the liturgy—in a manner honestly related to his symbols, his language, his sensitivities, and his aspirations. There has been practically nothing done in this neglected area. The real task is still ahead of us.[7]

To stimulate reflection and get rid of adherence to unimaginative routine one is tempted to start with a comparison, which at first glance may seem artificial and inappropriate, between liturgy and theater.[8] But it is not a mistake to traverse this unfamiliar territory in order to break down the barriers of formalism.

1. Technical progress has reached such a stage of development that it runs the risk of overwhelming human effort entirely. Technical progress manages man as much as and more than he manages it. Today, therefore, man is experiencing the need to rediscover the *sense* of his own destiny. And that is what dramatic art worthy of the name does. In this sense, its purpose is analogous to that of a liturgy which also provides such a sense of destiny. Add to that, that both theater and liturgy are cultural expressions; that is, they are actions involving the participation of the community of man.

This common vocation and structure share common dangers. The liturgy is threatened by the same defects as a certain kind of deliquescent theater: the theater of escape. The liturgy too can deteriorate into an escape. In that case all it gives man is a haven of oblivion, euphoria, estheticism, and security—instead of making him face his destiny. Unfortunately there is a liturgy of escape just as there is an escape theater, with this difference, that such liturgy is totally boring, whereas certain escape films do attract an audience. The liturgy has to coextend again with human realities, human activities, and human finalities.

2. This comparison calls for a corrective measure that is most important. If the liturgy, through its concern for and involvement with man's destiny, does have this one thing in common with authentic theater (or even with the psychodrama) it is also very different.

Liturgy does not operate at the same level. Like the theater it is a symbol, but it is not fiction. It purifies the symbols with which the theater is replete and gives them substance.

And it does more: whereas the theater necessarily includes a hard and fast distinction between actors and spectators, the liturgy admits only of actors: hence the dismissal in ancient times of the catechumens before the celebration of the mystery.

Finally and especially, liturgical signs effectively *accomplish* what they *signify*. They actualize the saving acts of Christ, his sacrifice. More precisely, Christ is consciously involved through the signs expressed in the liturgical community. There, he accomplishes the unity, growth, commitment, and witness that are signified ritually. The liturgy is thus an action of Christ as it is an action of the Church —an action that must radiate throughout the world in order to guarantee salvation. And today, to a great extent, salvation operates through development for the reasons we have already examined.

IN SEARCH OF MODELS

There must be an organic union and continuity between the liturgical action and development action.

How can that become a reality? Models are few and far between. The final liturgy celebrated by the Council on December 8, 1965 is valuable as a suggestion, not as an obligatory model. Similarly, the offertory of the early days, bound up as it was with the existence of rural communities in an agrarian civilization, corresponds less and less to what a contemporary Christian community is in a civilization of growing urbanization. In short, these references are valuable as witnesses of a living tradition, but we must go back to its origins.

Where must we look today in order to retranslate the same liturgical tradition for our times?

Secular life offers certain suggestions. Christ gave the liturgy the form of a meal. It is the concrete sign of a family bond, the bond of community and friendship, which unites and involves. Our contemporaries, mistrusting symbols as they do, are inclined to say that the meal "no longer has meaning today." And yet, more than they think, they do experience its communitarian significance. I am thinking here of a group of very dynamic men who one day had invited me to a weekly luncheon meeting. It was at the beginning of the Council. The conversation came around to change in symbols; some declared that a meal no longer had any significance or human sense today. I then asked naively what was the meaning of this weekly luncheon to which I had been invited. The conversation that followed brought out that the meal was precisely the bond that maintained the friendship of the group and humanized it by bringing it beyond the merely functional and administrative. For similar reasons, luncheon-debates, business lunches, exhibitions, congresses, and the like are often held these days so people can exchange ideas and plans over a meal. The living bond between a meal and a human project with the mediation of a dialogue goes back to what Christ did at the Last Supper. This is one idea.

Such an idea encounters experimentation that is without a doubt debatable, but also symptomatic and urgent. Think for example of the "Dutch agapes" of the *Shalom* group. It is an ecumenical group which is very committed to action for peace and development. These agapes are certainly arguable because of their doctrinal ambiguity, premature intercommunion, and because of a certain lack of sacrality even.

But the attraction that the formula exerts is due to the fact that a genuinely communitarian gathering furnishes the ambience for actions and words which, authentically human, are expressive of the community. The values of this attraction is beginning to be acknowledged. Several bishops in Europe and America have authorized, as controlled experiments, home Masses of this kind, which are capable of integrating both *human activity* and dialogue on the objectives of the Christian community gathered round the table.

The real problem is to rediscover in acts and in words *the sense of human activity and community exchange* that is lacking in the present liturgy. This dialogue, which in words and actions expresses and actualizes men's fellowship with God, should occur on several levels, each with its own particular needs. In the liturgy of the word, the dialogue ought to be full and free; less ornate and more hieratic in the prayer of the faithful, and more essential, ascending and vertical in manner during the canon. That the canon is a weighty monologue is more obvious in a vernacular liturgy, at least in the case of the Roman canon. To some extent that has been remedied by introducing shorter canons and the acclamations, which are certainly appreciable palliatives. But the solution would be to find, at that solemn point of the Mass, the expression that would bring together and involve the community as it really is, in the sacrifice of Christ.

These are merely points of reference. The restoration of unity between liturgy and life, between salvation and development can only be the subject of research at present. Such liturgical search ought to be conducted with a sense for its tradition and its norms, of course, but also with a sense of today's realities, of the forms and structures through which our age speaks, and of a certain communitarian spontaneity which will give life to tradition for contemporary man. This last point has pregnant consequences. Thus, for example, the Mass in the form of a meal around a table exercises a strong attraction among our contemporaries because it is an authentically human act and because it is the act of Christ himself and of the first Christians. But it can only be done effectively in small groups. This requirement is often more demanding than that of what is "allowed" or "forbidden." Too often that approach is merely a laxist substitution for the real requirement. A meal for a hundred or a thousand people is unwieldy and hard to bring off successfully, like those large banquets where there is very little human fellowship. For great assemblies the solution will have to take other forms and other ways.

As for the Eucharist in the form of a meal, there are risks. There is the danger of making an artificial and misplaced adaptation of a Mass ritual that was developed for a cathedral or of bringing the Eucharist down to the level of an ordinary or contrived meal. It is undoubtedly more fruitful not to begin hastily in "adapting the Mass." We should go back to the roots of the problem by restoring prayer to its communitarian dimension and by making it progress to a point where a demand for the Eucharist would arise. It would be better to foster this demand than to improvise anarchical Masses. The period in which the Church authorities are still in a waiting stage ought to be used for such prerequisite experiments which will aim at restoring the existence of common prayer itself.

The Eucharist is too important a matter for us not to stress the pitfalls. But difficulties ought not to lead to discouragement. As the Gospel says, "He who seeks, finds" (Matthew 7:8; Luke 11:10). And it is reiterated in the conclusion of *Populorum progressio*:

> We therefore appeal to . . . all men of good will, and using the words of Jesus Christ we earnestly implore them: "seek and you will find," open the ways by which men through giving and receiving mutual aid, through study in greater depth, through greater love, may organize a more brotherly way of life so that human society may be based on a truly human accord.

What is important is to restore the bond between the liturgical Easter and the Easter of development.

MISSION
AND
DEVELOPMENT

13

What has just been said about liturgy and development[1] could have served as the conclusion of this book, for it is the response to a major problem for Christians today: how to avoid falling into a secularism in which Christianity would fade away? But the connection between *mission* and *development*, or more precisely, between the missionary task of evangelization and the secular task of economic and cultural development, gives rise to the same connected and thorny problem.

Contrast of Ideas

The problem could appear artificial, for when we look at the two ideas it seems that mission and development are not in the same sphere.

1. Their finalities are different: on one side evangelization and on the other, a process of civilization. Mission aims at making pagans into "disciples" of Christ and at baptizing them (Matthew 28:19). Development's formal object is to elicit the economic advancement of peoples. The two ideas are heterogeneous in their finalities: the one spiritual, the other material; the one eternal, the other temporal; the one supernatural, the other natural; the one religious and the other secular.

2. The subjects of mission and of development are also different. On the one hand, the subjects of mission are non-Christians who

are to be baptized; on the other hand, all men, whether Christian or not, are subjects of development. Missionary activity is directed to consciences; development acts on structures.

3. Finally, the activities differ; development is an economic *praxis*; the missionary task is above all in the order of the Word: the teaching of pagan peoples (*cf.* Matthew 28:19).

The problem therefore could be one of choosing between completely different activities that are even alien to one another.

The "Movements" Concur

Yet these activities find themselves in concurrence today. They at times pose the problem of a choice. This was the question raised as far back as February 1947 when the Journées missionnaires de La Tourette Symposium brought together the pioneers of the development movement. With Lebret in the foreground, and people from the missionary movement, the worker-priests from the Mission de Paris and most prominently, A. Depierre, the symposium confronted the problem raised by the text of Pius XII. Among the chief questions[2] were: "Must we first evangelize or civilize?" "Must the Church transform society in order to be faithful to herself, or transform herself in order to open the ways of salvation to a new society?"

For two reasons the problem is still more acute today:

First, an awareness of human values was consecrated by the Council. The human is less and less looked upon as a means. It appears more and more paradoxical to build a hospital in order to give the sacraments to the dying, since a hospital's specific purpose is to care for the sick, for example. As a reaction against a dominating and possessive spirit that used human values as a kind of Trojan horse of religion, people have at times come to consider any *utilization* of the human as a subversion or an alienation. Whatever we may say of the excesses of yesterday and today, the option between the secular human tasks and those that are specifically religious is particularly acute. This is the whole problem of secularism.

Secondly, the problem is also raised from the viewpoint of history. In the sixteenth century a missionary movement arose in the Church as a result of the discovery of unknown lands and peoples. This movement gave rise to a multitude of personal sacrifices, vocations, foundations, and organizations. It catalyzed the forces of the

Church for the conversion of pagans. Today this movement is losing momentum. The missions no longer have the prestige they enjoyed in the past. They no longer catalyze vocations and personal generosity in the same way.

Undoubtedly many factors account for this: the attraction of novelty, of the adventurous, of the unknown has disappeared. The movement has hardened into a centralized, entrenched, and highly systematized ecclesiastical organization. The ecclesiastical administration has greater control in mission countries than elsewhere, and in direct proportion to their degree of financial dependence. The missionary movement is therefore at the point where organization is oppressive and impetus is declining. Development, however, tends to direct secular commitments toward the "mission countries." This new movement seems, then, to be turning forces and acts of generosity away from evangelization to the benefit of nonreligious activities. Here we find again a typical problem which had been already brought up at the Council: the concurrence within the Church of Counter-Reformation movements which were losing their force and compensating movements which appeared a few decades before the Council. The mariologists, for example, felt that the biblical, ecclesiological, and ecumenical movements, particularly, were supplanting the mariological movement. Similarly the eucharistic movement which originated in the seventeenth century as an exaltation of the Real Presence of Christ seemed to have been absorbed and even submerged by the liturgical movement which was focused on promoting the active participation of people. This shift in the current of human affairs was felt at the Congress of Bogotá where there was a very small attendance at the eucharistic activities. The public only turned out to see the pope. In all these cases, we are dealing with movements that tend to be mutually exclusive. They are considering the two quite different sides of the same coin—and each in isolation, as it were.

That problem was examined in the more general concerns at the Council over Schema 13. Does not dialogue with the world on its own ground run the risk of diverting the Church from the preaching of Jesus Christ? Does not the service of the world risk diverting her from the service of God?

There are frictions and tensions within the whole mythology that flourishes in such cases. The ecumenists have been accused of recreating the Protestant heresy within the Church; the liturgists of sabotaging the Real Presence; the architects of Schema 13 of converting the Church to the world cursed by Christ. We must rise above these chimeras and the excesses that give rise to these imagings. The old and new movements are less divergent than they seem, despite the backwash observed at their confluence. They are currents in the great river of tradition.

Reconciliations and Convergences

A problem certainly does exist, but it is less clear-cut than it seems at first sight for two correlative reasons.

1. The post-Tridentine "missionary movement" has recently experienced a substantial change, the result of a new impetus. The missionary idea, taken from the Gospel as its source, has rediscovered its universality. A mission is less and less conceived within the narrow bounds of an arbitrary geographical area, an area of closed administrative organization, and of narrowly defined religious activities. Right after World War II a new missionary movement was born out of a twofold realism with respect to human realities and the Gospel. Henri Godin's book, *La France, pays de Mission?* was in 1943 the manifesto[3] of that rediscovery. The new missionary movement, which originated outside the traditional movement, even then posed a problem of concurrence with the classic movement. It was not dedicated to missionary territories. It was discovering the necessity to evangelize in milieus that had become sociologically alien to Christianity in traditionally Catholic countries. Its very title was a provocation.

However, the movement renewed the sense of the missionary need as a need for the integral salvation of man, respecting his human values, his culture, his ideals, his pre-Christian or Christian virtualities. "Mission" understood in this way integrates the whole man and overcomes the dissociation between the religious and the profane, for it is not merely bringing men to the practise of Christian rites. It is a problem of converting them in their entirety, in the whole of their lives, beginning with aspirations that are already found in them, and with their human values and their cultures which must first be understood and then espoused, as Christ espoused mankind. What is important to our problem is that this movement rediscovered the existential unity of salvation: body and soul, individual and group, nature and super-nature. This comprehensiveness was all regained in a radical way and in the missionary field itself.

2. As for development as defined by Paul VI and as it is generally

defined by the Latins (which is more comprehensive than the pragmatic Anglo-Saxon concept), it is not merely economic growth. It is the
development of all men and the whole man, an integral humanism
called to self-transcendence through divinization, in accordance with
the model of God-made-man.

In short, the two movements have an understanding of man that involves both human values and the mystery of the Incarnation which is
the key to them. When they fulfill their authentic vocations, both
movements proceed from the heart of reality as it is lived and become
fully immersed within it so that they can return to its center.

At the same time, the great abstract distinctions which theoretically oppose *mission* and *development* because of the difference of
their subjects, their finalities, and their activities, are becoming increasingly unreal and outmoded in the field.

Those mutual oppositions are disappearing also because of the
ambiguity of the elements involved. Who today would claim to show
the supernatural outside of nature, or a human nature that was alien
to the supernatural?

Finally, the oppositions are disappearing as a result of recent
evolutions that tend to dispel the clear-cut distinction.

The idea of "mission" was quite clear at a time when there existed
a Christendom composed of Christians—and pagan lands filled with
pagans. The former had the mission of evangelizing the latter, and
that was that. But today, we have become aware that the countries of
"Christendom" have become mission lands that have to be evangelized. Not only unbaptized people live in them, but also the baptized
who are without faith or who are even partisans of a formalism from
which the Gospel seems to have disappeared. Latin America is an
unevangelized Catholic land. And if Protestant missions have met
with such success there it is because they proposed the Gospel to Christians who were hungry for it.

In this area, paradoxical discoveries have been made. For example, Bishop Fragoso[4] made this observation: "The grass-roots Christian communities working for the development of a particular group
of men do not rally all practicing Christians to their cause. Far from it.
And men who are outside of religion and even non-Christian become
involved in development with a perfectly evangelical spirit."

A like observation was made with regard to evangelizing groups working in a Parisian suburb a few years ago. An unbaptized woman, married to a Catholic divorcé (and therefore lost to the catechumenate), was spreading the Gospel in a most effective way. "The best militant of the group," one of the leaders said of her.

Where then is the mission frontier if persons unbaptized yet active in the catechumenate can be missionaries to people who are baptized but strangers to the Gospel? Certainly we should not argue from these extreme cases, since we would end by obscuring the whole issue, but these facts do prohibit oversimplifications.

As for development, as we have seen, it implies analogous ambiguities. Since it does involve a *human* development in search of *fullness,* it tends toward the transcendent last end of man, which will be fulfilled in the love of God.

Basically, these "oppositions" which are necessary from the point of view of a theoretical analysis, correspond to two poles of the same existential reality. And this is what makes either simplistic or hard and fast solutions impossible. Both development and mission aim at the human and the divine, the corporal and the spiritual, the temporal and the eternal, because these are not distinctly subsistent realities. There is a distinction, but there is also a convergence. There is a continuity on the level of spirituality and a discontinuity on the level of technology and of specific finalities.

There can be opposition, distortion, and divorce between these two poles when they become dissociated in a given Christian or in a Christian group. But such divorce is an anomaly which amazes people who are not touched by this deficiency. The life of the well-oriented Christian is harmoniously related to both poles, without being overwhelmingly confronted with those "heart-rending options," bandied about by a certain kind of Christian literature.

Father Lebret came to development from an apostolic and missionary orientation that he did not lose when he became involved in the structural reforms without which the men to be evangelized can not even be men. He sensed the convergence early and said as much at the Journées de la Tourette[5] in 1947: "Missionary action is opening up to the structural action (of development)."

This formula epitomized his own route. It implied the experience which he described at the very beginning in these terms:

> We must reach the people and not merely those at the fringe. This requires a community of destiny with the people, an option

for the people. Taking charge is a very difficult thing, and it requires that you put on a new skin, you become the other, and
you grow yourself (*Ibid.*).

And again Lebret wrote:

> The spiritual man plunges into an effort to take total charge
> ... [for it is] the man freed from stifling economic servitude and
> political pressures [who] is able to answer God's call (*Ibid.*,
> pp. 7–8; Poulat, *op. cit.*, p. 526).

People, he said, are looking for a "spirituality that will give value to
the universe," one that will free man who is crushed under the weight
of nature, ignorance, and work and will involve him in an undertak-
ing of personal and collective transcendence (Poulat, *ibid.*, p. 531).

It was in such a tradition that he found the basis of this faith in
man and in mankind's potential: "It is in full agreement with Saint
Augustine that we can propose to assume everything that is positively
human in the modern world and offer it in homage to God" (*Journées,
op. cit.*, p. 29; Poulat, *op. cit.*, p. 531).

He conceived the two categories of tasks on the basis of one humanism: "The work of the mission in a given area will be more
especially to evangelize the pagans and at the same time to endeavor to
transform the already existing Christian nucleus into a missionary
nucleus. Économie et Humanisme's task will be to work in a Christian spirit for the setting up of new structures in this region" (in Unis
pour ... Lettre aux communautés de la Mission de France, June 1,
1946, Poulat, *ibid.*, p. 532, note 12).

Authentic missionaries who are sent into mission territories discover this same humanism, this respect for human values without
which there can be no mission in keeping with the spirit of the Gospel.
This was the special theme of the 1968 meeting of bishop-delegates to
the missionary cooperative held at Vichy. Its subject was "Evangelization and Development" and this was the basic argument (*La Croix,*
Nov. 15, 1968, p. 9):

> Development is not the primary task of the missionary but
> it is inseparable from evangelization. You cannot speak of God
> to someone who is dying of starvation or living in subhuman con-
> ditions. This does not mean profiting from the situation to make
> "rice Christians." At the basis of missionary activity is a will to
> promote man in respecting his freedom and dignity. A person
> who chooses to become a Christian must do so with full aware-
> ness of what he is doing.

Differences and Coincidences

Certainly, the development movement is characterized by precise techniques and objectives that are proper to it. A Christian working in this area will not be unfaithful to these norms. But, rightly, he will think that development is in the service of man and that man has a divine calling. Development will be at the heart of his activity and of his research. He will perceive the "signs of the times" which give a *directional sense* to development; he will normally bear an evangelical witness. And without betraying development—quite the contrary— he will be more apt to situate it in line with its most authentic and ultimate finality.

In doing so, he will not overturn the order of criteria proper to economic development. Instead he will bring to it an illumination, an orientation, a dynamism, and a sense of the pressing need for action as a result of his own perception of the eschatological extension of the human plan.

This does not mean that he will set up and complete an a priori Christian plan and then subject men to it.

The Christian who works for development, in accordance with the proper acceptation of this notion, knows that man is humbly building an unpredictable future along untrodden paths and he can only make short-term plans. And he knows that a plan is adapted in accordance with the lessons of experience.

His influence will be an animating one, as the "leaven in the dough" (Matthew 13:33; Luke 13:20–21).

His key perceptions will be the following: that there is a light which illumines every man coming into the world (John 1:9); that it is good to heed that light even among non-Christians; that there is a forward movement of mankind oriented toward the "day and the hour" no one knows, "not even the Son, but the Father only" (Mark 13:32; Matthew 24:36).

Such Christians will detect the signs of an authentic hope. They will come to discern and to promote the values of fellowship among men, of brotherhood, and of participation, for these are the vital structures in which charity can blossom. This is the body called to be animated by this gratuitous gift of God. Indeed, the agape is not for self-seeking, it is for giving of self: "Do not let your left hand know what your right hand is doing" (Matthew 6:3); God is often un-recognized in our neighbor (Matthew 25:37 & 44). And no one knows, ultimately, whether he "possesses" this gift of God, first of all because we would be unable to "possess" it as an object, and then because God gives no certitude to man in this area, according to the normal rule of grace.[6]

For all these reasons, authentic Christians foster the flowering of the "human values" which have the nature of an evangelical prepara-tion or evangelical virtualities; and if they live the Gospel they attract people to it.

Similarly, the missionary who is faced with underdevelopment cannot remain indifferent to this phenomenon. He too must watch for the light that enlightens every man. He does not seek to "recruit" or "annex" but to baptize; that is, to liberate in order that men and human realities may flourish. He does not take a position against these realities, but within them. He first takes them upon himself and penetrates them, and in that way assists their evolution from within and in keeping with their own innermost nature.

Consequently, there is a differentiation between mission and de-velopment, in objectives and in techniques. And a tension exists be-tween these elements; but they also have a twofold coincidence be-tween them:

1. Mission and development coincide in the Christian himself, whether he is devoted to a specifically missionary activity in the classic sense of the word, or is involved in development. There is an existen-tial coincidence between the two finalities, secular and religious, in every Christian worthy of the name.

2. If we take them in all of their meanings, mission and develop-ment are directed to all men and to the whole man without dissocia-tion. Missionary activity cannot be foreign to a humanism that re-spects the people of all milieus and cultures; while the aim of de-velopment is a search for the human fullness which is accomplished in God.

In this dilemma, analogous to those we considered in Chapter 8, we have to separate in order to unite what coincides in keeping with human existence. Evangelizing and civilizing are not conflicting tasks. Civilization, the fruit of development, is the organic state in which salvation is accomplished. It can be favorable or unfavorable. Evange-lization, which is primordial, explains the meaning of salvation and the awareness of the strength received through grace to accomplish it.

And evangelization directs man to the objective means of this same salvation to which he is called. The essential object of evangelization is to save by releasing the yearning for love which God has placed in the heart of man who is created in his image. Here again, everything comes back to the problem of a Christian existence implying faith and charity, prayer and liturgy.

In our day, Christians, in an excessive reaction against the excesses of the past, have come to value the praxis over the word, the implicit over the explicit, the anonymity of God over too facile an objectivization. They retreat to the roots, the sources, the origins, just as people did periodically in the Church as a reaction against the artificial constructions and superstructures that proliferated. Everything is questioned most exhaustively because of the change going on in man himself, because of the amazing number and variety of new human projects, and because of the correlative exacerbation of the threats hanging over the head of mankind. Plans for development correspond to a basic line of research geared to the trends and needs of today. Christians committed to development must not lose themselves in it at the risk of endangering both the material objectives and their transcendent goal. At this point we could mention many known remedies and often repeated admonitions, but on a much deeper level the Christian must be fully attentive to the Holy Spirit. The movement he inspired from the lowest to the highest levels in the Church seems called to regenerate that fullness which Christians search for in hope, hesitantly but intensely.

A LAST WORD

14

The development movement is axial to the postconciliar stage of the world. It is one of the sign posts of a "Vatican III," which could also be a "Geneva I" if we think on an ecumenical level, or even a "New Delhi I." If we think on a human level we advert to our problem of "all men and the whole man."

The movement taking form is a gamble for the Church and for the world, a noble risk to take in a situation that seems dismal to the technicians. But what a group or a people can do, once they take their destiny into their own hands, is incredible. What will happen if this leap toward the good becomes world-wide?

Today, development calls for a profound conversion: a conversion from good intentions to scientific realism and effective action.

A conversion from chauvinism to universalism—from bilateral to multilateral aid.

A conversion from economic materialism (which may be worse with capitalism than with marxism) to cultural humanism: a humanism that is open to man's divinization.

If we consider the structures that have to be transformed, this conversion can also be called a "revolution"; if present structures do not allow us to foresee any real solution worthy of the name—as it now seems.

It is at this point that we have the debate between capitalism and socialism, and it would indeed be pretentious to attempt to arbitrate at a moment when such knowledgeable specialists as Gunnar Myrdal have just changed their views in the matter.

It would undoubtedly be simplistic to reject socialism categorically as being "intrinsically evil," because it originated in atheism or even in "collectivism," as the current slogans say. *Pacem in terris* and *Populorum progressio* have done away with these oversimplifications by distinguishing "doctrine" and "movement" on the one hand, and the principle of common utility (basic) and the rule of private property (relative) on the other.

It would also be simplistic in another way to radically reject capitalism also as "intrinsically evil."[1] That aphorism is justified in the teaching of the Gospels only in the degree that capitalism is defined by the law of profit and by the law of "unrighteous mammon" (Luke 16:9 & 11; 18:24; *cf.* Mark 10:23, 24).

In this debate, whose outcome seems impossible to predict, research is inevitable and necessary. And there is room for pluralism. For Christians, development requires a commitment that achieves the integration of faith and praxis, of word and action, in line with that unity sought by the Council when it went back to the very sources of the Incarnation.

What does development require of theology? First of all, a renewal in humility. Development involves interdisciplinary collaboration, and no discipline can play its part in it unless it is organically integrated. The theologian, then, cannot be a person who favors the builders of development with "theological fall-out from the stratosphere."

He must enter into the very life of the other disciplines; he must start from the heart of reality as it is lived, from activities in progress, and then reassess their meaning. Just as the economist takes account of the dynamism existing in his particular area of concern, so must the theologian take account of the dynamics of conversation and human involvement, of their meaning in relation to man's destiny and his divine vocation. He is called to fulfil this task in a way that is increasingly unpretentious in many areas—in research, in collaborations in which each person has to know how to subordinate himself to the whole, and in regard to cultural development which advances irresistibly in step with cultural pluralism and of which theology is an interdependent branch.

Theology, then, has to renounce its Greco-Latin ethnocentrism and enter into the proper genius of each culture. Still more radically, it must be aware of its immersion in cultural realities without which it could no more exist than a fish out of water, or a branch without a trunk or roots. To recognize this relativity does not mean denying the absolute of doctrinal truth. Instead it means measuring the conditions of access to it. The Absolute is not impaired by the vicissitudes of history; it is from history that man's question about the Absolute arises. God himself encountered men in history, in that very specialized human condition in which he gave to men the universal message of the Gospel.

The function of theology, therefore, should be to elucidate the meaning of charity at work in economic, political, and cultural structures and the significance of earthly values and their import on man's destiny. And that process of elucidation has to occur at the very center of the gestation and birth pangs that the contemporary world is suffering today. It implies a renovation and in a certain sense a reconversion of ecclesiology: from a closed to an open society, from the static to the dynamic, from the juridical to the vital, from the ecclesiastical to the cosmic.

In the spirit of the prophets, the Church would have to become again "a sign for mankind of a possible future willed by God." This requires creativity like that which characterized the plans made by the people of God when they shook off the yoke of oppression in order to march toward the promised land. And similar inventiveness and creativity again spring up on their return from the Babylonian captivity. Such dynamism is not dead. In 1968 it appeared again at the Medellín assembly, which spontaneously presented its integral development project as a new exodus.

May revelation, once again, inspire a great plan encompassing the whole of mankind.

It is from the depth of this modesty, this hope, that theology can still voice the word of transcendence in immanence, willed by the creative Word, within every man, and which became incarnate among men.

God took human enterprise seriously: the adventure of the animal who got up from all fours in order to master the earth and contemplate the heavens. He loved as a friend the being who was forming himself more and more freely and who finds himself today on the threshold of potentials which are still forbidden him.

But that is not all. At the same time as God gave man, through the interplay of cosmic evolution, intelligence, freedom, love, in one word a soul, God also completely and freely gave an extension of his temporal destiny in a divine dimension. He called mankind to an age capable of gathering together in him, in a simultaneity of fullness, the totality of his fleeting existence. In short, he calls man and mankind to an everlasting fulfillment.

We must surely take seriously the technical and temporal foundations of this plan, for God willed man's development from his material and bodily roots upward. A full understanding of development must take into consideration the call to fullness, as more than the absurd adventure of a being who blossoms and withers in a day like a wild flower.

Reference Matter

NOTES FOR
THE TEXT

Notes—Chapter 1

1. For a brief bibliography on development, see pages 235-238.

2. Fifty-fourth session of the Semaines sociales de France, Nantes, July 11-16, 1967; *DC,* September 1967, no. 1500, col. 1487-1506.

3. Resolutions of the Congress of the Laity on development in *DC,* November 5, 1967, no. 1504, col. 1880-1883.

4. The Institute for the Study of Developing Countries (Tiensestraat 41. University of Louvain, catalogue, 1968-1969, pp. 125-128). The object of this institute is the "organization and coordination of university teaching devoted to the developing countries. Its program provides students with a deeper knowledge of the countries of the Third World and of the problems of development" (p. 125). A Third World Council was also created by the University of Louvain (from June 4-9, 1968). An international symposium met in November on the initiative of these organizations for the study of a cooperative plan for Latin America.

5. This center, which does not have a really set name, was organized by Father Theodore Mulder and Father Philip Land of Justitia et Pax.

6. The CIDSE brought the following organizations together:

Australian Catholic Relief—AEC (Sydney, Australia)

Bischoppelijke Vastenactië (Utrecht, the Netherlands)

Catholic Relief Services (U.S.A.)

Comité catholique contre la faim et pour le développement (Paris, France)

Entraide et Fraternité (Brussels 4, Belgium)

Fastenopfer der Schweizer Katholiken (Lucerne, Switzerland)

Koordinierungstelle für Entwicklungshilfe des Sekretariates der Österreichischen Bischofskonferenz (Vienna, Austria)

Misereor (Aachen, Germany)

Organisation catholique canadienne pour le développement et la paix (Montreal, Canada)

7. On the secretariat for activities concerning social and economic development in the Society of Jesus, see the bulletin of the pontifical commission Justitia et Pax, no. 3, October 3, 1968, p. 11.

8. OECD-ICVA Directory: *Development Aid of Non-Governmental Non-Profit Organisations,* Edwin Eggins, project director (Paris: OECD, 1967), 1,378 pages. French edition, also 1967: *Aide du developpement. Organisations non gouvernmentales sans but lucratif. Organisations de cooperation et de developpement economique.* [OECD: Organization for Economic Cooperation and Development; ICVA: International Council of Voluntary Agencies.]

9. IRAM was founded in 1957 subsequent to a request made by Morocco to the Abbé Pierre. It is led by Y. Goussault and R. Colin. The headquarters were set up in Paris, 97 rue Réaumur. On the methods, see R. Colin, *"L'Animation, participation des masses et des cadres au développement,"* in *Vie Sociale* 11. *Les Dossiers de tendances,* no. 12, January 1966, pp. 33-48.

10. These gifts and good works continue, but there is a transition, a reconversion in the direction of less clerical forms.

11. On the first donations of Church lands in Chile, see below, Chapter 2, Note 11, page 222. Here are a few later initiatives, recorded in the mimeographed bulletin *Service des pauvres, Service d'humanité* (the dates listed below are those of the bulletin's publication, which rather closely approximate the dates of the facts mentioned):

August 1964, p. 7: The Vatican gives up land and buildings in Tunisia.

November 1965, second edition, p. 18: At Bogotá, the Fathers of St. Philip Neri hand over for land reform 2,000 hectares (4,940 acres) received as a legacy. The peasant farmers receive adequate training to become owners (*cf. Ecclesiae,* 1965, p. 1261).

November 1966, p. 8: The diocese of Salto (Uruguay) gives 270 hectares (666 acres) to eight young people to launch a cooperative.

September 8, 1968, p. 1: In Ecuador, the bishops of Quito, Riobamba, and Ibarra offer 49,170 hectares (121,449 acres) at a low price to 1,240 families. The operation was conducted with the aid of the Development Bank and the guarantee of the government (*La Croix,* May 16, 1968).

November 1968, p. 13: Archbishop Manuel Sánchez of Concepción (Chile) puts his episcopal residence, situated in the heart of the city on the Plaza de Armas, up for sale and moves to a more modest quarter of the city. He distributed 2,680 hectares (6,619 acres) of land belonging to the Church to 32 farming families, and provided for the technical assistance of C.O.R.A. (The Government Committee for Land Reform in Chile; *cf. La Croix,* August 19, 1968).

12. Other comparable facts will be found in *Service des pauvres, Service d'humanité*:

December 30, 1963, the refusal of subsidies for a church (*cf. ICI,* December 15, 1963, no. 206, pp. 23-24).

March, 1966, p. 13: the bishop of Yokohama stopped the plan for a large church building.

January 1968, p. 6: "When the Cardinal of Lima gave up the idea of building a cathedral, the polemics rebounded in Rio de Janeiro, in regard to Cardinal de Barros Câmara's project to build a cathedral . . ."

August 1968, p. 20: Message of the Jocistes on the occasion of May 1, 1968: "Let the leaders of the Church be less busy about constructing large buildings: seminaries, schools, cathedrals, and temples of stone, and be more concerned with the living temples who are men" (*Ecclesia*, 1968, no. 805).

13. *ICI*, May 1, 1968, no. 311, p. 96.

14. *Service des pauvres, Service d'humanité,* February 1968, p. 13 (after Jean Cardonnel, in *Dieu prend parti,* nos. 46-47).

15. CIAS edits the *CIAS Review* (Palpa 2440, Buenos Aires, 26). At this writing the magazine is in its seventeenth year, but the development theme has assumed growing importance.

16. In Asia and Africa, there are comparable organizations, although they are less numerous. For example: the centers at Dakar (founded by the Dominicans in the tradition of Lebret), Abidjan (Jesuits), Congo-Kinshasa (P. Beeckemans). And in the Philippines there is the East Asian Pastoral Institute of Fathers Johannes Hofinger and Alfonso Nebreda, S.J.

17. The social action department of CELAM is directed by Cardinal Eugenio de Araújo Sales of Salvador Bahía.

18. On the national commissions on Justice and Peace which are formed in a nonrestrictive and decentralized manner in many countries, in connection with the Roman commission (*cf.* following chapter, Note 9, page 222), see the bulletin of the pontifical Commission on Justice and Peace, no. 1, p. 7 and annexes; no. 2, p. 6; no. 3, p. 6. Commissions already exist in the following countries:

AFRICA: Algeria, Congo-Kinshasa, Cameroon (diocesan commissions with a national federation), Rwanda, Burundi, East Africa (on an international scale bringing together five countries), South Africa, and West Africa (in the process of foundation).

AMERICA: U.S.A. and Canada (in the process), Brazil (diocesan and regional commissions in Recife, São Paulo, and Pernambuco), Argentina, Venezuela where the commission directed by Carlos Acedo Mendoza has come up with publications and a considerable organization, schematized through an "organigram" realized in 1968 on the occasion of the visit of the secretary general to Rome.

ASIA: Ceylon, Indonesia, Japan, Laos, Lebanon, Malaysia, the Philippines. Plans projected in Cambodia and India.

EUROPE: Germany, England, Austria, Belgium, Denmark, Scotland, Spain, France, the Netherlands, Italy, Malta, Poland, and Switzerland.

OCEANIA: Australia and New Zealand.

19. The Mexican congress on development was originated under the inspiration of the *Carta pastoral del episcopado Mexicano sobre el desarollo e integración del país,* a pastoral letter issued at Mexico City for the first anniversary of *Populorum progressio,* March 26, 1968. After the opening session, the preparatory organization distributed several mimeographed documents on land reform, 71 pp.;

urban reform, 63 pp. and 15 plates; educational reform, 30 pp., etc.

20. J. Comblin, *Notas para una Teologia do desenvolvimento,* Movimiento familiar cristão, Belo Horizonte, March 1968, volume printed without pagination (32 pp.).

21. On the basic document of the Brazilian episcopate, adopted by 219 out of 248 bishops (May 4-10, 1967), see *ICI,* June 1, 1967, no. 289, p. 17. This document had been preceded by a manifesto of the ACO of the Northeast, accepted three months later by seventeen bishops from the region (*ICI,* nos. 262 and 271) and mentioned in a Catholic Action document dated May 1, 1967 (*ICI,* June 1, 1967, no. 289, p. 17).

22. On the movement of Bishop Helder Camara, see René Laurentin, *L'Amérique latine à l'heure de l'enfantement* (Paris: Seuil, 1969), pp. 94-97.

23. Henri Fesquet, *L'Église en état de péché mortel* (Paris: Grasset, 1968), p. 28. And the speeches of the pope in *DC,* September 15, no. 1524, col. 1549-1554.

24. A few of these manifestos were published in the Appendix of Laurentin's *L'Amérique latine,* pp. 195-229. These documents (a letter signed by Bishop Guzmán and a group of laymen, by 350 Brazilian priests, by 800 Latin American priests, by the leaders of the Latin American Christian labor unions) as well as the documents published in Laurentin's *Flashes sur l'Amérique latine* (Paris: Seuil, 1968), pp. 53-86, are merely samples. See again, for example, the statement of 50 priests approved by Cardinal Landázuri-Ricketts, in *ICI,* April 15, 1968, no. 310, p. 12.

25. *Revolución social en América latina,* open letter of July 18, 1968.

26. *II Conferencia general del episcopado latino-americano. Documento de trabajo, Medellín (Colombia), 26 agosto-7 septiembre,* a pamphlet of 26 pages. The document begins with an analysis of the demographic, economic, social, cultural, and political situation (pp. 7-12), before getting to the religious situation (pp. 12-15). With *Gaudium et spes* (no. 42), the document emphasizes that the Church's mission is "not of an economic, political, or social order (p. 21), but must in the historical context contribute to the temporal achievement of the continent."

27. These discourses are reproduced *in extenso* in *DC,* September 15, 1968, no. 1524, col. 1539-1570. See especially the discourse to farmers, August 23, col. 1455-1548; the allocution given during the mass of Development Day, col. 1549-1554, and the opening discourse of the second general conference of the Latin American episcopate, col. 1566-1569.

28. The preliminary introduction according to the first mimeographed edition at Medellín, September 1968, p. 2.

29. Letter of the bishops of Colombia on the occasion of the Eucharistic Congress, May 3, 1968, *DC* August 4-18, 1968, no. 1522, col. 1438-1439.

30. On the notion of movement and the postconciliar movements, see René Laurentin, *La question mariale* (Paris: Seuil, 1963), pp. 38-58; and *La Vierge au Concile* (Paris: Lethielleux, 1965), pp. 56-72.

31. On the grass-roots communities, see Laurentin's *L'Amérique latine,* a work focused on this point, especially Chapter 11, pp. 169-184.

32. On the first world conference organized at Geneva by the Church and

Society department of the World Council of Churches (July 12-26, 1966), see *DC*, July 15, 1966, no. 268, pp. 19-25, and September 1, 1966, no. 271, pp. 15-16.

33. It is known that the New Delhi conference was disappointing in the sense that the developed nations refused to commit themselves in any way at a time when their aid was diminishing and deteriorating into a full economic crisis. Yet this conference was not completely ineffectual:

1. The principle was accepted that each state was to *try* to give 1 percent of its income to development.

2. It was decided to bring about agreements on the natural resources market, since price deterioration is catastrophic for the underdeveloped countries. Since then, two agreements were reached, on cacao and on sugar. Others are in process.

34. The stages in the foundation of the joint committee of the WCC and the Roman Catholic Church on Society, Development, and Peace, are summed up in the report of the co-president, M. Kohnstamm, to the general secretariat of the World Council, published in *DC*, September 1, 1968, no. 1523, col. 1507-1513. *Cf.* the bulletin of the pontifical commission on Justice and Peace, no. 1, April 1968, pp. 4-6 and 11-12; no. 2, July 1968, pp. 1-4. The joint group is concerned with three areas: theology, peace, the economy.

35. Acts of the fourth assembly of the WCC. *Cf.* Annie Perchenet, *Chrétiens ensemble. Journal d'Upsal* (July, 1968), Paris: Desclée de Brouwer, 1968. *ICI,* August 1968, nos. 317-18, pp. 14-17; *DC,* September 1, 1968, no. 1523, col. 1473-1519; bulletin of the pontifical commission on Justice and Peace, October 1958, no. 3, p. 1.

36. At the grass-roots many initiatives of ecumenical collaboration are to be found as evidenced by the information bulletin *Service des pauvres, Service d'humanité,* December 1963, p. 34 (Taizé collection); *ibid.,* September 1965, p. 4 (fourth ecumenical fast at Montbéliard for the Greeks: 38,000 French francs collected); *ibid.,* p. 7 (collaboration of Catholic and Protestant youth for the garbage-disposal facilities in a Reims slum); etc.

37. "Propositions de la conférence de Beyrouth," published in the bulletin of the pontifical commission on Justice and Peace, no. 2, July 1968, p. 2.

Notes—Chapter 2

1. We shall return later to the encyclical *Populorum progressio,* published in *Osservatore Romano,* March 27, 1967; *DC* April 16, 1967, no. 1492, col. 673-704.

2. Allocution to the committee on world food, created in 1961 by the UN and FAO, in *DC,* June 4, 1967, no. 1495, col. 1005-10.

3. *DC,* November 19, 1967, no. 1505, col. 1946-47.

4. *DC,* February 4, 1968, no. 1510, col. 201-203.

5. *DC,* February 18, 1968, no. 1511, col. 349-55.

6. *DC,* March 17, 1968, no. 1513, col. 535-44.

7. The constitution *Gaudium et spes,* December 5, 1965, in *Enchiridion Vaticanum,* Bologna, ed. Dehoniane, 6th ed. 1967, pp. 778-965.

8. *Le Figaro,* December 9, 1966, and *Bilan du Concile* (Paris: Seu'l, 1966), p. 194.

9. The Commission on Justice and Peace, foreseen by no. 90 of the constitution *Gaudium et spes,* was created by Paul VI on January 6, 1967 (*Motu proprio Catholicam Christi Ecclesiam*), *DC,* February 5, 1967, no. 1487, col. 193-96. For details of this foundation, see René Laurentin, *L'Enjeu du Synode* (Paris: Seuil, 1967), p. 196, note 73.

10. On June 15, 1968, for example, Paul VI received the Justice and Peace commission in audience; see *DC,* July 21, 1968, no. 1521, col. 1294-95.

11. On the giving of Church lands and the action of Dom Manuel Larraín in regard to development, see the bulletin *Service des pauvres, Service d'humanité,* June 21, 1963, pp. 7-8 (*cf.* ICI, August 1962, no. 173, p. 16) and March 1966, pp. 2-4. A translation of the article of A. Bonato, "L'Expérience de réforme agraire au Chili," in *Orientamenti Sociali,* December 1965, where one finds the whole genesis of the Chilean experiment.

12. *Le père Lebret (1897-1966), Symposium,* mimeographed by IRFED. And the book of F. Malley, *Le père Lebret. L'économie au service de l'homme* (Paris: Cerf, 1968).

13. François Perroux, *Les Mesures des progrès économiques et l'idée d'économie progressive,* ISEA progress report, series 1, 1956; cf. Louis Joseph Lebret, *Dynamique concrète du développement* (Paris: 1967, p. 35).

14. Concerning the mission-development problem, Father Lebret expressed what he thought during the mission days at la Tourette, in February 1947, L'Arbresle (Rhône): Économie et Humanisme, 1967, 60 pp., excellently analyzed and quoted by Emile Poulat, *Naissance des prêtres-ouvriers* (Paris: Casterman, 1965), pp. 525-36. See Chapter 13 of this book page 200.

15. Pierre Teilhard de Chardin, "Le Christique," text written in New York in March 1955 and published in [*Pierre*] *Teilhard de Chardin. Images et Paroles* (Paris: Seuil, 1966), p. 210.

Notes—Chapter 3

1. Development according to Marx: We shall quote from the *Communist Manifesto* (1848), after the French translation of C. Andler (Paris: Rieder, no date), pp. 21, 22, 31, 32, 34, 35, 39, 41, 43, 48, 50, 55, 57, 58, 67, 68, 69, 70, 73. And the texts mentioned by J. Y. Calvez, *La Pensée de Marx* (Paris: Seuil, 1956).

2. *Das Kapital,* French translation, Molitor XII, p. 38, quoted by Calvez (see the preceding note): and the Roy translation III, pp. 12-13, quoted by Calvez, *op. cit.,* p. 313; cf. pp. 485 and 491: "In the development of productive forces a stage is reached where there arise productive forces and means of circulation which can only be pernicious in the existing circumstances, and are no longer productive forces, but destructive forces (the machine theory and money) . . ."

Marx also speaks of the development of capitalist production, *Das Kapital,* Roy translation III, p. 32, Calvez, *op. cit.,* p. 313; cf. p. 329.

3. Actually Marx is speaking here more precisely of movement in connection with a development: "Undoubtedly private property propels itself through its

simple economic movement towards its own suppression. But it does so only through an unconscious development independent of itself which is produced against its will, and which is conditioned by the nature of things; it does so only by producing the proletariat qua proletariat, i.e., conscious destitution . . . the conscious dehumanization of its own dehumanization and therefore suppressing itself. The proletariat executes the judgment that property brought against itself by producing the proletariat, it executes the judgment that salary brings against itself by producing wealth in the other and destitution in the one who receives it." (*Heilige Familie,* in *Nachlass* 3, pp. 132-33; Calvez, *op. cit.,* pp. 495-96).

4. For Marx, money is only the form of developed value (i.e. a nonimmediate return), in line with other forms of value in the value of exchange. *Das Kapital,* Roy translation, I, p. 14, Calvez, *op. cit.,* p. 285. This, Marx notes, "is the whole mystery of money"; on the "development of contradictions" which results from it, see Calvez, *op. cit.,* p. 291, note 67, and p. 295 where other quotations are found.

5. Letter to Weidemeyer, March 5, 1852, in *Études philosophiques,* Editions sociales, p. 118. Calvez, *op. cit.,* p. 499, note 39; *cf.* p. 521 and *Communist Manifesto, 1848,* p. 72. (See note 1 on page 222 of this book.)

6. *Das Kapital,* Roy tr., III, p. 155; Calvez, *op. cit.,* p. 329. See also *Das Kapital,* II, p. 165-66, Calvez, p. 310-311: "The only real way whereby a mode of production and the social organization corresponding to it go to their dissolution and their metamorphosis is the historical development of their immanent antagonisms."

Similarly, Engels, who applies the same schema to the farmer: "The suppression of the private ownership of the soil does not imply the re-establishment of the old primitive common ownership: what it does imply is the establishment of a more developed form, a far superior one, of common possessions which instead of becoming an obstacle to production, will on the contrary give it for the first time its full impetus." (*Anti-Dühring,* I, 214. Calvez, *op. cit.,* p. 271, note 30).

7. *Das Kapital,* 2nd ed. Hamburg III, 2nd part, p. 255. Calvez, *op. cit.,* pp. 474-75.

8. Laurentin, *L'Amérique latine,* Chapter Eleven, pp. 138-46.

Since then I have received some more precise information on this "brain drain." According to the data supplied by U Thant, 20,760 foreign technicians have been attracted to the United States in 1967 alone. Ten years ago the yearly figure was only 2,500. This comparison allows us to measure the sizable growth of the procedure that deprives Norway each year of 23.8 percent of her young engineers; Switzerland 22.4 percent and Greece 20.7 percent.

9. Pius XII, Christmas message 1941, published only in Italian in *AAS* 34, 1942, pp. 16-17.

10. *Pacem in terris,* no. 124, *AAS* 55, 1963, p. 290.

11. Perroux, in *La Croix,* April 19, 1967.

12. *Ibid.*

13. Saint Bernard, *De consideratione,* Liber 2, cap. 8, no. 18, PL 182, 753, AB, scolds Pope Eugene III about the "gaudy purple" of the pontifical vestments: "Therefore rip off that finery, accursed since the beginning (Genesis 3:7); tear away that leafy cloak that hideth ignorance, but not the wound from the physician. Destroy the illusion of fleeting honor and the sparkle of thine ill-crowned

glory, and consider thyself in thy nakedness, for naked thou camest forth from thy mother's womb (Job 1:21). Wert thou then bedecked with kingly diadem? Wert thou glittering with gems or silken flowers, or crowned with feathers . . . ? etc."

"Peter is here, and we have no knowledge that he hath ever sauntered about bedazzled with gems or silk, neither covered with gold nor astride a white horse, nor escorted by soldiers, nor shut up within a bevy of ministers. Albeit, he thought himself well able to fulfill his mission of salvation (cap. 3, no. 6, PL 182, 776 A).

Eugene III was a Cistercian and a former pupil of Bernard.

Notes—Chapter 4

1. A high official wrote recently to Father Cosmao: "Can there be a theology of development? Does this not lead to a fresh look at the problem of the relations of God and men . . . ?" (V. Cosmao, *Signification et théologie du développement,* report of October 23, 1967, mimeo., p. 23).

2. André Feuillet, *Le Christ, sagesse de Dieu, d'après les Épîtres pauliniennes* (Paris: J. Gabalda, 1966) and Stanislas Lyonnet, *Saint Paul et le Gnosticisme. L'Épître aux Colossiens,* in *Studies in the History of Religions* (Supplement to *Numen* 12. *Origins of Gnosticism* (Leiden: Brill, 1967), pp. 538-51, esp. pp. 542-47.

Notes—Chapter 5

1. Right after World War II, in his work on the Bible, André Laurentin had made a rather novel study which was stolen from him along with his briefcase before it could be published. Since then, there have been many studies; A. M. Dubarle, "Le Concept de l'homme dans l'Ancien Testament," in *Sacra Pagina* (Paris: J. Gabalda, 1959) pp. 532-36.

2. Stanislas Lyonnet, *Saint Paul et le Gnosticisme. L'Épître aux Colossiens,* in *Studies in the History of Religions* (Supplement to *Numen* 12. *The Origins of Gnosticism* (Leiden: Brill, 1967), pp. 538-51, and *L'Église peut-elle dialoguer avec le monde?,* mimeographed pamphlet of 23 pp., no place or date (Rome: Biblicum).

3. Instead of saying in keeping with the texts of the Epistle to the Romans (8:21) that creation will be "freed from slavery and *corruption,*" the Council (*Gaudium et Spes,* no. 39) said "that it will be freed *a servitute vanitatis* (from the slavery of vanity). The word "vanity" was taken from the preceding verses (8:19).

Lyonnet, "Redemptio cosmica, secundum Rom 8, 19, 23" in *Verbum Domini,* 44, 1966, pp. 225-42 well demonstrated that the two notions cannot be assimilated. Vanity has a moral meaning (*cf.* Ephesians 4:17; Romans 1:21; 1 Peter 1:18) and refers to the past: to the consequences of sin. Corruption has a physical meaning: the condition of the body which is destined to die (1 Corinthians 15: 42, 50; *cf.* Romans 1:23; Colossians 2:22; 2 Peter 2:12). The resurrection of Christ, the first-born of all creatures who was raised for us, frees our mortal bodies from that corruption.

In what sense does Paul understand this liberation of the entire cosmos in respect to corruption? Not in the sense of a magical action on the material world where man would then be sheltered from every evil or evil influence, in line with the view of the Gnostics. What Paul is considering is man's salvation. But when faced with the Platonist perspective whose sarcasm he felt on the Areopagus (Acts 17:32), he teaches that the salvation of man is the salvation of the whole man. This salvation implies his bodily redemption in Christ who rose in his body. And this body cannot be separated from the rest of material creation. Creation is not some sort of a pedestal upon which man, and the preeminent Man, Christ, would have been set up like a statue, but rather the stem of which man is the flower (Isaiah 11:1). Thus the world is not vain.

4. Lyonnet, first article mentioned in note 2 above, pp. 541-47 and "Redemptio cosmica sec. Rom. 8, 19, 23," in *Verbum Domini* 44 (1965), pp. 234-35.

Notes—Chapter 6

1. On the poor in the Bible see the basic study by Cornelis van Leeuwen, *Le développement du sens social en Israël avant l'ère chrétienne* (Assen: Van Gorcum, 1955), Bibliography, pp. 231-35. M. Froidure, *Conflits sociaux et Parole de Dieu,* typed thesis, le Saulchoir, 1966. J. L. Vesco, "Les lois sociales du livre de l'Alliance (Exode 20: 22-32)," in *Revue thomiste* 68, 1968, pp. 241-66. This latter article is limited, as its title indicates, to the first legislation of Israel in the code of the Covenant, prior to the institution of the kingdom. The study was undertaken in reference to *Populorum progressio,* with concern for showing that the Bible is "skilled in humanity" (pp. 241 and 264), according to Paul VI's expression. The article begins with these significant words: "The development of peoples is considered attentively by the Church . . ." This article therefore belongs to the dossier gathered in Chapter 1 on the Christian development movement.

2. On this subject, see the "Ostrakon of the Coat," published by J. Naweh, in *Israel Exploration Journal* 10 (1960), pp. 129-39.

3. Concerning the return from exile considered as a new exodus by the prophets, starting with Deutero-Isaiah, the references are conveniently grouped together in Note *d* for Isaiah 40:3 in the Jerusalem Bible.

4. According to the notions of the Chanaanites whose land Israel conquered, Baal was the master of the earth and made it fertile. This role was attributed to Yahweh (we find traces of this in many texts; Deuteronomy 10: 12-14, etc.), but it was purified. Yahweh assumes the role of Baal, but he transcends it; he no longer wants to be treated like Baal, according to the strict teaching of the prophets beginning with Hosea (who lived in the eighth century before Christ): 2: 18; *cf.* 2: 11-13, 16-17; Jeremiah 23:27, etc.

5. Deuteronomy 32:8: this archaic text has not been free from certain contrary implications. Qumran confirmed that the reading should be "sons of God" and not "sons of Israel" which is a late correction of the Hebrew text. It nevertheless refers to apportionment of the land.

6. Doctrine of the Greek Fathers on the relativity of property. Basil of Caesarea, *Homilia in divites* 50, 7, PG 31, 276 B-C. Gregory of Nyssa (+394), *Homilia contra usurarios,* PG 46, 476 D; John Chrysostom (+407), *in epist. I ad Tim., Homilia* 13, 4, PG 62, 562-63, etc.

7. Doctrine of the Latin Fathers: Ambrose, *De Nabuthe Jezraelita*, PL 14, 731 C, 734 B, and 747, mentioned in the encyclical *Populorum progressio*, no. 23, note 1: "It is not from your own possessions that you are generous to the poor. You are giving to him what belongs to him. For what is given in common, for the use of all, is what you have arrogated to yourself. The earth is given to everyone, and not only to the rich." In Ps 118, Sermo 8, no. 22, PL 15, 1303 CD: *Cum praesertim Dominus Deus noster terram hanc possessionem omnium hominum voluerit esse communem et fructus omnibus ministrare, sed avaritia possessionum jura distribuit. De officiis ministrorum*, Pars. I, cap. 28, no. 131-132, PL 16, 62 A, particularly forceful: *. . . Ipsum quod putant philosophi justitiae munus, apud nos excluditur . . . Evangelii auctoritate . . .* (no. 132) *. . . Formam justitiae putaverunt ut quis communia id est publica pro publicis habeat, privata pro suis. Ne hoc quidem secundum naturam, natura enim omnia omnibus in commune profudit; sic enim Deus generari jussit omnia, ut pastus omnibus communis esset et terra foret omnium quaedam communis possessio. Natura igitur, jus commune generavit, usurpatio jus fecit privatum.* Saint Augustine (+431) *Homilia 23, in Genesi* PL 35, 1347: *Jure divino Domini est terra et plenitudo ejus* (= Ps. 23:1). *Pauperes et divites Deus de uno fecit, et pauperes et divites una terra supportat.* St. Gregory the Great (+ 604) *Pastoral. 3*, cap. 21, PL 77, 87 A: *Cunctis hominibus terra communis est, et idcirco alimenta quoque omnibus communiter profert. Incassum ergo se innocentes putant qui commune Dei munus sibi privatum vindicant.* Isidore of Seville (+ 636), *Etymologiae.* In accordance with the "right of nature," possession is common to all (*communis omnium possessio*).

8. Gilles Couvreur, *Les pauvres ont-ils des droits?* (Rome: Gregoriana, 1961) is the basic work in this area.

9. Couvreur, *ibid.,* pp. 2-4; *Cf.* DTC 3, 589-90 and J. de Sousberghe, "Propriété de droit naturel," Thèse néo-scolastique, in *Nouvelle Revue théologique,* 72 (1950), pp. 580-607, which would call for some nuanced interpretation.

10. CT 9, 61:26, Sub-commission, *de ordine morali* 11.

11. This adaptation of laws to structure is verified in the Bible. Deuteronomy 15 uses again for a trade society what Exodus 23 had prescribed for an agricultural society.

12. This passage from *Populorum progressio* (no. 23) is a quotation of a letter addressed by the Cardinal Secretary of State in the pope's name to the Semaine sociale de Brest, "L'Homme et la Révolution urbaine" (Lyon: Chronique sociale, 1965), pp. 8-9.

Notes—Chapter 7

1. Pius XI, *Quadragesimo anno,* 1931, nos. 66, 111, and 117. Pius XII, *Allocution to the Congress of International Exchange,* March 7, 1948, DC 1948, col. 62. On this point see J. Calvez, *Populorum progressio,* Paris 1967, Introduction, p. 9.

2. This point was excellently treated by Msgr. Philippe Delhaye at the Louvain symposium on Latin America, November 6, 1968.

3. The principle of subsidiarity had been formulated by Pius XI in *Quadra-*

gesimo anno, May 15, 1931, AAS, 23, 1931, p. 203. Pius XII applies it to the life of the Church in *Allocution to the Cardinals,* May 20, 1946, AAS, 38, 1946, p. 145. See R. Laurentin, *Le premier Synode,* p. 290.

4. Calvez, *Populorum progressio,* Introduction, p. 15; and the more developed study by Yves Congar in *L'Église dans le monde de ce temps,* t. 2, coll. Unam Sanctam, no. 65b, (Paris: Cerf, 1967), pp. 483-516.

5. *Message of Paul VI to the world,* given to the press on December 4, *DC,* January 3, 1965, no. 1439:

"We are entrusting you with our special message to the world. Let nations stop the armament race and instead devote their resources and their energies to brotherly assistance of the developing countries.

"Let each nation having 'thoughts of peace, and not of affliction and war' devote at least a part of its military expenses to a world fund for the solution of the numerous problems that are present for the underprivileged (food, clothing, housing, medical care)."

6. *Allocution* of October 4, 1966, in *DC,* November 6, no. 1481, col. 1840: "In our time peace is called development."

7. This point has been developed by Msgr. Paul Poupard, who was one of the editors of the encyclical, and charged with presenting it to the press, "De l'aide au développement solidaire," in *Masses ouvrières,* no. 246, January 1968, p. 22.

8. This is what is shown in a comparative textual analysis by Msgr. Philippe Delhaye (in *Bijdragen, Tijdschrift voor Filosofie en theologie,* Nijmegen, 29, 1968, no. 4, pp. 351-68).

   a. Four times the encyclical *Humanae vitae* (HV) interprets the constitution *Gaudium et Spes* (GS) in a restricted sense:

   no. 49, par. 2 = HV no. 11

   no. 52, par. 3 = HV no. 24: on scientific research

   no. 48, par. 4 = HV no. 25 where the mention of love is suppressed

   no. 51, par. 3 = HV no. 14: the condemnation of abortion is extended to any interruption of the generation process that has already begun: a formula which the conciliar commission had discarded.

   b. One text is modified: GS, no. 51, par. 3 spoke of the "objective criteria drawn from the nature *of the person and his acts.*" HV no. 10 substitutes the word *marriage* for the word *person,* which does away with the personalist views of the Council.

   c. The encyclical returns to the formulas imposed on the commission in the name of the pontifical authority.

   GS, no. 50, par. 1 = HV no. 9: on the ends of marriage.

   GS, no. 51, par. 1 = HV no. 24.

   But it does not mention the complementary element which was the doctrine proper to the conciliar assembly: importance of ends other than fecundity, the risk of continence for conjugal fidelity.

   There is not complete coincidence therefore between the two documents, and there is need for integrating them, concludes Delhaye.

9. A review of the encyclical *Populorum progressio,* published in *La Croix,* April 22, 1967, p. 5.

Notes—Chapter 8

1. *Cf.* above, p. 103.

2. On this, see the article of G. M. Cottier, "L'athéisme religieux," in *Nova et Vetera* 43 (1968), p. 36-55.

3. On the nonreligious Christianity of Bonhoeffer, see René Marlé, *Dietrich Bonhoeffer* (Paris-Tournai: Casterman, 1967) where Bonhoeffer asked, "How do we speak of God—without religion, i.e. without the temporally conditioned presuppositions of metaphysics, inwardness, and so on?" and his own reply, "We are moving towards a completely religionless time; people as they are now, simply cannot be religious any longer (p. 132).

4. The evidence given by young Christians involved in the May 1968 revolution in Paris is very typical. Some examples were published by Robert Davezies, in the collection *Mai 68 La rue dans l'Église,* Paris: l'Épi, 1968.

5. A discourse published in its entirety in *DC,* December 4, 1960, no. 1341, col. 1503. The editor was Msgr. Bernard Lalande. Between this discourse of Cardinal Feltin and the letter to U Thant (May 26, 1966), in which Paul VI first uses the formula "development, the new name of peace," there was an intermediary link, Manuel Larraín, bishop of Talca, Chile, president of CELAM (+ 1966).

6. Paris: Aubier, 1965 (Theologia 4).

Notes—Chapter 9

1. R. Laurentin, *Bilan du Concile,* Paris: Seuil, 1966, pp. 75-76. Bernard Lambert, "La Problématique générale de la Constitution pastorale," in *L'Église dans le monde de ce temps,* t. 2, coll. Unam Sanctam 65 b (Paris: Cerf, 1967), pp. 131-70. Certain fathers and experts distinguished very many senses of the word "world." This is not the place for these analyses.

Let us point out, with S. Lyonnet, in *Verbum Domini 44,* 1966, p. 226, that according to the Council it is the figure of this world and not the world itself that is deformed by sin.

2. S. Lyonnet, *L'Église peut-elle dialoguer avec le monde?,* mimeographed pamphlet of 24 pages, undated (Rome: Biblicum, ca. 1966).

3. Max Weber, *Die protestantische Ethik und der Geist der Kapitalismus,* 1904, English translation, New York: Scribner's, 1958, p. 91.

4. Quoted in J. Comblin, *Teologia do desenvolvimento,* Belo Horizonte, 1968, p. 12.

5. José Maria González, "Le Chrétien et la Révolution," IDOC, no. 68-22, June 2, 1968, pp. 3-4.

Capitalism as a socio-economic and political structure is defined by the four laws that condition its economic evolution and its transformation:

—The first of these laws (and the chief one) is the struggle for profit. *Capitalist economy is a market economy in the sense that production is not to satisfy*

the needs proper to the immediate producer, but to put things on the market. And this market selling does not come from an intention to serve mankind; it has no other objective than gain, which we call profit. The search for profit is the goal of the capitalist business man. To this primordial right to seek profit are added three others:

— Competition *among capitalists for better sale of production*

— *The* concentration *of monies in an ever decreasing number of hands.*

— *Finally, the* progressive reduction of the profit rate *in order to guarantee first place among competitors.*

Envisioned in its essence, as it has just been defined, capitalism must be considered from the viewpoint of Christian morality as intrinsically evil in its structure.

This conclusion is a striking reminder of the strong terms Pius XI used to characterize Marxist atheism.

6. ASS 37, 1905, p. 237: The question posed was:

— *Utrum liceat parvas imagines chartaceas B.M.V. deglutire ad inopetrandam?*

The response of the Holy Office, which met on July 29, 1903, was:

— *Dummodo vana omnis observatio et periculum in illam incidendi removeatur, licere.*

7. Comblin, *op. cit.,* p. 15.

8. Fernand Boulard and Jean Remy, *Pratique religieuse urbaine et régions culturelles,* Collection de sociologie religieuse, Paris: Editions ouvrières, 1968, p. 179.

9. Comblin, *op. cit.,* p. 17.

Notes—Chapter 10

1. A short list of works on violence: G. Zananiri, "L'Église et la Violence" in *Ami du clergé,* 78 (1968), no. 42, October 17, pp. 611-16. *À la recherche d'une théologie de la violence,* symposium of P. Blanquart, L. Bernaert, P. Dabezies, A. Dumas, Casamayor, P. Lecocq (Paris: Cerf, 1968). M. J. Le Guillou and G. Blaquière, "Réflexions chrétiennes sur la violence" in *Évangile et Révolution* (Paris, Centurion, 1968). A. Tirot, "Difficulté de parler de la violence," *Terre entière,* May-August, 1968, no. 29-30, pp. 140-154.

2. Yambo Ouologuem, *Le Devoir de violence* (Paris: Seuil, 1968) (Prix Renaudot). Even novels today include violence in their titles.

3. Roger Schutz, *Violence des pacifiques,* Taizé, 1968.

4. On the Abidjan Conference, see *ICI,* April 15, 1968, no. 310, p. 10, col. 1. Three Catholic representatives of the pontifical commission on Justice and Peace participated in this conference which concluded: it is not possible to "blanketly condemn recourse to force . . . In certain circumstances, violence or a threat are justified because they elicit drastic measures destined to ameliorate unbearable situations."

5. On the Uppsala Assembly, see *ICI,* August 1968, no. 317-318, p. 15; and A. Wenger, *Upsal* (Paris: Centurion, 1968) especially pp. 137 & 167.

6. On the Lambeth Conference, see *ICI,* no. 319, p. 19: "We must recognize as a new element . . . the concept of a just revolution . . . In certain extreme situations . . . Christians, while ardently desiring peace, may consider taking part in violence to be a lesser evil" (*cf. Le Figaro,* August 21, 1968; *La Croix,* August 18-19, 1968).

7. A report on the ecumenical conference at Beirut, organized jointly by the Church and Society department of the WCC and the Justice and Peace commission of the Roman Catholic Church, on the subject of development, in *ICI,* May 15, 1968, no. 312, p. 8. "Note de la commission théologique de la Féderation luthérienne mondiale sur l'usage de la violence" in *Le Monde,* September 10, 1968. This note measures the newness of the problem and suggests that Christians, if they take part in a revolution, should "humanize" violence.

8. Documents of section 3. Développement économique et social, par. 15. A. Wenger, *op. cit.,* p. 137; *cf.* Documents of section 4, *Justice and Peace,* no. 30; *ibid.* p. 167; *ICI,* August 1968, no. 317-318, p. 15.

9. Ad Lucem held an international colloquium on violence at Namur in August 1967 (*La Croix,* August 24, 1967).

Several Christian groups, Témoignages chrétiens, Christianisme social (Protestant), Économie et Humanisme, La Lettre, Frères du monde, Terre entière, IDOC, and the Commission on Religions of the African Cultural Society, held at Paris, March 23-24, 1968, a colloquium which resulted in a manifesto, and then a book, issued in October with the title: *Christianisme et révolution,* Éditions La Lettre (*Témoignages chrétiens,* October 1968). IDOC dissociated itself from the manifesto, in view of its strictly informational task (*La Croix,* April 2, 1968).

Manifestos were multiplied on the occasion of Paul VI's trip to Bogotá, see Laurentin's *L'Amérique latine,* pp. 146-51.

10. *La Croix,* February 3-9, 1968.

11. Emmanuel Mounier, *Révolution personnaliste et communautaire,* Paris: Éd. Aubier-Montaigne, 1935 reproduced in the collection E. Mounier, *L'Engagement de la foi,* Paris: Seuil, Vol. I, 149.

12. *Ibid.,* p. 223. *Oeuvres complètes,* vol. 1, p. 849.

13. *Ibid.,* p. 388 (this text dates from 1933), coll. *L'Engagement de foi,* pp. 223-24.

14. Mounier's theses were influential among the Christian members of the underground in 1940-45; they had come from the pacifism that had characterized the Catholic Left between the two wars.

15. G. Zananiri, in *Ami du Clergé,* 78 (1968), October 17, p. 616.

16. *Ibid.*

17. On the law of concentration and its mechanisms, see R. Laurentin, *L'Amérique latine,* pp. 138-45.

18. Paul VI, Allocution to the Sacred College, December 1967, *Osservatore Romano,* January 5, 1968.

19. The texts of the three discourses at Bogotá against violence are quoted in Laurentin, *op. cit.,* pp. 148-49.

20. *Populorum progressio,* no. 31, where the pope takes a position against revolutionary insurrection, but admitting this exception: "Except in the case of

obvious and prolonged tyranny, which would seriously endanger the basic rights of the person and dangerously harm the good of the country" (alluded to in the text, page 156).

21. On the positions taken at the Medellín assembly, see Laurentin, *op. cit.,* pp. 150-54.

22. On the prohibition against the catechumens taking arms as an employment, consult the *La Tradition apostolique de Saint Hippolyte,* Bernard Botte, (Münster Westfalen: Aschendorffsche Verlag, 1963), p. 37; and the texts which are the sources of this reconstitution: *Testamentum Domini,* 16-17, ed. I. E. Rahmani ("Si autem volunt illi in Domino baptizari desinant militia vel potestate; sin nimus, ne admittantur"); *Ordo Ecclesiae Sahidicae,* 18, 19, 20; the *Constitutions of Hippolytus,* 10. Michel Dujarier, *Le Parrainage des adultes aux trois premiers siècles de l'Église* (Paris: Cerf, 1961) demonstrated that the respect for life was one of the criteria for admission to the catechumenate during the first centuries.

23. Pius XI, Apostolic Letter *Nos es muy* to the Mexican episcopate (March 28, 1937) in *DC,* April 10-17, 1937, col. 985-1001, esp. 993-94: general principles concerning the civil activity of Mexican Catholics.

24. Discourse on the anniversary of *Populorum progressio,* March 27, 1968, *DC,* April 21, no. 1515, col. 679. *Cf.* the discourse of June 24, *DC,* 21 July 1968, no. 1521, col. 1626.

25. *Cf.* Laurentin, *op. cit.,* pp. 150-54.

26. A. Dumas, in the book mentioned above, in note 1, pp. 14-19.

27. Roger Schutz, *Violence des pacifiques,* Taizé, 1968, p. 206.

28. Albert Camus, *The Rebel,* (New York: Knopf, 1968).

29. Michael Aucouturier, *Pasternak par lui-même* (Paris: Seuil, 1963), p. 156.

30. "The development movement must, practically out of necessity today, elicit acts of violence, connected with the more acute sense of injustice and the immense growth of aspirations (a 'revolution of rising expectation,' as people say)," André Tunc, professor at the Faculté de droit et de sciences économiques at Paris, in *La Croix,* October 18, 1968, last page.

Notes—Chapter 11

1. G. Sebregondi, "Le Développement harmonisé. Notes pour une théorie," in *Économie et Humanisme,* no. 84, March-April, 1954, pp. 66-76.

2. Lebret, *Dynamique concrète du développement,* pp. 75-83.

3. *Ibid.,* pp. 335-41.

4. *Ibid.,* p. 78.

5. *Ibid.,* p. 83.

6. Volume mentioned in the preceding notes and the bibliography on development on pages 235-238 of this book.

7. Lebret, *op. cit.,* p. 50.

8. Perroux in *La Croix,* April 19, 1967, p. 4.

9. *Ibid.*

Notes—Chapter 12

1. *Participation:*

For the Bible, see particularly: 1 Corinthians 9: 12, 23; 10: 17, 21, 30; Hebrews 3: 1, 14; 5:13; 6:4; 2:14 (with the words *metécho, métokos*) and 1 Corinthians 10: 16, 18; 2 Corinthians 6:14 (with the root *koinón*, which the Vulgate renders similarly by the words *particeps, participio, participatio*). Elsewhere, it translates *koinonia* by *communio.*

For the liturgy, let us recall the old offertory prayer: *Ejus divinitatis esse consortes qui humanitatis nostrae fieri dignatus est particeps.*

For the Council, see the Table of Contents in the Centurion edition, under the word *participatio,* pp. 885-86, which groups the references under subtitles: Participation in God, in Christ, in the Church, in the liturgy, in society, in culture, in international life, and also: participation of the Word of God in human solidarity (*Gaudium et Spes,* no. 32). See also the *Indices verborum . . . Concilii Vaticani* II, published by the Istituto per la scienza religiosa di Bologna, (Firenze: Valecchi, 1968-1969) concordance of words used in each text of Vatican II.

2. Elements of this are found in Yves M. J. Congar, *Jalons pour une théologie du laïcat* (Paris: Cerf, 1953) pp. 330-40. [English edition: *Lay People in the Church,* translated by Donald Attwater, Newman Press, 1967.] Among others, he mentions Saint Cyprian, *Epistle 14,* 1, 2, and 4: *"Nihil . . . sine consensu plebis";* cf. *Epistle 34,* 4, 1: *"Tractanda . . . non tantum cum collegis meis, sed cum plebe ipsa universa";* cf. *Epistle 32.*

3. On the sacrifices of praise and the Christian life considered as worship, see among others Romans 12:1; 15:16; Philippians 2:17; 3:3; 4:18; 2 Timothy 1:3; Hebrews 9:14; 12:28; 13:15; 1 Peter 2:5.

4. René Laurentin, *Bilan du Concile* (Paris: Seuil, 1966), pp. 244-56; especially pp. 246-48.

5. *Ibid.,* p. 194.

6. Previously mentioned in Chapter 4.

7. Liturgy and symbology (the study of the systems and the processus of signs and symbols). In a mimeographed note where he shows the gulf between the sign and the thing signified in the liturgy, J. Hameline makes these suggestions:

A symbological approach, without forgetting what the other disciplines have to offer, and without pretending to account for the phenomenon in all its dimensions, would permit us to study in their functioning . . . ritual expressions and communications, the processus of sense production (integration levels of sense units, procedures of cut-off and openness through metaphor and metonymy, the effect of masking and neutralization, secondary expressions, etc . . .) and to determine the total architecture of the representative field in which ritual and liturgical phenomena are inscribed and act as signs . . .

Among other things, we would study the integration mechanisms in significant totalities, the possible effects of "masking" or of nonsignification through a transformation of the indicative classes (example: host, flat, white, and round), the eventuality of semantic neutralization giving rise, through the reduction of significant differences between certain ritual elements, to the appearance of a new sign-bearer with an at times very pronounced and very inclusive sense (the Book, the Text, the Recitation . . .). The different modalities of language-communication, rhetoric and poetics in liturgy, the iconography, and the decor would be subject to special study. In a second stage, leaving the area of symbology, a wider view, appealing to the data of religious psychology, could envision the study of the general mechanisms of symbolization, ritualization (formal or informal), of the role of representative mediations and systems of expression in religious identification and the sense of belonging, particularly of semanticization in the secular and sacred field.

8. André Laurentin, "Théâtre et Liturgie," statement made at L'Arbresle in July 1967, published in the symposium *Art, Geste et Liturgie* (Paris: Centurion, 1969).

Notes—Chapter 13

1. Concerning the missionary problem, a Bibliography will be found in the *Encyclopedie de la foi* (Paris: Cerf, 1966), pp. 3, 89-90, 95.

2. The "Journées missionaires de la Tourette," February 1947. (L'Arbresle, Rhône: Économie et Humanisme, 1947), 60 pp., analyzed by Emile Poulat, *Naissance des prêtres ouvriers* (Paris: Casterman, 1965), pp. 525-36.

3. Henri Godin and Yvan Daniel, *France pagan?* Translated and adapted by Maisie Ward (New York: Sheed and Ward, 1949); originally published as *La France, pays de Mission?* (Lyon: Editions de l'Abeille, 1943).

4. On this interview with Bishop Fragoso, see René Laurentin's *L'Amerique latine*, pp. 111-16.

5. "Journées missionaires," p. 29; Poulat, *op. cit.*, pp. 531-32.

6. Denzinger-Shönmetzer, no. 1534, 1540, 1565, 1566.

Note—Chapter 14

1. Previously cited in Note 5 of Chapter 9, p. 228 of this book.

BIBLIOGRAPHY

A complete bibliography of development would count thousands of books and articles, so this is but a selection: 1. Some of the more recent basic works; some of them include bibliographies; 2. Some commentaries on **Populorum progressio;** *3. Theological works on development; a category still few in number; 4. Some journals that deal with development.*

General Books

ALBERTINI, J. M. *Les Mécanismes du sous-développement.* 3rd ed. Paris: Editions Brière, 1968.

AUSTRUY, J. *Le Scandale du développement.* Paris: Rivière, 1965.

BOREL, P. (ex-director of IRFED). *Les Trois révolutions du développement.* Paris: Editions ouvrières, 1968.

CASTRO, JOSUE DE. *Le Livre noir de la faim.* Paris: Editions ouvrières, 1961. *The Black Book of Hunger,* Boston: Beacon, 1969.

—— *Géopolitique de la faim.* Paris: Editions ouvrières, 1962.

FURTADO, CELSO. *Development and Underdevelopment.* Berkeley: University of California Press, 1964.

GANAGE, E. *Economie du développement.* Paris: PUF, 1962.

—— *Développement économique.* Paris: PUF, 1963.

—— *Institutions et Développment:* Paris: PUF, 1966.

GENDARME, R. *Pauvreté des nations.* Paris: Editions Cujas, 1963.

HIRSCHMANN, ALBERT O. *The Strategy of Development.* New Haven: Yale University Press, 1958. This has been published in Spanish, and in French: *Stratégie du développement economique.* Paris: Editions ouvrières, 1964.

KINDLEBERGER, C. P. *Economic Development*. 2nd ed. New York: McGraw Hill, 1964.

LACOSTE, Y. *Les Pays sous-développés*. Collection "Que sais-je," 1959.

—— *Géographie du sous-développement*. Paris: PUF, 1965.

LEBRET, L. J. *Dynamique concrète du développement*. Paris: Editions ouvrières, 1961; reprinted in 1967.

—— *Economie et Civilisation*. Tome 1. *Niveaux de vie, Besoins et Civilisations* (in collaboration with A. Piettre, A. Sauvy, and R. Delprat). Paris: Editions ouvrières, 1956.

LEWIS, W. ARTHUR. *Theory of Economic Growth*. London: George Allen; New York: John Wiley, 1957.

—— *Development Planning:* The Essentials of Economic Policy. New York: Harper and Row, 1966.

MOUSSA, PIERRE. *Les Nations prolétaires*. Paris: PUF, 1960; *Underprivileged Nations*. Boston: Beacon, 1963.

MYINT, H. *The Economics of the Developing Countries*. London: Hutchinson, 1964; New York: Praeger.

MYRDAL, GUNNAR. *Planifier pour développer*. Paris: Editions ouvrières, 1963.

PERROUX, FRANCOIS. *La Coexistence pacifique:* II. *Pôles de développement*. Paris: PUF, 1958.

—— *Les Techniques quantitatives de la planification*. Paris: PUF, 1965.

—— *L'Economie des jeunes nations*. Paris: PUF, 1962.

SAUVY, A. *Le "Tiers-Monde": Sous-développement et Développement*. Revised, augmented edition by A. S. Paris: PUF, 1961 (*cf*. Balandier).

Editions of and Commentaries on Populorum progressio

MONTVALON, R. DE. *Trois encycliques sociales: Mater et Magistra, Pacem in Terris, Populorum progressio*. Paris: Seuil, 1967.

PAUL VI. *Encyclique Populorum progressio sur le développement des peuples*. Introduction and commentaries by L'Action populaire. Paris: Spes, 1967.

—— *Le Developpement des peuples, Populorum progressio*. Introduction by Vincent Cosmao (adjunct director general of IRFED). Paris: Centurion, 1967.

RIGA, PETER J. *Church of the Poor: A commentary on Paul Sixth's Encyclical on the Development of Peoples*. Techny, Ill.: Divine Word, 1968.

Theological Works

ALFARO, J. *Hacia una teología del progreso humano*. Barcelona: Herder, 1968.

ALVES, RUBEM A. *A Theology of Human Hope*. Washington: Corpus Books, 1969.

COLONNESE, LOUIS M., ed. *Human Rights and the Liberation of Man in the Americas*. Notre Dame, Ind.: University of Notre Dame, 1970.

COMBLIN, JOSEPH. *Teología do desenvolvimento*. Belo Horizonte, Brazil: Movimento familiar cristão, 1968.

HOUTART, F. and VETRANO, V. O. *Hacia una teología des desarrollo.* Buenos Aires: Latinoamericanos libros, 1967.

LA CHAPPELLE, P. DE (adjunct secretary of the pontifical commission Justice and Peace). "Nouvelle dimensions des responsabilités chrétiennes: Le Développement des peuples." *Lumen Vitae* 23 (1968) 60-70.

LARRAIN, MANUEL. "Lettre sur de développement." Edited by *Pax Christi.*

MUNBY, DENYS, ed. *World Development: Challenge to the Churches.* Introduction by Barbara Ward Jackson. Washington: Corpus Books, 1969.

Peruvian Bishops' Commission for Social Action. *Between Honesty and Hope: Documents from and about the Church in Latin America.* Maryknoll Documentation Series, Maryknoll, N.Y.: Maryknoll Publications, 1970. Translation of *Signos de Renovación,* published in Lima, Peru, 1968.

SODEPAX. *In Search of a Theology of Development.* Papers from a consultation at Cartigny, Switzerland, November 1969; *Toward a Theology of Development,* an annotated bibliography prepared for SODEPAX (Committee on Society, Development, and Peace, Ecumenical Center, Geneva) by Gerhard Bauer.

Symposium on the Theology of Liberation, Bogotá, March 6-7, 1970, *Aportes para la Liberación.* Bogotá: Presencia, 1970.

VAN BAELEN, L. O.F.M. CAP. *Morale du développement: Le Probleme des pays en voie de développement.* Preface by Professor L. Janssens. Lyon: Editions Xavier Mappus, 1967.

Works of Spirituality

LEBRET, L. J. *Action marche vers Dieu.* Paris: Editions ouvrières, 1949.
—— *Dimensions de la charité.* Paris: Editions ouvrierès, 1958.

Journals

Communautés. Archives internationales de sociologie de la coopération et du développement, 7, avenue Franco-Russe, Paris; director, Henri Desroche.

Community Development Journal, quarterly, Oxford University Press.

Croissance des jeunes nations, 163, boulevard Malesherbes, Paris. Informative magazine for the general public.

Développement et Civilisation, IRFED, 47, rue de la Glaciere, Paris.

Economic Bulletin for Asia and the Far East, quarterly, United Nations.

Economic Bulletin for Latin America, quarterly, United Nations.

Economie et Humanisme, 88 quai Clemenceau, 69-Caluire. Founded by Lebret, directed by Father Viau.

Economie et Société, Cahiers de l'ISEA, Librairie Droz, 11 rue Massot, Geneva, Switzerland; director, F. Perroux.

Journal of Developing Areas, quarterly, Western Illinois University, Macomb, Ill. 61455.

Projet, Action populaire, 5, rue Marcheron, Vannes.

Studies in Comparative International Development. Monographs appearing serially, twelve per year, published at Rutgers University, New Brunswick,

New Jersey, distributed by Sage Publications, Inc., Beverly Hills, California 90212.

Tiers-Monde, L'Institut Tiers-Monde, 58, boulevard Arago, Paris.

Tiers-Monde: Problemes des pays sous-developpés, 1, place Paul Painlevé, Paris; director, François Perroux.

Trimestro económico, Fondo de Cultura Económico, Mexico.

Literature

To encourage readers to seek out autobiographies, novels, and personal reports, we add a few titles that may be surprising. These works help us see from within what the problem of human development means and convince us that development is not understood by way of analyses alone. Literature and art can express in depth what it means to live within it.

CHEIKH HAMIDOU, KANE. *L'Aventure ambiguë.* Paris: Julliard, 1966.

LEWIS, OSCAR. *Children of Sanchez.* New York: Random House, 1961; Modern Library, 1969. This American sociologist, working in Mexico, collected biographies in underdeveloped areas and in this book tells the story of a whole family.

OUSMAN SEMBENE. *Le Mandat.* Paris: Editions africaines. An excellent film of great human and documentary value was made from this in 1968.

SUAVET, THOMAS. *Actualité de L.-J. Lebret.* Paris: Editions ouvrières, 1969.

TURNBULL, COLIN. *The Lonely African.* New York: Simon and Shuster, 1962. Monograph on typical "decultured" Africans, whose way of life is imported from the West. The author is a specialist in African anthropology.